GOVERNORS OF EMPIRE

ALSO BY AMAR FAROOQUI

Early Social Formations (2001)

Smuggling as Subversion: Colonialism, Indian Merchants and the Politics of Opium: 1790–1843 (2005)

Opium City: The Making of Early Victorian Bombay (2006)

Sindias and the Raj: Princely Gwalior, c.1800–1850 (2011)

Zafar and the Raj: Anglo-Mughal Delhi, c.1800–1857 (2013)

The Establishment of British Rule: 1757–1813 (2014)

The Colonial Subjugation of India (2022)

GOVERNORS OF EMPIRE

THE EAST INDIA COMPANY'S
CHIEF FUNCTIONARIES IN INDIA

Amar Farooqui

ALEPH

ALEPH

ALEPH BOOK COMPANY
An independent publishing firm
promoted by *Rupa Publications India*

First published in India in 2025
by Aleph Book Company
161-B/4, Gulmohar House,
Yusuf Sarai Community Centre,
New Delhi 110049

ISBN: 978-81-19635-28-3

1 3 5 7 9 10 8 6 4 2

CONTENTS

INTRODUCTION

Among the many propagandist exercises of the empire in its heyday was the publication of a series entitled *Rulers of India*, intended to glorify prominent governors-general and a few other colonial officials who had served in India. The series was an initiative of the Oxford University Press (Clarendon Press). Its general editor was the well-known colonial administrator and ideologue, W.W. Hunter. The series was not confined to British 'rulers of India'; it also included a few pre-British rulers. This was part of the programme in the closing decades of the nineteenth century to develop Oxford University Press (OUP) as a commercial concern. Bartholomew Price, secretary to Delegates of the Clarendon Press, and his successor Philip Gell, played a crucial role in transforming OUP into a business venture. This was also the time when the Indian empire began to figure seriously in the plans of OUP, as a market and as a theme for its publications. Since the late 1870s, it had been publishing the *Sacred Books of the East* series under the editorship of Max Müller, who also provided some inputs for the proposal that the Delegates had been considering for a series that eventually came to be published under the title *Rulers of India*.

The scheme might have been inspired partly by the *Statesmen Series* being brought out by W.H. Allen of London. W.H. Allen had a large list of publications on India, as for instance J.W. Kaye's best-seller, *A History of the Sepoy War* in three-volumes, and its expanded version *Kaye's and Malleson's History of the Indian Mutiny* in six-volumes. The *Statesmen Series* was not confined to Britain, or the empire, and included volumes on political figures from other parts of Europe as well. A biography of Benjamin Disraeli (*Lord Beaconsfield*) came out in 1888, and of Lord Palmerston in the same year. In 1889, a volume on Lord Dalhousie was published as part of the series; it was authored by Captain L.J. Trotter who would be commissioned to write the volume on Warren Hastings in the *Rulers of India* series. The genre had been popularized in Britain by writers such as Trotter—mostly amateur historians, many of whom were retired colonial bureaucrats or military officers. They catered to the appetite that the Victorian reading public had acquired for popular histories and biographies. There was simultaneously a growing demand for books on India, the demand spurred by interest in the 'mutiny'. The appetite for 'mutiny' literature in the latter half of the nineteenth century seemed insatiable.

Hunter, who had spent twenty-five years in India as a civil servant and returned to England following his retirement in 1887, was approached by Gell in 1889 for assuming responsibility for the *Rulers of India* series as its editor. Hunter was associated with several official documentation projects while working in India, including the multi-volume *Imperial Gazetteer of India* which first came out in 1881. He also had numerous publications to his credit, including *The Annals of Rural Bengal* and the controversial *The Indian Musalmans: Are They Bound in Conscience to Rebel Against the Queen?*. Hunter agreed to be editor of the series. He was to receive £75 for each volume in his capacity as editor, while the author of each volume would receive £25. The desired length for each work was two hundred pages or less. This would ensure that the volumes were modestly priced. Rimi Chatterjee, in her detailed study of the project, notes that 'The series was thus meant to be slim and school-bookish rather than ponderous and scholarly … To some extent Gell's views and Hunter's coincided: they both saw the merits of short books that assumed an average level of interest and erudition in their readers.'[1]

The Delegates had conceptualized this as 'a series giving the salient features of Indian History in the Biographies of

---

[1]Rimi B. Chatterjee, *Empires of the Mind: A History of the Oxford University Press in India under the Raj*, New Delhi: Oxford University Press, 2006, pp. 208–09.

successive Generals and Administrators'.[2] However, the series became essentially a history of Britain's empire in India in the era of the East India Company (EIC). Of the twenty-eight volumes that were eventually published, a few were on pre-British Indian rulers such as Ashoka, Akbar, Mahadji Sindia, and Ranjit Singh (seven in all). Twelve volumes were devoted to governors-general, from Warren Hastings to John Lawrence and Lord Mayo. There was of course a volume on Robert Clive, while the lives of five colonial bureaucrats or army officers were the subject, respectively, of another six volumes. The Portuguese colonial enterprise was represented by Afonso de Albuquerque (d. 1515), and the French undertaking in India by Joseph-François Dupleix. The Dupleix volume was among the first set of volumes which came out in 1890, the others being volumes on Warren Hastings, Lord Cornwallis, and Lord Dalhousie. In India, the volumes on Ashoka (published as a supplementary volume in 1901), Akbar, and Mahadji Sindia, rather than the volumes on British 'rulers', were the bestsellers. Chatterjee remarks that 'Hunter's experience of India and the Indians ought to have made it clear to him that the life of Akbar was a better prospect than that of Henry Lawrence'.[3]

In other words, for Hunter the series was an opportunity to narrate the story of the growth and expansion of the empire from its beginnings to its high point in the last quarter of the nineteenth century (Mayo was governor-general from 1869 to 1872, when he was assassinated). Four of the eight Indian rulers belonged to the late eighteenth or early nineteenth centuries, whose histories were closely intertwined with those of the EIC. All colonial bureaucrats and military officers are pre-revolt figures, as are the governors-general—barring two: Lawrence and Mayo. Lawrence was an employee of the Company for thirty years, played a crucial role in the suppression of the revolt, and then became governor-general in the early years of

[2]Ibid., p. 207.
[3]Ibid., p. 217.

direct Crown rule. Together, these volumes acquaint the reader with the history of the empire established by the Company, through biographies of 'great' men who contributed to the creation of that empire and its consolidation. Later, a condensed version of the *Rulers of India* volumes was issued by OUP for the Indian market in four volumes, with the title *Sketches of Rulers of India* (1908), edited by G.D. Oswell (principal of Rajkumar College, Raipur, 1894–1910). Each volume in this series comprised abridged versions of several books of the original series, grouped chronologically.

Almost all the volumes of *Rulers of India* were authored by colonial administrators or army officers who had served in India. Hunter used his contacts among these officials to commission these works. Eric Stokes has observed that, 'It was Macaulay on his return from India who had read the English mind aright, and realized that the one form in which the strange and unattractive subject of British-Indian history could be made palatable was that of biography.' As the Victorian public saw it, the function of the historian 'was to inform and exhort by presenting the national character in its highest examples, and by narrating the lives of Britain's great men he was to demonstrate how individual character moulded history'.[4] It is not surprising that the Delegates should have preferred to rely on this model, even though Gell clarified to Hunter that the volumes were not intended to be personal biographies. The authors were to concentrate on what the 'rulers', implying British 'rulers', had done for India. There is very little in these volumes on the social background of the 'rulers', or their lives after they returned home except a few cursory remarks.

---

[4]E. T. Stokes, 'The Administrators and Historical Writing on India', C. H. Philips (ed.) *Historians of India, Pakistan and Ceylon*, London: Oxford University Press, 1967, p. 385. Thomas Macaulay wrote numerous biographical essays on historical and literary figures. Two of his most well-known essays on the formative phase of the British empire in India are his lengthy biographical essays on Clive (1840), and Warren Hastings (1841). Both these were reviews of biographies of the two EIC officials.

Nonetheless, the individual biographies of the governors-general, their social milieu, and their fate *after* their career in India had ended, is of historical interest because it allows us to situate these figures within a larger context and view them as part of the longer history of colonialism. Standard textbook accounts rarely dwell on these aspects, depicting the governors-general in isolation, their tenures in a disjointed manner, and removing them from their context. The omnipotent governor-general, it would appear, came from an alien world and, having spent a few years in India, went back to it. Only the brief Indian sojourn is, one would suppose, worth talking about.

This book provides a glimpse of the world of the governor-general, from the time that the designation was introduced in 1773, when gains from the initial colonial conquests were being consolidated and there were demands in Britain for better management of these territorial acquisitions in the interests not only of the shareholders of the EIC but of the ruling elite of Britain as a whole, to the period immediately after the brutal suppression of the revolt of 1857. The designation continued to be used down to the end of colonial rule, and for a few years beyond that until India became a republic in 1950. Lord Mountbatten was the first governor-general of independent India, with George VI (r. 1936–52) as king.[5] He was succeeded by the veteran Indian nationalist, C. Rajagopalachari in June 1948. Rajagopalachari relinquished office in January 1950, and the office itself was abolished when India became a republic. The governor-general had held the additional title of 'viceroy', as the deputy of the British monarch, since 1858. The latter

---

[5]The Indian Independence Act, 1947, provided for dropping the title *Indiae Imperator*, emperor of India, from the several borne by the king. The title was introduced by the Royal Titles Act of 1876, which had made Victoria empress of India. According to section 7 (2) of the Act, 'The assent of the Parliament of the United Kingdom is hereby given to the omission from the Royal Style and Titles of the words "Indiae Imperator" and the words "Emperor of India" and to the issue by His Majesty for that purpose of His Royal Proclamation under the Great Seal of the Realm.' The proclamation was issued on 22 June 1948, and the 'king-emperor' became merely 'king'. Mountbatten's term ended on 21 June 1948.

title was discontinued in 1947.

I have tried to present the history of the colonial period, till the revolt, through portraits of ten successive chief functionaries of the Company posted in India. Of these, nine had the designation of governor-general. These are figures representative of a particular phase of colonial rule and/or style of governance. John Lawrence (1864–69) has been included as he was the last Company employee to become governor-general, and this takes the story of the empire down to the early 1870s when Lawrence passed away. The EIC itself ceased to exist in 1874.

It would be inaccurate to regard the governors-general as rulers of India. Till 1858 they were functionaries of the Company, even if their appointment was controlled by the British cabinet, as it was from the 1770s–80s onwards. The politics of appointment was, as we shall see, a complicated affair, reflecting the complex sharing of power between the British government, directors of the EIC and, in a limited way, the monarch or the royal family. The arrangement was an evolving one throughout the period of this study. The Court of Directors ruled exclusively till 1773, and after that in conjunction with the cabinet. Nevertheless, the views of the directors about who should be governor-general could not be disregarded. The approval of the Court of Directors was not a mere formality.

Governors-general spent a few years in that position, usually about five years. Lord Ellenborough was in India for two years, from 1842 to 1844; Warren Hastings was governor-general for nearly twelve years, Lord Moira for ten, and Dalhousie for eight.

These were mighty figures in India. Yet on their return, they had to work hard to remain politically relevant. Most were unsuccessful. At best, they might be occasionally consulted about colonial policy relating to India. Otherwise, they lived in quiet retirement. It is worth looking at their lives in Britain following their return (the EIC did not allow any governor-general to linger on in India once he had relinquished charge) to understand the nature of the power they wielded. Warren Hastings lived for thirty-three years after he went back to

England, and died in his eighty-fifth year, almost forgotten by his contemporaries. The 'great' conqueror Lord Wellesley lived for thirty-seven years after his recall in 1805, dying at the age of eighty-two. Wellesley failed to realize his political ambition of heading the government, or at least being an important member of the cabinet (he was in the cabinet for a fleeting moment). Even in later years, at the turn of the century, an imperial colossus—as represented in colonial historiography—like Curzon had to suffer disappointment after he abruptly resigned following a tiff with the commander-in-chief of the army in India, H.H. Kitchener, and returned home. In England, his career made very slow progress and did not advance beyond that of foreign secretaryship, a position he attained fourteen years after he returned home. He had at one time aspired to be prime minister.[6]

Just a small number of biographies of governors-general have been added to the enormous output on the history of modern India in the past fifty years or so. Percival Spear came out with his authoritative *Master of Bengal: Clive and His India* in 1975. Nirad Chaudhuri's meticulously researched and eminently readable *Clive of India* was published in the same year. Lord Bentinck has been fortunate in having the historian and musicologist John Rosselli as his biographer. Rosselli's *Lord William Bentinck: The Making of a Liberal Imperialist* (1974) is a comprehensive account of Bentinck's life, including his years in Italy as colonial civil and military administrator, a phase often mentioned in passing in accounts

---

[6]As a typical example of the misleading characterization of governors-general as independent actors, ignoring the colonial context, one might cite a journalistic piece, an article by the American foreign policy expert A. Weiss Mitchell, 'The Curzonian Imprint on Indian Foreign Policy', *Hindustan Times*, 13 June 2021—an example I have taken at random. In this the author, while discussing Curzon's foreign policy, portrays him as a great champion of India, and as a viceroy who looked forward to the time when 'a confident, self-governing India would become a major source of stability ...', as if Curzon, arch-imperialist, could have pursued an independent policy, unrelated to the interests of British colonialism, and without any reference to London.

relating to his tenure as governor-general in India. Iris Butler in her life of Lord Wellesley, *The Eldest Brother* (1973), utilized valuable new source material which was not available to earlier biographers. S. Gopal published a biography of Lord Ripon in 1953, focussing on his viceroyalty (1880–84). He later produced a massive three-volume biography of Jawaharlal Nehru (1975–84), and wrote an intimate biography of scholar-president Sarvepalli Radhakrishnan (who also happened to be his father) in 1989, but did not return to the genre of biographies of colonial administrators.

Interest in the lives of governors-general seems to have waned after the 1970s, with the exception of Warren Hastings, who continues to be a favourite.[7] The only significant addition to the list of biographies of governors-general in recent years is Richard Middleton's *Cornwallis: Soldier and Statesman in a Revolutionary World* (2022).

There is scope for a work on the lives of governors-general which places them against the backdrop of the social and political history of India and Britain in the epoch of Company rule, and is therefore also a history of the EIC. This is what this book attempts to do. To some extent, it is a companion volume to my *Colonial Subjugation of India* (2022), but it can be read independently.

This is a book about individual lives. The biographies allow us to grasp concretely the foreignness of British rule. Governors-general were products of British society, and their eventual destination was Britain. They had no long-term stakes in India, and embarked on their homeward journey the moment their tenures ended. None of the British 'rulers of India' settled in India; no governor-general came to Calcutta or New Delhi with the objective of making India his home. Britain was obviously home for them. Of the long line of governors-general between 1773 and 1948, just two are buried in India: Cornwallis and

---

[7]For a discussion on trends in writings on Hastings, see Alfie Banks, 'The Imperial Afterlife of Warren Hastings, 1818–1947', *The Journal of Imperial and Commonwealth History*, Vol. 50, No. 3, 2022, pp. 498–531.

Lord Elgin, simply because they happened to die in a foreign land while in office.[8] The remains of Mayo, the only other governor-general whose death occurred while in office, and the only governor-general whose life had a violent end at the hands of an assassin, were taken to Ireland and interred in Naas (County Kildare). Governors-general and senior Company officials did not intermarry with Indians. A few of them did have Indian families, as for instance John Shore. Shore lived with 'native' women and had progeny from them. These families were abandoned when they went back to England. Further, this practice had come to an end by the beginning of the nineteenth century.

The colonial state was a machine for extracting surpluses from India and transferring them to the metropole. This is what made the colonial state 'colonial'. All governors-general of the Company era and under the Crown, as well as the governors of Bengal (Fort William) between 1757 and 1773, were expected to ensure that the machine functioned efficiently. They represented only one component of the extractive apparatus, the others being the EIC establishment in London, and the British government.

The directors of the EIC exercised firm control over their chief functionaries in India. In the early period of its existence, the Company had elaborate mechanisms in place for enforcing discipline aboard its ships. The personnel who manned these ships were required to strictly follow instructions given to them when they set out on their long trans-oceanic voyages, and were liable to be penalized even for minor infractions. The higher-level personnel were enjoined to record in minute detail everything that transpired during the voyage. This meant that the directors were aware of happenings on each ship while

---

[8]The Elgins, senior (8th earl) and junior (9th earl), belonged to a prominent political dynasty which is virtually unknown in so far as standard textbooks on the history of modern India are concerned. Two Elgins, father and son, were governors-general in India. The 8th earl died in India in 1863. The 9th earl was governor-general in the latter half of the 1890s.

it was abroad. Officers and ordinary sailors had to finally return to Europe where they had their families. They could be punished for disobedience or misconduct, and could therefore not afford to defy their employers.

It is incorrect to suppose, as has often been suggested, that the vast distance which separated Company officials posted in India from headquarters in London, provided them with the opportunity to act independently. Every action was closely scrutinized, and had to be approved by the Court of Directors in order to be considered valid. Hardly any freedom was allowed to the EIC's chief functionaries for acting independently, though they might appear to be larger-than-life figures. Clive, on the morrow of Plassey, had to resort to subterfuge to function as the head of the Company's establishment in Bengal. His authority was regularized only after orders were received from London. Given that the relevance of the governors-general was ultimately linked to their place in British society and politics, they had to be very attentive to the state of affairs prevailing at home. Their roots were in Britain, not India. A closer look at their lives would confirm this.

Colonial ideologues sought to conceal the intrinsic foreignness of British rule by labelling their immediate predecessors, the Mughals, as foreigners. The notion that India endured several centuries of 'foreign' rule during the medieval period was firmly planted by colonial administrators and ideologues in the early decades of the nineteenth century. Lord Ellenborough (governor-general, 1842–44) proclaimed in 1842 that 'the insult of eight hundred years', had been 'avenged' when British troops on his orders transported the so-called 'Gates of Somnath' from Afghanistan to India. In speaking of the 'insult of eight hundred years' he was referring to the incursions of Mahmud of Ghazni, especially his foray into Gujarat in 1025 during which he plundered a temple located at Somnath. In colonial historiography Mahmud's incursions are supposed to have marked the beginning of 'Muslim invasions', laying the foundations of 'foreign' rule during the medieval period. When it was discovered much later that these gates had nothing to do with Somnath, they were quietly dumped in the Red Fort of Agra, where they can still be seen. The damage, however, was done; the seeds of religious discord were sown.

Ellenborough was a prominent Tory politician who presided over the Board of Control several times. The board was the body which, from 1784 onwards, monitored the Company's administration on behalf of the British parliament. Ellenborough was president of the board when the bill for divesting the Company of its authority to govern the Indian empire was being drafted in 1858. In 1842, soon after he assumed office as governor-general, Ellenborough had put together an armed force, the 'Army of Retribution', for marching through parts of Afghanistan in order to salvage imperial prestige following the crushing defeat inflicted on British forces in the First Afghan War (1839–42). It was against this backdrop that he issued the statement which portrayed the British as saviours of Indian subjects of the empire, rescuing them from foreign rule!

Already by this time the medieval period had come to be denoted in colonial writings as the 'Muslim period'. The typical colonial understanding of India's medieval past is summed up in a widely-read work published at the turn of the century, Stanley Lane-Poole's *Mediaeval India Under Mohammedan Rule* (1903). It might be worthwhile to quote the opening sentences of Lane-Poole's Preface:[9]

> The Mediaeval Period of Indian history, though it does not exactly correspond with the Middle Age of Europe, is not less clearly defined. It begins when the immemorial systems, rule, and customs of Ancient India were invaded, subdued, and modified by a succession of foreign conquerors who imposed a new rule ... These conquerors were Muslims, and with the arrival of the Turks ... at the beginning of the eleventh century, India entered upon her Middle Age.

---

[9]Stanley Lane-Poole, *Mediaeval India Under Mohammedan Rule*, 712-1764, London: T. Fisher Unwin, 1926, p. iii.

From that epoch for nearly eight hundred years her history
is grouped round the Mohammedan rulers...

The denigration of the Mughals, and Muslim rulers of
the subcontinent generally, characterizing them as foreign
oppressors, would become crucial for communal assertions
about India's past by the end of the century. The view that
all Muslim rulers were foreign invaders has been central to an
idea of India based on exclusion. This view continues to be
perpetuated by right-wing political formations, very aggressively
in recent years, for mobilization along communal lines.

It did not matter that Mughal rulers from Akbar onwards
were born and brought up in India; that they lived out their
lives and died in India; and that they are buried in India. The
last Mughal emperor, Bahadur Shah Zafar, never stepped out
of Delhi, where he spent over eighty years of his life till he
was exiled to Rangoon after the revolt of 1857, dying there in
captivity in 1862. His remains were interred in an unmarked
grave. Mughal rule had never extended to Burma.

Without going into the complex historical problem of how
we are to define 'foreignness' in the context of pre-modern
societies before the emergence of modern nation-states with
their well-defined borders, it is important to emphasize the
specific character of colonialism as a system of exploitation, of
extraction of wealth which is then transferred to the metropole.
The ruling elites of the metropole, in this case Britain, were
the main beneficiaries of this system, using it to augment their
own wealth manifold. The Industrial Revolution in England,
which gathered momentum in the latter half of the eighteenth
century, could not have been sustained without the resources
pumped out of Bengal and Bihar especially after the battles of
Plassey (1757) and Baksar (1764), and transferred in various
ways to the metropole. While Britain grew rich and became the
foremost capitalist economy in the world, India became poor.
The pioneers of economic nationalism, Dadabhai Naoroji and
R.C. Dutt studied a mass of official statistics and were able to

demonstrate that British rule had systematically impoverished the Indian people through a mechanism whereby their resources were drained away continuously. This was made possible by the political and military control which was exercised by the colonial state. It unleashed its full military might to brutally suppress the revolt of 1857, amounting to a reconquest of the empire. The drain could then continue for another ninety years.

∽

A note on spellings: names of places in the Indian subcontinent are mostly those commonly used in the latter half of the twentieth century, when Cochin (Kochi), Bombay (Mumbai), and Madras (Chennai) began to be renamed. Renaming is an ongoing process. The names and spellings used in the book are those with which people of my generation have been familiar. English language spellings of these places have been used. Many of these names and spellings were in use prior to 1947. Some spellings such as 'Cawnpore' (Kanpur), 'Jubbulpore' (Jabalpur), 'Simla' (Shimla), and 'Poona' (Pune), were changed soon after Independence or a little later in the century. The current official name of the respective places has also been provided to make it easier for readers to identify them, except places which have been renamed in the past few years. The erstwhile names and English spellings of the latter are often still in everyday use. Archaic spellings, such as 'Behar' (Bihar), or 'Oudh/Oude' for Awadh (region/Mughal suba/kingdom/colonial administrative unit) have been avoided, unless required by the context. Moreover, Awadh corresponds to the pronunciation, and is used widely in scholarly writings. Subedar has been preferred to subadar or subahdar, being closer to the pronunciation. Punjab has been used instead of Panjab, as it continues to be used officially. Names and places outside the subcontinent follow the same principles. Ceylon and Sri Lanka are used interchangeably. For names such as Sindia (Śinde), which has several variants, the spelling closer to the pronunciation has been preferred.

I

SHIPS AND FACTORIES

In August 1608, a ship named *Hector* arrived on the shores of Surat, in present-day Gujarat. This was the first ship belonging to the English East India Company (EIC) to reach India, and had also been a part of the inaugural trading venture of the EIC—the first fleet of ships sent forth to the Indian Ocean in 1601, an undertaking made possible by the rapid expansion in England's shipping industry. The growth of English shipping in the preceding years must be viewed against the backdrop of the Anglo–Spanish conflict of 1585–1604. The conflict provided excellent opportunities for growth, and a great deal of the expansion took place due to private initiatives. At this time, the Royal Navy, though exceptionally effective on the high seas, was still quite small in terms of numbers. In the closing years of the reign of Elizabeth I (r. 1558–1603), the core of the navy consisted of thirty-four queen's ships, which could, along with a few other ships of the naval force, be deployed in warfare far more efficiently than the formidable Spanish Armada. The relatively smaller dimensions of the English ships gave them greater manoeuvrability and speed, while their superior artillery gave them better firepower. At the same time, given the small size of the royal fleet, England had to rely on private shipping to augment its military capability in the fight against Spain. The latter was far too powerful an enemy for Elizabeth to be able to carry on a sustained struggle against it with the limited resources at the disposal of the Crown.

In the latter half of the sixteenth century, the presence of privately-owned English armed vessels engaged in raiding ships on the high seas had been growing in the Atlantic Ocean. These ships often targeted royal Spanish ships carrying treasure from the Americas to Europe. Many of the predatory expeditions had the tacit—or even formal—support of the state, and quite a few were organized by prominent figures at the court. Foremost among these was Francis Drake, who was the first English navigator to have sailed around the globe in 1577–80. He was part of a group of elites that promoted armed shipping ventures known as privateering. The group included Walter Ralegh (Raleigh), one of the pioneers of English colonization in North America. Privateering referred to the officially sanctioned assault on vessels of enemy states by private ships, and their plunder. As the war with Spain gathered intensity, it became legitimate for private English ships to prey on Iberian shipping.[1] Technically, privateers could obtain 'letters of reprisal' in the High Court of Admiralty, authorizing them to attack and pillage enemy vessels as recompense for losses suffered by English ships in Spanish harbours when they were impounded in 1585. In the midst of mounting tensions between the two countries, Philip II of Spain (r. 1556–98) had suddenly in that year closed Spanish ports to English ships. Very soon, in England, 'proof of loss [required for issuing letters of reprisal] became little more than a legal fiction and ventures of reprisal were promoted by men who had never dreamed of trading in Spain'.[2] Privateers also attacked neutral vessels, so that, usually, there was hardly any distinction between piracy and privateering. Besides, many of the naval expeditions during the war were semi-official operations, involving both privateers as well as royal ships.

Privateering inflicted substantial damage on Spanish shipping. It has been estimated that 'the English captured well over a thousand Spanish and Portuguese prizes during

---

[1]Almost the entire Iberian Peninsula, comprising mainly Spain and Portugal, was part of imperial Spain between 1580 and 1640. Portugal in these decades was under the Spanish crown.

[2]Kenneth R. Andrews, *Trade, Plunder and Settlement: Maritime Enterprise and the Genesis of the British Empire, 1480-1630*, Cambridge: Cambridge University Press, 1984, p. 245.

the war, losses which must have contributed as much as any other factor to the catastrophic decline of Iberian shipping' by the beginning of the seventeenth century.[3] More importantly, privateering gave an impetus to oceanic maritime enterprise in England. Ships had to be built, equipped and armed; financial resources had to be mobilized; men had to be recruited; goods acquired in plundering voyages had to be sold; fleets had to be victualled; and competent officers had to be found who were adept at navigating as well as fighting, and could 'manage the whole course of an expedition from the fitting out to the safe delivery of privateers and their prize'.[4] The experience gained by traversing vast distances in the Atlantic along routes extending to the Americas and the Caribbean in the west, or southerly to the Azores Islands, the Canary Islands, or Morocco and its vicinity, was invaluable for the difficult long-distance voyages to the Indian Ocean and beyond.

Privateering also made available resources that could be channelled into financing costly overseas commerce, and it is no coincidence that the EIC was formed just as the war with Spain was drawing to a close. Nor is it surprising that many privateering magnates played an important role in organizing the Company and directing its operations in its formative phase. James Watt, who was governor of the EIC from 1601 onwards and is referred to by Kenneth Andrews, the leading authority on English privateering, as 'the prince of privateering promoters',[5] was an active participant in the commerce-raiding of the last two decades of the sixteenth century, as were many of his other associates, all of whom were London-based merchants. These were the men (101 in all) who came together in September 1599 to petition the privy council, a body that advised the monarch, for exclusive privileges to trade in the East.

Once the queen's 'gracious acceptance of the voyage' was known (she would have been consulted informally), a committee

---

[3]Ibid., pp. 248–49.
[4]Ibid., p. 253.
[5]Ibid., p. 252.

was constituted 'to tender a petition to the privy council, requesting a warrant for the Adventurers to proceed in the voyage ... to prepare a grant of privilege upon such points as shall be reasonable and fit for such a trade'.[6] The proceedings relating to the grant of the charter were briefly suspended due to ongoing negotiations with Spain. Permission to the Company to conduct trade in the East Indies would have undermined the Iberian (Portuguese) monopoly over the all-sea route between Europe and Asia via the Cape of Good Hope. After some delay, and following the failure of the negotiations, the consortium received its charter which was granted in December 1600, with the all-important provision that, 'None of the Queen's subjects, but the Company, their servants, and assigns, [were] to resort to India without the Company's licence upon pain of forfeiting ships and cargoes, half to the Queen and half to the Company, with imprisonment till the offenders give £1,000 bond not to trade thither again.'[7] The charter named '[the] Earl of Cumberland, and two hundred and fifteen knights, aldermen, and merchants', to whom privileges were granted for the 'discovery of the trade for the East Indies'.[8] The charter was valid for fifteen years. It concluded with the stipulation that 'If this charter shall not appear profitable to the crown and realm it may cease after two years' notice; if otherwise, the Queen promises at the end of this term [of fifteen years] to grant the Company a new charter for another fifteen years'.[9]

Arrangements for the inaugural voyage were more or less in place by the time the charter was finalized. The EIC's first fleet consisted of five ships under the overall command of James Lancaster, who was closely associated with Watt and was also one of the original directors of the Company. He

---

[6]W. Noel Sainsbury (ed.), *Calendar of State Papers, Colonial Series, East Indies, China and Japan, Volume 2, 1513-1616*, London: Longman, Green, Longman & Roberts, 1862, pp. 102–03.
[7]Ibid., pp. 117–18.
[8]Ibid., p. 115.
[9]Ibid., p. 118.

had honed his skills in privateering undertakings during the Anglo–Spanish war and had, in the process, acquired the abilities required for leading trans-oceanic expeditions. Moreover, the flagship of the fleet, the *Red Dragon* (initially named *Scourge of Malice* or *Malice Scourge*), was a well-known privateer, as were two other vessels—*Ascension* and *Susan*. The powerful, 600-ton *Malice Scourge* was bought by the fledgling EIC from the Earl of Cumberland, a leading Elizabethan courtier, for £3700; another £1000 were spent on its repair. The ship had been built in 1595 and was equipped with thirty-eight guns. The 240-ton *Susan* had been purchased from Paul Bayning for £1600 on the condition that it would be bought back by him for £800 on its return.

The fleet, which set sail from England in April 1601, confined its trading activities mainly to the Indonesian archipelago (Acheh and Pariaman in Sumatra and Bantam in Java). The ships procured spices, including pepper and cloves, from Indonesian markets, plundered a Portuguese ship, which provided some cotton textiles for purchasing spices in Bantam, and returned to England in 1603. The cargo of pepper unloaded by these ships caused a glut in the London market, thereby depressing prices of the commodity, although the Company did manage to earn some profit. The profit was sufficiently attractive for the EIC's stockholders to continue investing in the Eastern trade. For the time being, however, the inadequate demand for pepper, combined with the outbreak of plague in London, made it difficult for the EIC to raise sufficient capital for sending another expedition to the Indian Ocean. It had already squandered some of its resources in sponsoring a voyage to discover a north-western route to the East Indies. The Company had been approached by a navigator named George Weymouth with a proposal to organize a voyage to search the hitherto elusive sea route to East Asia ('Cathay') through the northern extremity of North America. Given the enormous length of the all-sea route via the Cape of Good Hope and the control that the Portuguese exercised over it, the directors of the Company were prepared to finance Weymouth's exploratory journey. The expedition was a failure.

The Cape route had been used regularly by the Portuguese for the Europe–Asia trade since the successful voyage of Vasco da Gama from Lisbon to the Malabar coast, and back, in 1497–99. Once da Gama's ships had demonstrated the feasibility of the Cape route, the Portuguese crown had established a monopoly over it. This monopoly was enforced by violent means. Portuguese ships were heavily armed, and the crews could be deployed to conduct warfare, engage in piracy, attack, and capture ships, and plunder the cargo. This had an adverse impact on traditional Asian sea-borne commerce. Wherever they were unable to—or did not seek to—supplant Asian traders, they attempted to earn revenues from the trade by levying duties. Vessels had to obtain a pass (cartaz) to be allowed to ply unmolested. The duty was a form of 'protection' money, guaranteeing that the Portuguese would not harass them and that they would be secure from attacks by hostile ships. The Portuguese had set up a string of fortified outposts extending from Hormuz in the Persian Gulf, to Goa, Daman and Diu on the west coast of India, to Malacca (Melaka) at the entrance of the South China Sea, for controlling sea routes, and their ships patrolled the high seas to regulate shipping in the Indian Ocean. Moreover, the Portuguese monopoly over the Europe–Asia trade through the Cape route implied that European competitors were prevented from partaking a share of it. The Portuguese found it increasingly difficult to enforce the monopoly towards the end of the century. Dutch and English intrusion began to undermine Portuguese control, which, in any case, was not very effective in Southeast Asia.

Between 1601 and 1613, the EIC's voyages were separately capitalized. The outlay on a voyage was exclusively for that voyage alone. Separate accounts would be maintained for each venture, and the books for that venture were closed when the ships returned and the cargo had been sold. The proceeds would be distributed among those shareholders who had subscribed to the voyage after deducting expenses, marking the conclusion of the venture. Every shareholder did not necessarily subscribe to or invest in each voyage. At times, the capital for two voyages might be merged, as happened with the capital for the third and fifth expeditions; the ships of the fourth voyage were lost at sea. The separately capitalized early voyages, with their consecutive serial numbers, began to overlap as the Company endeavoured to send out at least one fleet annually.

The voyages for the years 1609–13 were very profitable, the capital yielding returns between 122 and 234 per cent. In 1613, terminable joint-stocks were instituted. These joint-stocks were for a series of voyages spread over several years, in place of investment in a single voyage as was the initial practice. For instance, the second joint-stock operated for a duration of fifteen years, from 1617 to 1632, and the third joint-stock from 1632 to 1642. The capital could be paid in instalments, for instance, eight equal instalments in the case of the second joint-stock, which were to be paid over eight years (originally, the second joint-stock was to last for eight years). The accounts would be settled at the end of the series, and a fresh series would be set in motion.

A permanent joint-stock came into existence only as late as 1657. This is when 'The New General Stock' was formed, coinciding with the grant of a fresh charter to the Company under the Protectorate. The 'Protectorate', established under the leadership of Oliver Cromwell ('lord protector'), is the term used for the regime in England between 1653 and 1659. England was a republic from 1649, the year in which the Stuart king Charles I was executed, to 1660, when the monarchy was restored. The EIC's monopoly over trade between England and the East Indies had been undermined due to the formation of several competing companies in the years that preceded the establishment of the Protectorate. The 1657 charter restored the monopoly, and the stock of the rival companies was merged with that of the EIC. The merged general stock (the permanent joint-stock) lasted till 1709, when the 'old' or original London

Company was united with another competitor, the 'new' or English EIC, which had begun to challenge the monopoly status of the London EIC in the last quarter of the seventeenth century. Some very tricky financial adjustments had to be carried out to protect the interests of stockholders of the two companies. The amalgamation led to the formation, in 1708–09, of the United Company of Merchants of England Trading to the East Indies. Henceforth, this was the entity that would operate in the East Indies, going on to create an empire in India, which it governed till 1858.

∽

In August 1611 the *Globe*, yet another EIC ship, arrived on the Coromandel Coast. It sailed past Nagapattinam (in present-day Tamil Nadu), where the Portuguese had a settlement, and proceeded northward along the coast, briefly halting at Pulicat (also in Tamil Nadu). The *Globe* had reached the Bay of Bengal after an uneventful journey lasting seven months. It was the EIC's second ship to reach India and the first to seriously engage in trade in the subcontinent for an extended period. Six Asian voyages (including that of the *Hector*) had preceded it, making the trading expedition of the *Globe* the seventh 'adventure', as these expeditions were then called.

When the EIC's agents first began their activities in India, they had to concurrently deal with the Mughal authorities, officials of Golconda, and those of Vijayanagara, depending on the part of the subcontinent where they were operating. It is at times assumed that they only had to deal with Mughal officialdom, whereas their contacts with Golconda and Vijayanagara were vital when they first made their appearance. Surat was the leading Mughal port in the early seventeenth century, while Pulicat was a Vijayanagara port. Masulipatam (Machilipatnam in present-day Andhra Pradesh), where the EIC established its first factory on the Indian subcontinent, was part of the Golconda kingdom. A factory refers to a complex for conducting trade. It would have an office, warehouses, and living quarters for European employees. The Portuguese, whose presence on India's west coast and the Coromandel dated back to the early years of the sixteenth century, were quite well-entrenched in these areas by the time the EIC made its appearance a century later. It required time and effort to overcome the hurdles created by them. This was the case in Surat, where Portuguese connections with local officials made things difficult for the English. We have already noted that the Portuguese exercised control over Nagapattinam, for which reason the *Globe* had by-passed this port in the Vijayanagara territory, making its way northward along the coast. They also had a settlement in Pulicat at the northern extremity of Tamil Nadu, since the early sixteenth century. The Dutch, in turn, had just acquired a toehold at this port (in 1609–10) when the EIC tried to obtain permission for trading there. In fact, the Dutch East India Company (VOC, Verenigde Oostindische Compagnie, i.e., United East India Company), which was incorporated two years after the EIC (in 1602), was already ahead of the latter at the time of its foray into the Bay of Bengal.

Dutch endeavours to open up trade with Asia via the Cape of Good Hope preceded those of the EIC by a few years. In 1595, an exploratory expedition was sent to Asia by a company based in Amsterdam. The expedition's fleet of four ships was commanded by Cornelis de Houtman and was destined for the Indonesian archipelago. Here it combined senseless violence, especially on the island of Madura adjacent to Java, with the purchase of some spices. The violence was unprovoked, was not directly related to the purchase of spices, and can be seen as an attempt to generally intimidate Asian seafarers and traders. Three of the four ships returned with their cargo in 1597. Even though the sale of goods brought back by the fleet did not yield much profit, the expedition did demonstrate the feasibility of successfully conducting trade using the Cape route by challenging the Portuguese monopoly. Whereas in the historiography on Dutch seaborne trade the voyage of Houtman is regarded as a landmark event, contemporary Javanese sources do not mention this encounter. Nevertheless, the Dutch sailors seem to have misbehaved at most of the royal courts where they appeared, giving rise to widespread antagonism, which they countered with armed force. This was to remain the norm for the VOC, as it had been for the Portuguese, which in turn would be the path followed by the EIC. Between 1595 and 1602, sixteen exploratory expeditions were launched by companies based in Amsterdam, Rotterdam, Middelburg, and other places in the Netherlands. These companies, which existed for the duration of a venture, were liquidated after the ships returned, the commodities were sold, and the accounts had been settled.

Among the causes of the war between England and Spain was military intervention by Catholic Spain in the Netherlands, primarily to stamp out Protestantism but for political reasons as well. The Netherlands was predominantly Protestant, its Protestantism deeply influenced by Calvinism. English support to the Dutch was partly actuated by its own commitment to Protestantism.

The Anglo–Spanish War provided opportunities for Dutch merchants to attempt to procure Asian commodities directly, rather than relying on the Portuguese as they had done hitherto. Moreover, Spanish occupation of Portugal, the upheavals of war, and the decline of Antwerp as the pre-eminent commercial centre of north Europe disrupted existing supply networks. Amsterdam greatly benefitted from the decline of Antwerp, replacing it as the commercial capital of north Europe. The financial infrastructure now available in the city facilitated the mobilization of capital for equipping voyages to Asia. These developments coincided with the spurt in information in the Netherlands about sea-routes linking Europe and Asia, about spice markets, and political conditions in regions where trade could be carried on. A lot of the critical information about these matters had been jealously guarded by the Portuguese, who did not allow potential competitors to have access to it for most of the sixteenth century. In this context, a key work that appeared in 1595–96 was the famous *Itinerario* of Jan

Huyghen van Linschoten, published in Amsterdam. The work consists of three distinct books.

Van Linschoten, who was of Dutch origin, had moved to Spain as a young boy against the backdrop of the prevalent state of unrest in the Netherlands, and subsequently found a job as an assistant or scribe in the establishment of the archbishop of Goa. This allowed him to spend five years in Goa. While in Goa, he was able to assemble a vast amount of information about Portuguese commerce in Asia, including sea routes, ports, and political and social conditions, both from the documents and classified nautical maps to which he had access due to his connections with the establishment of the archbishop, as well as through his conversations with seafarers and traders who visited Goa. The second book of the three-part *Itinerario*, entitled *Reys-gheschrift* ('Travel Account'), contains vital information relating to sea routes and navigation and is largely a compilation of extracts from Portuguese texts that van Linschoten appears to have copied in Goa while employed in the archbishop's office. It is for this reason, namely the hard information it contained, that the *Reys-gheschrift* was the first to be printed. The print version was made available in 1595, just in time for the departure of the fleet commanded by Houtman, for which its contents served as a valuable guide. The two other books of *Itinerario* were published in the following year.

One startling fact revealed by van Linschoten was that the Portuguese position in Southeast Asia was not very strong. This was precisely the region in which the Dutch were to concentrate their activities. The Indonesian archipelago in Southeast Asia was the main source of spices, namely, pepper, cloves, nutmeg, and mace, sought by European traders. The production of the last two was confined to the tiny Banda Islands, while the Moluccas or Maluku (also known as the Spice Islands) produced cloves. The VOC eventually limited the cultivation of cloves to just two small islands in the Moluccas, Amboyna/Ambon and Ternate, eliminating its production in other parts of the Spice Islands. It also took control of the Banda Islands, brutally crushing local resistance by virtually wiping out the entire population. Pepper was grown quite widely in Southeast Asia and on the Malabar Coast, and the Dutch never managed to acquire a monopoly over it, though they did succeed in taking over the major producing areas.

Without the aid of van Linschoten's information, it would not have been easy for the early Dutch mariners to undertake their oceanic journeys to the east. This is also true of the English pioneers. In its historical consequences, the publication of *Itinerario* was a great misfortune for Asian people, whose colonization was speeded up by the information it disseminated. An English translation of the work, published in London, came out in 1598. English voyages of the early 1590s to the East Indies had not been successful and had been beset by problems due to insufficient information. These voyages included an expedition of James Lancaster in 1591–94, which ended in disaster. On the other hand, Lancaster's first voyage for the EIC, commencing in 1601 after the publication of *Itinerario*, was successful; the instructions given to him were quite precise. Whereas the importance of van Linschoten's *Itinerario* for the progress of English sea-borne commerce in Asia via the Cape can hardly be exaggerated, Andrews has pointed out that the 'deplorable record' of the 1590s was indicative not only of 'the inadequacies of English shipping and seamanship in the late sixteenth century', but also of 'a certain lack of interest in the establishment of a commercial sea-link with the East'.[10] Privateering in the Atlantic Ocean and the plunder of Spanish treasure were more attractive options. The current demand for spices too was limited. Supplies obtained through trading links with Europe and with Turkey (the older, eastern Mediterranean route was not abandoned) were adequate for the English market. Interest in the writings of van Linschoten waned during the seventeenth century as knowledge about sea-routes and commercial intelligence rapidly accumulated in the

---

[10]Andrews, *Trade, Plunder and Settlement*, p. 237.

early decades, rendering the *Itinerario* somewhat redundant and showing it to be inaccurate in many instances. Yet the work had played a key role in breaking the Portuguese stranglehold over the Europe–Asia seaborne trade in the years between its publication and the end of the first decade of the seventeenth century.

The Houtman expedition was followed by another Dutch shipping venture under the direction of Jacob Corneliszoon van Neck. This venture occupies an important place in the history of the formative phase of Dutch and English trades and colonial expansion. The fleet commanded by van Neck had eight vessels. It embarked on its journey in 1598 with instructions to proceed to the Indonesian archipelago. After passing the Cape of Good Hope, van Neck's ship and two other vessels of the fleet were separated from the other ships during a storm and had to seek shelter on the east coast of Madagascar. The other five ships, under van Neck's lieutenant Wybrand van Warwijck, took a detour and landed on the coast of Mauritius. Subsequently, Mauritius would become one of the halting stations for Dutch ships, even as the Cape emerged as the principal station, on the route between the Netherlands and Asia. Mauritius, like the Cape, was used for replenishing supplies for the long oceanic journeys to and from the Netherlands. Van Warwijck's landing marked the beginning of the process that led to the depletion of the island's natural resources, with disastrous consequences for its environment. The elimination of several species of animals that occurred as a result, is exemplified by the extinction of the flightless dodo (*Raphus cucullatus*) within a few decades of van Warwijck's stopover in Mauritius.

The fleet was reunified at Bantam after a few months. Half the fleet then returned to Europe with its cargo of spices in mid-1599. The remaining four ships went further east to the Moluccas and the Banda Islands, and after obtaining supplies of cloves, nutmeg, and mace, two of the ships reached Amsterdam in May 1600, and two in August. The goods brought back by the ships together realized a profit of 300–400 per cent after costs had been deducted. This was regarded as an outstanding commercial achievement, and soon, several more Dutch fleets were sent out to trade in Asia, totalling fourteen fleets by 1602. The remarkable success of the expedition aroused great interest in England. Van Neck's journal (daily register) of the voyage was quickly translated into English by William Walker and published in 1601. The journal attributed to van Neck was 'based on two anonymous journals kept on two of the ships that remained in the East Indies (returning in 1600) after van Neck himself had sailed home in 1599'.[11] Walker's translation was dedicated to Thomas Smythe, the first governor of the EIC. The text would have been available to Lancaster and his fellow mariners before they set out on their voyage. The 1599 petition of London merchants addressed to the privy council contains several references to the recently-arrived ships of the Dutch second voyage (the four vessels that reached Europe in July 1599). It states that the petitioners, 'induced by the success of the voyage performed by the Dutch nation, and being informed that the Dutchmen prepare for a new voyage, and to that end have bought divers[e] ships in England, were stirred up with no less affection to advance the trade of their native country than the Dutch merchants were to benefit their commonwealth, and have resolved to make a voyage to the East Indies'.[12] Significantly, the first batch of the expedition's ships had returned home a few weeks before the petition was drafted, and the remaining ships returned a few weeks before the EIC was granted its charter.

The Dutch fleets sent out between 1595 and 1602 were put together by several short-lived companies formed during the period. These were forerunners of the VOC. The Houtman and van Neck voyages were, for instance, organized by the

---

[11]Anthony Payne, 'Hakluyt and the East India Company: A Documentary and Bibliographical Review', *Journal of the Hakluyt Society*, February 2021 (online), p. 48n166.
[12]'Minutes of an "Assembly of the Directors of the voyage" [to the East Indies]', 25 September 1599, Sainsbury (ed.), *Calendar of State Papers, 1513-1616*, p. 102.

Verre Company (or Compagnie van Verre, 'Far Distant Lands Company'). The companies undertook the entire range of activities relating to each voyage: procuring and equipping ships, recruiting crews, mobilizing and managing finances, purchasing silver for buying commodities in Asia, selling the cargo upon the return of the fleet, and distributing the proceeds from these sales to shareholders. Shareholders were required to pay cash up front, and their liability was limited to the extent of their investment. Once the account books for these initial voyages were closed, the company would cease to exist. These business concerns avoided investment in fixed capital. The assets created while a venture was in progress would be disposed of when the company was wound up. The actual management of the company was entrusted to its directors, who charged fees for looking after the affairs of the company while a venture was in progress. A subsequent voyage would be a fresh undertaking with similar arrangements. Both the VOC and the EIC operated on the same principles during the early years of their existence, with the difference that they were not wound up at the end of a single voyage. Unlike the EIC, which was a cohesive corporation of London-based merchants, the VOC had a more complex structure, allowing the participation of investors from several parts of the country, and reflected the peculiar constitutional features of the Netherlands.

The Netherlands was a republic at this time, a confederation of seven provinces formally known as the Republic of the United Netherlands. As a political entity, the Republic of the United Netherlands (or Seven United Netherlands) lasted for nearly two centuries, c.1580s–1790s. Today, the Netherlands is a constitutional monarchy. Before the 1790s, as a republic, it was governed by a federal assembly, the States-General, with the constituent provinces being virtually autonomous. The States-General may be regarded as the central governing organ of the republic. Given the chaotic situation created by the extraordinarily large number of competing commercial voyages to Asia at the turn of the seventeenth century, which had led to a glut in the Dutch spice market and pushed up prices in Asia, measures were initiated under the supervision of the States-General to form a company that would bring together the numerous businesses engaged in the trade. These initiatives culminated in the formation of the VOC in 1602. The Company consisted of six chambers, each representing those cities in which the early companies had been based, namely, Amsterdam, Rotterdam, Zeeland, etc. Each of these chambers had its own managerial organization headed by its own board of directors. The overall supervision and management of the Company was placed in the hands of a central body of seventeen directors, the 'Heeren Zeventien' or Heeren XVII (Gentlemen Seventeen). The VOC's business was apportioned among the six chambers according to a fixed formula by which Amsterdam had half the share, Zeeland had one quarter, and the rest one-sixteenth each.

The VOC was established through a charter given to it by the States-General. This gave it a monopoly over the trade between the Netherlands and Asia for twenty-one years, as well as authority to administer its settlements, fortify them, engage in war, and negotiate treaties. In other words, the Company had quasi-governmental powers, a feature common to monopoly trading concerns of this era. The EIC, too, had attributes of sovereignty. The States-General retained the power to monitor the Company's affairs and intervene in them as and when required. Besides, the Heeren XVII directors were closely associated with the States-General, and there was a close link between the Company and the government, a link which gave a growing number of investors the confidence to buy the VOC's shares. The first set of overlapping voyages was to run for ten years, at the end of which, the capital was to be returned to the shareholders, who had the option of investing their capital again for the remaining years of the monopoly. The uncertainties of the undertaking prompted such a stipulation. As we have seen, the EIC's charter provided for its cessation with two years' notice should the ventures turn out to be unprofitable. It was difficult to predict at the outset whether the companies would be profitable in the long run. It took the EIC more than half a century to stabilize its finances, by which time the VOC was already the dominant force in Asian waters.

England and the Netherlands were on the same side during the Anglo–Spanish conflict, and England continued to be sympathetic to the Dutch cause at the beginning of the seventeenth century in the struggle against Spain. Yet, the VOC and the English company were engaged in a fierce and violent conflict for several decades in Asia. The VOC had the upper hand in this conflict and was able to exclude the EIC from Southeast Asia. There was much that the EIC learnt from the practices of the Dutch, especially the aggressiveness with which they enforced their monopoly, and involvement in the intra-Asian trade, profits from which could be used for purchasing goods for the European trade. Initially, the Dutch were reluctant to have a confrontation with the English in Asia due to their ongoing conflict with Spain, but it became difficult to avert a confrontation since the policy of the VOC, from the late 1610s onwards, was to maintain high profit levels by preventing European rivals from having any access to Indonesian spices. It ruthlessly resorted to armed force to achieve this objective.

To begin with, the VOC's immediate priority was to dislodge the Portuguese. The first few fleets were specifically instructed to attack Portuguese ships while proceeding to the Indian Ocean. The Portuguese were already in a vulnerable position by the end of the sixteenth century. Their ability to regulate the seaborne traffic of the Indian Ocean had declined, and their pepper trade was facing a crisis by the end of the century. The situation worsened with the regular unloading of Dutch (and English) pepper cargoes, which pushed down prices and ended the dependence of European distributors on Portuguese pepper. The English and the Dutch both had an interest in ending the Portuguese monopoly, and in the 1620s they collaborated to oust the Portuguese from their strategically located stronghold of Hormuz in the Persian Gulf. It is not surprising that the VOC had to spend a large proportion of its capital on military operations, so much so that some of its shareholders in Amsterdam were concerned about the implications of continuous warfare for their fortunes. Eventually, the VOC supplanted the Portuguese, established its monopoly over the Cape route, closed Southeast Asian producing areas to European rivals, and disrupted traditional maritime trading networks with its extensive involvement in intra-Asian trade. The inroads made by the English company, in the face of Dutch hostility, and its successful intrusion in Indian markets—where Dutch stakes were not as high as in Southeast Asia—contributed to weakening the VOC's influence by the closing decades of the seventeenth century, creating historical conditions for the EIC to widen the scope of its activities in Asia, centred on the Indian subcontinent.

∽

Among the diverse tasks that personnel aboard the EIC's ships (these ships came to be referred to as 'East Indiamen') had to perform were diplomatic, political, and military functions. This was especially true in the seventeenth century when the Company was still developing its commercial networks. The ship's captain was expected to combine maritime expertise with business acumen, military abilities, and a basic grasp of politics and diplomacy. Experienced captains would already have acquired mercantile knowledge through earlier seafaring ventures. This would be augmented by relevant Company records. These records accumulated with time as the voyages proceeded, making the archive richer and the information more precise. Trade, however, involved negotiating with authorities of Asian states, which in this period were in a position to withhold consent for commercial dealings or special privileges and to enforce discipline if there was any attempt to disregard their injunctions. Consequently, the success of an expedition depended to a large extent on the captain's talent for diplomacy. Lancaster's account of his visit to Acheh (present-day Aceh, Indonesia) in the journal for the first voyage describes in minute detail the courtly ceremonial amidst which Elizabeth's letter addressed to the sultan of Acheh was delivered. The account demonstrates familiarity with the main aspects of the sultanate's diplomatic protocol. Lancaster's audience with the sultan was preceded by lengthy deliberations with court officials, during which the credentials of Lancaster and his associates were verified; the purpose for seeking audience with the sultan was ascertained, and some of the initial formalities were taken care of. Incidentally, the English were assisted in their preliminary dealings with the court by two Dutch merchants who were temporarily residing in the town to purchase goods. A representative of the English delegation was then sent to the sultan to request permission for Elizabeth's letter to be presented to him by the captain: 'This messenger was very kindly entertained by the king who when he had deli[v]ered his message gladly granted his request, and communed with him about many questions: and after caused a royall [sic.] banquet to be made him.'[13] A robe of honour was conferred on him before he was dismissed. Subsequently, an official of the court had a meeting with Lancaster and demanded to see the superscription of the letter. He seems to have been satisfied after examining the superscription, 'he read the same, and looked very earnestly upon the seale, tooke a note of the superscription, and did likewise write her ma[j]esties [sic.] name.'[14] The official had initially suggested that the letter be handed over to him to be transmitted to the sultan. The suggestion was unacceptable as, according to Lancaster, he was authorized only to deliver it himself directly to the ruler.

The commander had convinced the court that he was the emissary of an eminent royal personage and was therefore eligible for an audience with the sultan, and entitled to ceremonial which accorded with his status. An important device for expressing the high status of the bearer of the royal letter

---

[13]Clements R. Markham (ed.), *The Voyages of Sir James Lancaster to the East Indies...*, etc., London: Hakluyt Society, 1877, p. 75.
[14]Ibid., p. 76.

was the design and style of the letter itself. Miles Ogborn has drawn attention to the care that was taken to produce such letters. The object itself had to be impressive:[15]

> This was a matter of creating a particular sort of valued and valuable object through the combination of a heraldic writing style, decoration with colourful illuminated borders, elaborate capitals and gold lettering, and the appropriate parchment fixed with the authenticating and authorizing armoury of the royal signature and seals. These letters were objects whose materiality was meant to display their political valence and economic value.

According to Lancaster's journal, the court sent six elephants to convey him and the letter to the palace. The letter was ceremonially carried on the biggest of these elephants, placed in a basin of gold, and covered by a silk cloth. Following consultations spread over several days, the English were granted permission to trade on a recurring basis.

The inaugural contact with Surat during the third EIC voyage in 1608, mentioned at the beginning of this chapter, was essentially of a diplomatic nature. Shortly after the *Hector* arrived at the port, the commander of the ship, William Hawkins, proceeded to Agra to deliver the letter sent for the Mughal emperor by Elizabeth's successor, James I (r. 1603–1625). The letter was addressed to Akbar, 'Kinge of Cambaya or Suratt', the EIC's officials not having learnt of Akbar's death (in 1605) at the time of drafting it. Meanwhile, the *Hector* sailed onwards to Bantam. Hawkins's antecedents are obscure, and nothing is known of his experience as a navigator or merchant. The EIC's records suggest that he was chosen primarily for his supposed diplomatic capabilities, including his familiarity with the Turkish language and court protocol. Hawkins reached Agra in April 1609 and stayed in the Mughal dominions for about

---

[15]Miles Ogborn, 'Writing Travels: Power, Knowledge and Ritual on the English East India Company's Early Voyages', *Transactions of the Institute of British Geographers*, Vol. 27, No. 2, 2002, p. 160.

two and a half years, during which he repeatedly petitioned emperor Jahangir (r. 1605–1627) for the grant of a farman (royal decree) that would allow the Company to regularly trade at Surat. The permission was withheld, and the request for a reply to James's letter was declined. On the whole, however, he was treated courteously and with considerable generosity at the court. Hawkins left Agra towards the end of 1611, departed from Surat in January 1612, and travelled to England via Bantam, but was not destined to return home. He died in 1613, shortly before the ship carrying him from Bantam to England reached its final destination.

It would take the Company another five years to acquire a stable presence in Surat. A factory was initially established there in 1613, which made some headway in trade largely due to the efforts of Thomas Aldworth, the agent who held charge of it. Aldworth was modestly successful despite complications created by the violent actions of English ships in the Arabian Sea mainly directed against the Portuguese. This was a show of strength intended to threaten the Portuguese and impress the Mughals. Several Indian vessels were caught in the crossfire between the EIC and the Portuguese, including a prestigious Mughal ship belonging to a leading member of the royal family. The dislocation caused by the Company's intrusion made local Mughal authorities wary of dealing with the English. This would have been at the cost of their largely cordial relationship with the Portuguese, a relationship marked by ups and downs since the Mughal annexation of Gujarat in 1573. At the same time, the English were able to demonstrate their superior naval strength in confrontations with the Portuguese. This made a section of Mughal officials receptive to the EIC's request for permission to trade at Surat. It is worth emphasizing that Portuguese power in the Indian Ocean was beginning to decline in the last quarter of the sixteenth century.

In 1614, the EIC decided to organize what its directors hoped would be seen as a high-powered diplomatic mission to the Mughal court. It was felt that sending a 'mere merchant' might not be the best way to negotiate an agreement with the Mughals for trading privileges. Following a lengthy debate among key functionaries of the EIC, it was resolved to request James I to extend his support to the project. The Company was to bear the expenses and pay the salary of the emissary deputed for the purpose. Some of the directors had expressed their reservations over involving the king in the matter as they feared this might open the way for royal intervention in the Company's affairs. Eventually, a consensus was reached on the issue, and the search began for a suitable person.

Thomas Roe, the person finally chosen as envoy, came from a background quite different from that of the navigators and merchants employed by the Company for its routine diplomatic and political dealings in Asia. Roe had been linked to the royal court since the time of Elizabeth, and the association continued under her successor. He was well educated and had recently entered Parliament as a member of the House of Commons. He had some experience of seafaring and travel, having sailed to South America and explored its coast. Roe was facing financial problems when the EIC approached him for the undertaking, and he readily agreed to its request. James I approved of the choice made by the directors, and the court provided the necessary diplomatic documents of state, including the letter of credence and, most importantly, James's letter addressed to the Mughal emperor. Roe was travelling aboard the Company's ship as its employee, performing also the role of commercial representative of the king of England. It was made clear that he would have nothing to do with the commercial aspects of the voyage or anything related to the navigation of the fleet, nor would he engage in trade on his own account. Considering his high rank as the bearer of the king's letter, this created a somewhat anomalous situation in terms of the order of precedence. The expedition was commanded by William Keeling, who was admiral of the third EIC voyage that had brought the *Hector* to the shores of India's west coast. He seems to have shown proper deference to the emissary, while the latter refrained from any kind of interference so that the journey was completed smoothly. Roe departed from England in February 1615, arrived at Surat in September, and reached Ajmer at the end of the year. The emperor was holding court at Ajmer at this time, and Roe was granted an audience in January 1616. He stayed on in the Mughal dominions till February 1619, returning home without having obtained the trade 'capitulations' that would have given the Company special trading concessions for an extended period of time.

The EIC was seeking 'capitulations'—formal agreements that would allow it to trade freely within the Mughal empire on the payment of customs duties at concessional rates. It was also seeking permission to establish factories. The award of 'capitulations' referred to the practice in the Ottoman empire of granting some privileges to non-Ottoman European merchants, which entitled them to reside and trade in the Ottoman territories. The 'capitulations' (ahdname) were usually in the form of formal agreements with European states or their representatives that granted these privileges and allowed the merchants to be governed by their own respective laws. The French were granted their first capitulations by the Ottomans in 1569, the English obtained them initially in 1580, and the Dutch in 1612; the Venetians had long traded in the Ottoman territories on the basis of capitulations. These capitulations were renewed from time to time, at times with additional stipulations. The English, for instance, could trade by paying customs duties at the rate of 5 per cent. Subsequent capitulations reduced the tariff to 3 per cent. The capitulations could be supplemented by farmans issued for specific purposes. The ahdnames and farmans constituted the legal framework within which traders of European states operated in Ottoman territories. The capitulations, with their provisions for extraterritorial jurisdiction, were to play a major role in undermining the Ottoman state from the late seventeenth century onwards.

While the Mughal authorities were willing to issue farmans that would allow the Company to carry on its commercial activities, Roe soon realized that there was no possibility of getting the court to agree to 'Articles of treaty on equall tearms [sic.]', i.e., on terms of equality.[16] Things worked differently in the Mughal empire. The farmans themselves required complicated negotiations and intense lobbying. Roe finally managed to secure two farmans. One of them granted the English general permission to trade within the Mughal dominions. This did not imply that they could carry on trade anywhere they wished to in the empire. Rather, it was understood that Surat was to be their main place of business. We do not know more about the provisions of this farman. The second farman related specifically to the port of Surat and was negotiated through Khurram (who would succeed Jahangir in 1628 as Shah Jahan). The Company, according to the terms of this farman, could engage in commercial activities at the port; it was exempted from paying tolls and could maintain a factory but could not buy or build any structure for the purpose. Moreover, the EIC's servants would be subject to their own laws, within certain parameters. No duties were to be levied on the import of jewels. Subject to several restrictions, a few Company personnel could carry arms. Roe had to give a written undertaking stating that the arms-bearing personnel would not pose any threat to the residents of Surat.

In the detailed journal he maintained of his voyage and his stay at the Mughal court, Roe projected himself as having been accorded a high status by Jahangir along with the recognition of his position as the ambassador of James I. This was only partially correct. It has been pointed out that Roe does not receive any mention in the emperor's memoirs, the *Jahangirnama*. On the other hand, the visual evidence from Jahangir's reign suggests that Roe's sojourn did not go entirely unnoticed. There is a well-known painting from c.1616 portraying a court scene in which Roe is depicted as

---

[16]William Foster (ed.), *The Embassy of Sir Thomas Roe to the Court of the Great Mogul, 1615-1619*, Vol. 2, London: Hakluyt Society, 1899, p. 346.

one of the participants. In yet another famous painting (c. 1615–18) known by the modern title 'Jahangir Preferring a Sufi Shaikh to Kings', attributed to the court painter Bichitr, the representation of James I is based on a portrait presented by Roe to the Mughal emperor. Whereas Roe is absent from the *Jahangirnama*, the visual evidence suggests that there was some interest in him at the court, at least momentarily. It is pertinent that the paintings are contemporary with Roe's stay at the court. The art historian Mehreen Chida-Razvi has presented a nuanced understanding of how the emissary was perceived at the court: 'In the two paintings it is possible to see that there was a curiosity and awareness of the English at Jahangir's court not reflected within the *Jahangirnama*.' She suggests that the embassy had 'an impact on Jahangir's wider world view', perhaps making it somewhat more eclectic.[17]

The Surat factory would grow and flourish in the subsequent decades. It remained the headquarters of the Company's operations on the west coast, to be supplanted by neighbouring Bombay by the end of the century. On the other side of the subcontinent, on the south-east coast, the Company had been operating at Masulipatam since 1611, when the *Globe* was anchored at the port. This became the main base of its commercial activities in the Coromandel till the late 1630s. The first set of merchants sent by the EIC to the Bay of Bengal, travelling aboard the *Globe*, also had to combine commercial with diplomatic and political roles. The ship was commanded by Anthon Hippon, who had been employed by the EIC for its earlier voyages, including the third voyage which had brought Hawkins to Surat. Hippon was employed as master of the *Red Dragon* on that expedition (the fleet of the third voyage consisted of three ships). A ship's master had responsibility for all technical aspects of navigation and steering, and exercised direct control over the crew in matters related to sailing.

---

[17]Mehreen M-Chida-Razvi, 'The Perception of Reception: The Importance of Sir Thomas Roe at the Mughal Court of Jahangir', *Journal of World History*, Vol. 25, No. 2, Issue 3, 2014, p. 284.

The arrangements for the *Globe's* expedition are representative of the care and precision with which the EIC's directors spelt out the functions of the mariners and commercial agents who were entrusted with the management of its voyages. As was the norm, the captain was issued a royal commission which authorized him to exercise control over the crew, gave him disciplinary powers, and the sanction to invoke martial law if necessary. The Company itself had no powers to invoke martial law at this stage. Three principal merchants were appointed for the seventh voyage, the *Globe* expedition. These included two Dutch merchants, Peter Floris and Lucas Atheunis. The proposal for a direct voyage to the Bay of Bengal and thence to several markets in Southeast Asia which were hitherto unexplored by the English, came from these two merchants. Floris and Atheunis had spent a few years on the Coromandel Coast, particularly in Masulipatam, and had traded privately in Southeast Asia. Floris knew some Telugu, the main language spoken in the Masulipatam region, and had visited Golconda city a few years earlier. He and Atheunis had connections with the VOC as well. When we look at their qualifications, 'we are entitled to infer that they formed a well-matched team'.[18] The two were quite knowledgeable about prospects of trade in the East Indies. They had altered their surnames while working for the EIC, perhaps because, in terms of recently introduced Dutch legislation, it was illegal for them to serve an English company operating in Asia. By the end of the 1610s, the EIC itself stopped engaging Dutch employees for its business in the East. To conclude the personal story of Floris, we may mention that he passed away in 1615, two months after his return to England. W.H. Moreland has painstakingly reconstructed the lives and careers of Floris and Atheunis in his introduction to Floris's journal of the voyage. The journal, originally written in Dutch, was translated into

---

[18]W. H. Moreland (ed.), 'Introduction', *Peter Floris: His Voyage to the East Indies in the Globe, 1611-1615*, London: Hakluyt Society, 1934, p. l.

English for perusal by the EIC directors.[19] The biographical details sketched by Moreland are invaluable for illuminating many aspects of the EIC's practices in the first fifteen years of its existence. The journal, like the journals of other voyages, is a product of Company policy to maintain a comprehensive record of each expedition, the business transacted during the voyage, and commercial or political information gathered on every trip. To ensure accuracy, and to guard against the omission of vital details, the key personnel were required to contribute jointly to the drafting of the material. The orders of the directors were:[20]

> That continual and true journals be kept of every day's course and navigation during the whole voyage, with a true relation of everything that passeth, and this not only to be done by the several captains, masters, pilots and masters' mates, but also by the merchants and pursers: and that some of the principals in each ship, may confer together at convenient times, ... to the end that, if any have forgotten, what another observed the same may be added, so as perfect a discourse may be set down to be presented to the Governor and Company, when God shall grant them a safe return, to be kept for better direction of posterity.

Minute attention to detail was essential for organizing a voyage due to the risks involved, and the large investment which each voyage entailed. The expedition would be on its own for two to three years, if not more, before returning home. Therefore, the instructions had to be exhaustive, providing for several eventualities. These would be set out in the commission drawn up by the directors for the commander (also styled as general).

---

[19]This contemporary translation is reproduced with some stylistic changes and extensive annotation in Moreland, *Peter Floris: His Voyage to the East Indies*.
[20]Cited in Richmond Barbour, 'The East India Company Journal of Anthony Marlowe, 1607–1608', *Huntington Library Quarterly*, Vol. 71, No. 2, 2008, p. 269. These instructions were part of the commission for the third voyage. I have used modern spellings and capitalization while citing the text from Barbour.

The commission specified the objectives of the voyage, the route it was to follow, and the places it was to visit; laid down rules and regulations; and established the chain of command. A separate set of documents, each document placed in a sealed box, contained orders for appointing a successor (or subsequent successors) to the commander (or his successor commanders) in case he or they expired during the journey. The procedure was stated in the Company's commission. The boxes were to be opened according to their numerical order and only if such a situation arose. Significantly, according to the instructions given by the directors, Hippon, in his capacity as commander (he was both captain and merchant for the voyage), was to have no say in the actual conduct of business, which was exclusively the concern of the chief merchants, and he was bound by their advice regarding the ship's itinerary in Asia.

Hippon died in July 1612. This required the first box to be opened in the presence of all officers to find out the Company's instructions about the successor. It so happened that the person named as successor, Robert Browne, had already died within a month of the ship's arrival on the Coromandel coast. Therefore, the second box had to be opened. In view of Hippon's expertise as a navigator, no separate master of the ship had been appointed for the *Globe*. The new commander, Thomas Essing, however, required the assistance of a master. It seems that the directors had not foreseen this contingency. The officers, including the merchants and factors who had assembled to learn of the deceased commander's successor, constituted the ship's council according to the provisions of the commission for the voyage. Collectively, they selected the ship's master for the remaining duration of the voyage. It may be mentioned in passing that the commission contained precise instructions for handling money and other belongings left behind by deceased members of the crew.

Essing expired in May 1614 while the ship was at Masulipatam for a second time, after visiting other ports, and was bound homewards. This created a crisis as there were no further instructions regarding the order of succession. In fact, no suitable replacement seemed to be available. The crew urged Floris to take over command of the ship, which he declined for the time being. Quite reluctantly, he named one of his subordinates, John Skinner, as the skipper and got the crew to agree to this arrangement. The problem was that Skinner was in an inebriated state most of the time, while another officer whose name had also been considered for the position was unpopular with the crew. The only other competent person, George Chauncey, was too young. Thus, Floris was henceforth de facto captain of the ship. Realizing that the temporary vacuum at the top had made the crew increasingly unruly and that it needed to be disciplined to avoid trouble for the remaining part of the journey, he decided to mete out harsh punishment to two malcontents. This was an attempt to vigorously enforce his de facto authority. The two sailors had been engaged in a duel, something that was strictly prohibited by the Company. The penalty imposed by Floris almost amounted to an execution. They were sentenced to keel-hauling ('thrice to be drawn under the ship's keel'), after which assuming they survived each of them was 'to be nailed with a knife through their hand at the main mast, and there to stand till they pulled it quite through their hands'; further, they would have to forgo six months' wages.[21] Keel-hauling was a brutal punishment in which the condemned person was suspended overboard by ropes and then passed under the bottom of the ship to be hauled up on the other side. It carried the risk of the person being dashed against the ship's bottom, which could, at times, be fatal. The sentence, however, was not carried out. A high official of the Golconda kingdom posted at Masulipatam interceded on behalf of the condemned men and urged Floris to pardon them, 'wherein I made very great refusal, yet at length being agreed of his

---

[21]Moreland, *Peter Floris: His Voyage to the East Indies*, p. 125. Spellings have been standardized in all quotations from the original text.

great importunities ...I have yielded to it'.[22] This episode firmly established Floris's authority.

As we have already noted, the diplomatic and political functions of the key commercial personnel travelling aboard the *Globe* were as much—if not more—important than buying and selling. Trading was closely intertwined with negotiations with local officials or their superiors and often meant appealing to rulers or members of the royal family for better terms. We find Hippon, Floris, and their associates interacting at all these levels in their endeavour to trade profitably at Masulipatam. Floris's account of the EIC's initial reception on the Coromandel Coast offers us a glimpse of the inner workings of local officialdom in its dealings with overseas traders.

Upon arrival at Pulicat, the ship had been met by two boats—one sent by the shahbandar and the other by inquisitive servants of the VOC. The designation shahbandar had come to be applied by the Portuguese in the sixteenth century to the 'superintendent' of a port in parts of Asia and was used in this sense by the Europeans. From the shahbandar's representatives, the English sought a document promising safe conduct (the document was often simply referred to as a 'safe-conduct') so that some of the EIC men could go ashore to seek permission to trade at the place. Once the safe-conduct had been delivered, the chief merchants proceeded to the town to take care of formalities for commencing their enterprise. They were informed that sanction had to be obtained from the Vijayanagara queen Kondamma, to whom a share of the revenues and port duties of Pulicat had been assigned. Kondamma and Bayamma of the powerful Gobburi family were wives of the Vijayanagara ruler Venkatapati Raya (r. 1585–1614) of the Aravidu dynasty. They jointly controlled the port, with the day-to-day administration being in the hands of Kondamma.[23] The Gobburi family held

---

[22] Ibid., pp. 125–26.

[23]Moreland describes Kondamma as 'the lady appointed as Governor by the Queen who held Pulicat for what may be described as her privy purse'. Moreland, *Peter Floris: His Voyage to the East Indies*, p. 10n4. According to Sanjay Subrahmanyam

sway over Pulicat and its surrounding area.

The Dutch had already obtained an authorization from Venkatapati whereby they had been granted an exclusive right to trade at Pulicat. When the English sought an audience with Kondamma, the shahbandar, who had been cooperative at first, informed them that this would not be possible. Dutch intrigues perhaps had a role in Kondamma's refusal. The English were told that Kondamma could not override the permission granted by Venkatapati to the Dutch and that the king alone could allow them to trade at Pulicat. They were, therefore, advised to go to Vellore, where the royal court was at this time. Since this would have taken up almost two months for an uncertain outcome, it was decided to abandon the attempt to conduct business at the port. Having been formally given leave to depart by the shahbandar, to whom a gift was sent consisting of three yards of cloth and a looking glass, the ship headed for Masulipatam via the port of Petapoli or Peddapalli (in present-day Andhra Pradesh), which lies en route. There is an interesting postscript to the first Pulicat encounter. A few months after the *Globe* returned to Masulipatam (December 1613) following its trip to various Southeast Asian ports, a message was conveyed to the English on behalf of Bayamma, inviting them to trade at Pulicat. They were assured of requisite facilities and the grant of privileges if they would conduct their business at the port. To this message, Floris responded by asking for a safe-conduct, particularly drawing attention to the manner in which the English had been treated at Pulicat on their previous visit. Simultaneously, a representation to this effect was made to the royal court at Vellore. The safe-conduct was issued and sent through four royal messengers who delivered the document along with 'a white cloth where [the king's] own hand is printed

---

and David Shulman, 'the control of customs and other revenues [of Pulicat] was vested by Venkatapati in Bayamma and Kondamma', who 'were wives of Venkatapati'. Sanjay Subrahmanyam and David Shulman, 'The Men Who Would Be King? The Politics of Expansion in Early Seventeenth-Century Northern Tamilnadu', *Modern Asian Studies*, Vol. 24, No. 2, 1990, p. 237.

in sandal or saffron, as also one of the Queen of Pulicat and diverse letters. The king's letter was written upon a leaf of gold'.[24] Floris records that, 'My man Wengali had been in person before the king and spoken to him, the king laying his hand upon his head presenting him with a [gift] so that I am assured that there is no deceit in this'.[25] Unfortunately for the English, while consultations about arrangements for Pulicat were in progress, news arrived of the death of Venkatapati in October 1614. In the upheavals that followed, the VOC was successful in stabilizing its position in Pulicat to the detriment of the EIC's interests. Such was the importance of the port that for a few decades, the Portuguese were engaged in a fierce conflict with the Dutch to evict them, but failed to do so. It became the main centre of the VOC's operations in the Coromandel till 1690, when their headquarters were shifted to Nagapattinam, from where they had dislodged the Portuguese in 1658.

To resume the story of the EIC's initial arrival at Petapoli, since this was a Golconda port, the English now had to deal with Golconda officials. The situation for the Company was more favourable in this kingdom. The merchants promptly received a safe-conduct and were permitted to trade by the 'governor' on the payment of duties at the rate of 3.75 per cent. Browne and Atheunis were to be temporarily stationed in Petapoli while the ship went on to Masulipatam (Browne passed away during his stay here). They were furnished with a bale of cloth, some lead, and 8000 Spanish silver reales or 'pieces of eight', which was the most widely accepted 'foreign' currency in Asia. The proceeds from the sale of the two commodities were to be used, in addition to the silver coins (which were indispensable for the EIC's commercial ventures), for purchasing cotton textiles for southeastern markets where the varieties produced in the Masulipatam region were in great demand. Profits from the trade in these cotton goods would then be invested in the

---

[24]Moreland, *Peter Floris: His Voyage to the East Indies*, pp. 126–27.
[25]Ibid., p. 127.

purchase of spices for the English market.

Cotton manufacturers of northern Coromandel produced an assortment of textiles catering to very specific tastes. Indian traders were well informed about the types that could be sold in a particular region, and the producers were able to fine-tune their designs for the highly diversified market. It took the EIC time to familiarize itself with the intricacies of the trade. While entering into contracts for apparel at Masulipatam, the *Globe* merchants had made a minor error when itemizing the designs for their order, due to which a small portion of their stock remained unsold. They were unable to find buyers for some of their cargo due to a slight deviation in the pattern for a lot intended for one of the markets in the Malay region.

The procedure for acquiring a safe-conduct had to be repeated at Masulipatam. Here, Floris was welcomed by some of his 'old friends', and negotiations commenced to fix the rate of customs duties. The rate agreed to was four per cent, both inwards and outwards, with no further charges. These were the rates fixed for the Dutch in 1606. A council was assembled aboard the vessel to consider a proposal for approaching high officials of Golconda to obtain formal authorization for all English 'ships that should come hereafter with a patent of his Majesty and commission from the Company in London', permitting them to trade at Masulipatam on a regular basis. The proposal was approved, as was the suggestion that a valuable gift be offered for the purpose 'at the general charges of the Company'.[26] Meanwhile, orders had been placed with local weavers for the different types of cloth pieces to be carried to Java and beyond. The ship was to call at Bantam, which was the EIC's principal station in Asia, and then proceed eastwards. Here it was to procure its main cargo of pepper. The sale of textiles brought from Masulipatam and Petapoli was sufficient to recover the reales which had been reserved for pepper purchases in Bantam and which had already been

---

[26]Ibid., p. 15.

used up for the settlement of customs duties in the Coromandel. Masulipatam had a large hinterland with a flourishing agrarian economy of surplus rice production, which sustained the weaving and dyeing industry concentrated in the countryside around the port town. The rise of the port may be dated to the 1580s. Its growth was facilitated by the policies of the Golconda sultanate, especially under Muhammad Quli Qutb Shah (r. 1580–1612), which encouraged shipbuilding and seaborne trade. The financial involvement of members of the royal family and the aristocracy in shipping and in long-distance trade in the Bay of Bengal and the Indonesian archipelago gave an impetus to the growth of commercial networks linking Masulipatam to Southeast Asia. The Narsapur river port, located on the Godavari River, close to Masulipatam, emerged as a major shipbuilding centre by the beginning of the seventeenth century. On its second halt at Masulipatam, the *Globe* was sent to Narsapur for repairs, where over a hundred workers, including twenty-five carpenters and caulkers, were engaged in mending the damaged parts and fixing the leaks it had sprung, and seem to have done their job satisfactorily.

As the ship prepared to depart from the port on its onward journey, there was an ugly incident in which Floris and his associates displayed their readiness to resort to violence in settling disputes with local officials and textile dealers. Their transactions with a key official, the local governor posted at Masulipatam, had led to a disagreement over the repayment of a debt by the official. Floris claimed that the official owed the English 5000 pagodas, the gold currency widely used in the region for such transactions. Once the preparations for departure had been completed, and the ship was scheduled to sail, Floris became desperate. In his desperation to realize the money, he worked out a plan to kidnap 'the Governor or his son'.[27] The crew endorsed the plan, which required bringing firearms ashore, something they were forbidden to do. This was

---

[27]Ibid., p. 133.

indeed a daring scheme considering that the *Globe* was a lone ship in a distant port situated in a powerful kingdom about which the English did not as yet have sufficient information, notwithstanding Floris's stay in the capital city a few years earlier. Such audacity was inconceivable without the experience of maritime plunder and privateering possessed by the crews of English ships. In an angry exchange with the governor before the abduction, Floris had haughtily declared, 'I would show myself to be a captain of the King of England'.[28]

The official's son was captured and taken hostage without much difficulty as the armed guards of the customs house were taken completely by surprise, certainly not expecting such conduct given the tenor of the interaction between local officials and the merchants aboard the ship. The guards tried to intercept the boat in which the boy was being transported and would have succeeded had not the abductors viciously fired at them as they fled to the ship. Nearly three thousand people lined up on the waterfront, helplessly watching the boat escape. Negotiations were soon initiated with the governor, with the principal VOC official on the Coromandel Coast, Wemmer van Berchem, acting as intermediary. Eventually, the matter was resolved amicably. This did not prevent Floris from dispatching an impolite letter to the royal court, 'praying them ... to do [the English] quick justice, or else more evil would follow'.[29] Be that as it may, the Golconda authorities exercised strict control over their premier port and permitted the English and the VOC (which was far more influential and active) to trade at Masulipatam without ceding any territory. The English factory in the town became the EIC's chief commercial establishment on the coast. In the late 1620s, tensions with Golconda officials and Dutch rivalry compelled the Company to shift its commercial activities southwards along the coast, to Armagon (Dugarajapatnam, near Nellore in present-day Andhra Pradesh), and later still to

---

[28]Ibid., p. 135.
[29]Ibid., p. 138.

Madras (now Chennai), which became its main factory in the Coromandel. There was an interlude during which Masulipatam again became the main Coromandel station for a few years. All these factories were subordinate to the headquarters in Bantam.

Since its inception, the Masulipatam factory was able to maintain regular overland communication with the Surat factory and other west coast stations such as Broach (Bharuch). We have several references in Floris's journal to the correspondence between him and Aldworth, who was stationed at Surat. Moreover, English ships calling on the Coromandel Coast had the alternative of sending letters or instructions they might be carrying for Surat across the peninsula using the land route. These links allowed Company personnel to overcome their isolation in the initial years of the EIC's presence in the subcontinent.

The problems which the Company encountered in operating in Masulipatam, Armagon, and some of the other locations where it had agencies, led to the search for a suitable place in the Coromandel for conducting business without too many constraints, and within easy reach of textile manufacturing localities. In 1639, Francis Day, the factor at Armagon, was deputed to survey the area south of Pulicat for identifying such a place (Pulicat is situated south of Armagon). In the report he presented to his superiors after touring the area, Day commended the countryside near the site which would become the city of Madras, for the abundance of cotton weavers and 'painters' (craft workers who created the printed designs on cloth for southeastern markets), and the relatively cheaper supplies there as compared to northern Coromandel. What is more, the chieftain who exercised control over the area was willing to grant privileges to the English. Day had already obtained a document giving concessions to the Company for trading in 'Medrasspatam', and authorizing it to erect fortifications.

During the 1630s, portions of northern Tamil Nadu were ruled by warrior chiefs, or nayakas, of the Damarla warrior clan, which had recently become powerful in the tract. The Damarla nayakas were nominally subject to the authority of the Vijayanagara monarchs. Northern Tamil Nadu along with the adjacent parts of Andhra had become the core area of the kingdom towards the end of the sixteenth century. The dwindling power and eclipse of Vijayanagara during the reign of the Aravidu king Venkata III (r. 1632–42), the penultimate Vijayanagara ruler, provided the English with a favourable opportunity to establish a settlement at Madras. Within a few years, the kingdom would cease to exist. The grant for Madras was negotiated with the Damarla chieftain Venkatadri and his brother Ayyappa, sons of Damarla Chennappa, and brothers-in-law of Venkata. Their keenness to assign a patch of land to the English may have been a reflection of their vulnerability in the area. The original instrument of 1639 was executed by Venkatadri. In the following year, the factory at Armagon was abandoned, with its staff relocating to Madras. Work on the fortifications began forthwith. It was completed in a few years, and the fortified factory was named Fort St George. The fort and the settlement that came up around it grew into the city of Madras. In the 1650s, Madras was upgraded to the status of a presidency (a Company territory governed by a council chaired by a senior official designated as president or governor), and after some further administrative reorganization, it became the EIC's main commercial, administrative, political, and military centre in the subcontinent in the last quarter of the seventeenth century. Madras was superseded by Calcutta after the conquest of Bengal.

༄

On the other side of the subcontinent, Surat had replaced Bantam as the EIC's headquarters in Asia in the 1630s, and till the end of the third quarter of the century, it was the Company's main commercial station in India. The acquisition by the English in the 1660s of the group of islands which collectively came to be known as Bombay, further strengthened their position on the west coast. The islands had been in the possession of the Portuguese since the first half of the sixteenth century. They were transferred by the Portuguese to the English crown in 1665; a few years later, the EIC acquired them from the crown. Between the 1660s and the end of the eighteenth century, this island cluster was transformed from a minor Portuguese outpost to a major English settlement, and eventually a city of great consequence on the western coast of India.

Bombay was one of the several territorial possessions of the Portuguese Estado da Índia on the west coast, lying between Goa in the south and Bassein, Daman, and Diu further north.[30] Portuguese records dating back to 1534, when they formally acquired these islands from the sultan of Gujarat, refer to revenues from three distinct administrative units—Mahim, Bombay, and Mazagaon—which constituted Portuguese Bombay. This administrative organization took into account the peculiar geographical configuration of the island cluster. Most probably, this arrangement was inherited by the Portuguese from the Gujarat sultanate when they took over the islands, and they continued with it. There were three, or by another reckoning four, separate islands comprising Portuguese Bombay: Colaba, Bombay including Mazagaon, Worli, and Mahim. Timothy Riding has recently argued that the notion of seven original islands comprising Bombay was a product of the nineteenth-century historiography of the city, which ignored or was ignorant of the longer history of land reclamation and contestations over Bombay's geography.[31] The Portuguese insisted that the islands were distinct and that only

---

[30]The Portuguese commercial enterprise in Asia was conducted on behalf of the crown by the Casa da Índia, a state organization with headquarters in Lisbon. During the course of the sixteenth century the widely dispersed Portuguese colonial possessions in Asia came to be collectively designated as the Estado da Índia (State of India) with Goa as its headquarters. The Estado da Índia functioned under the supervision of the Casa da Índia.
[31]Tim Riding, "'Making Bombay Island': Land Reclamation and Geographical Conceptions of Bombay, 1661-1728', *Journal of Historical Geography*, Vol. 59, 2018, pp. 27–39.

Bombay proper had been given to the English crown, while the English interpretation emphasized their unity, holding that the area enclosed by the islands was temporarily submerged under water, especially at high tide, but otherwise constituted a single unit. Eventually, the EIC was able to get its way on this question and successfully resisted the prolonged attempt of the Portuguese to assert a claim over the island of Mahim. It may be mentioned that, in the seventeenth century, the Portuguese retained possession of the large island of Salsette, north of Bombay, and Bassein, further north along the coast.

Riding has mainly focused on the dispute between the English and the Portuguese over defining the geography of Bombay. However, there were contestations of a slightly different order involving the Mughals, the Sidis, and the English. During the era of Aurangzeb (1658–1707), the Bombay group of islands was regarded as an appendage of Surat. The Sidi coastal warlords, who were part of the Mughal war machine while retaining a great deal of autonomy, exercised regular or, at times, transitory control over a string of islands along the Bombay coast, including Mazagaon, where their fleet was stationed for a few months annually. A portion of the Bombay cluster was thus part of the Sidi area of operation, even as a Portuguese resident of Bombay, Alvares Peres da Tavora, described as 'lord of Mazagaon,' held the lease for the Mazagaon estate, paying when the EIC took over an annual rental to the Portuguese government for it.[32]

In the 1680s, at a time when the EIC's position on the west coast was still not very secure, it became involved in an armed conflict with the Mughals. The outcome of the conflict was disastrous for the Company, which might have lost Bombay forever. Margaret Hunt's important research has shed light on the consequences of the EIC's misadventure and the erasure of the episode from the historical record. As she notes, the

---

[32]S. M. Edwardes, *The Rise of Bombay: A Retrospect*, Mumbai: Times of India Press, 1902, p. 78.

conflict has 'figured little in histories of the early East India Company, even though it helped precipitate one of the worst crises in the entire history of the Company'.[33]

At the beginning of 1689, the head of the Company's Bombay establishment, the enormously unpopular John Child, ordered an offensive against Mughal shipping in the Arabian Sea, mainly vessels carrying military supplies of grain. This was part of a larger policy of aggressive engagement in the subcontinent dictated by the directors. These attacks called forth harsh measures to curb the Company's piratical raids. The Mughal imperial authorities ordered a blockade of Bombay, resulting in large-scale destruction and depopulation of the settlement. The blockade and occupation of Bombay, lasting for fifteen months—from early 1689 to the middle of 1690—was carried out by a large force led by the Sidi chief, Yaqut Khan, whose main base was the island fortress of Janjira, located off the Konkan coast, south of Bombay. The Europeans and their Indian and Creole Indo-Portuguese dependents were confined to the fortified area at the southern tip of Bombay Island. Many soldiers deserted the Company, going over to Yaqut Khan, further weakening the English. Ultimately, the Company had to surrender unconditionally to the Mughals. Aurangzeb issued orders imposing a huge indemnity as the price for allowing the Company to resume its trade and admonished it for its defiance of Mughal authority.

The English had to approach the emperor as supplicants to plead for pardon. Alexander Hamilton, a participant in the events of 1689–90 and fiercely critical of John Child's leadership, described with considerable glee the humiliation suffered by the Company's representatives at the Mughal court; they were admitted to the emperor's presence, 'their Hands being tied by a Sash before them'. Aurangzeb reprimanded them and then 'pardoned their Faults, on Condition that Mr.

---

[33]Margaret R. Hunt, 'The 1689 Mughal Siege of East India Company Bombay: Crisis and Historical Erasure', *History Workshop Journal*, Vol. 84, Autumn 2017, p. 150.

Child should leave India, in nine Months and never come back again'.[34] Such an order of expulsion relating to the Company's chief functionary affirmed that Bombay was not beyond the scope of the emperor's authority. Whatever the perceptions of the Portuguese or the English, from the point of view of the Mughal state, they had no sovereign rights over the islands. These islands were part of the territories of the Mughal empire. Nevertheless, the Mughal court was not disinclined to consider favourably the Company's application for permission to resume its trade.

The Mughals, the Sidis, and the Marathas all recognized the value of the harbour. Contemporary accounts state that the Sidis were regular visitors to the islands between the 1660s and 1680s. Aurangzeb, too, kept an eye on the islands. It would be difficult to speak of the history of Bombay in this period without reference to the Mughals. Both Hunt and Riding do not appear to attach much importance to the place that Bombay occupied in the regional layout of Mughal territories on the west coast. Hunt seems to suggest that the Mughal action in 1689–90 had nothing to do with Bombay directly; the English on this occasion were merely caught in the Mughal–Maratha crossfire. While engaged in one of its campaigns in the region, the Mughal army had set up camp on the coast close to Bombay. The vessels attacked by the English were carrying supplies for the army, resulting in swift retaliation by the Mughals. As far as the imperial authorities were concerned, the Mughals had not conceded their prerogative to intervene in matters pertaining to Bombay, a prerogative exercised on several occasions, and their interests overrode those of the English. When, for instance, Bombay became the arena of an intra-Sidi feud in the 1670s, again because the imperial fleet was in the Mazagaon harbour, the emperor ordered that command of the naval force be handed over to Yaqut Khan, and the incumbent Sidi chief had to comply

---

[34]Alexander Hamilton, *A New Account of the East Indies*, Vol. 1, New Delhi: Asian Educational Services, 1995 p. 224.

promptly. Aurangzeb intervened decisively to ensure that no harm was caused to the imperial fleet.

The balance of power shifted decisively in the first quarter of the eighteenth century, making it easier for the Company to ignore the Mughal court. The English utilized the location of Bombay and the advantages of its excellent harbour to expand its seaborne trade. With prudent management of the somewhat limited resources of the islands, the Company gradually built an infrastructure in the eighteenth century that attracted merchants, shipwrights, artisans, sailors, and other migrants to the settlement. Bombay also changed spatially due to a long process of reclaiming land from the sea and filling of swamps, in the course of which the group of islands became the city of Bombay. Till 1687, the EIC's affairs in western India were governed by a council based in Surat. The headquarters was shifted to Bombay in 1687. This administrative reorganization marked the beginning of the Bombay presidency. All the establishments of the EIC in western India henceforth became part of this presidency.

∽

In eastern India, the EIC, following in the footsteps of the VOC, had set up factories in Orissa (present-day Odisha) in the early 1630s, at Hariharpur (Jagatsinghpur) on a tributary of the Mahanadi River, and another at Balasore. Shortly thereafter, its operations extended to Bengal. The Company established a factory at the port of Hugli in 1651. By the end of the century, it had acquired talluqdari or revenue collection rights over three villages located near Hugli. From 1690 onwards, these villages—Sutanuti, Govindapur and Kalikata—became the base of their commercial activities in the Mughal suba (province) of Bengal. The villages were to be the site of their headquarters in eastern India, Fort William. The fort (named after William III, better known as William of Orange) and the settlement around it grew into the city of Calcutta (present-day Kolkata). Calcutta was also made a presidency and later became the capital of the Company's empire. During the Mughal campaign of the late 1680s against the EIC, its establishment had been ejected from Bengal for disobeying the orders of the subedar (provincial governor) pertaining to trade. The Company's servants claimed general exemption from the payment of customs duties and other charges for goods entering via factories in Orissa and Bengal, whereas, according to Mughal stipulations, they were exempted from the payment of customs duties only if these had already been paid at Surat. Since some of the Mughal officials, including high nobles who had their own commercial interests, had earlier acquiesced in the EIC's evasions, accepting its erroneous interpretations of farmans or parwanas/nishans (orders issued by superior officials or nobles) in this matter, the Company had frequently managed to avoid these duties and now insisted on continuing with the practice. The situation changed when the imperial court expressed its displeasure over the laxity shown by its Bengal officials. Firm instructions were issued for compliance with its orders, making local connivance increasingly difficult. The Company's persistent refusal to pay duties on goods which were not exempt and the strict enforcement of the directives of the imperial court caused a breakdown.

The factory at Hugli had to be abandoned, and the staff was forced to move downstream to the village of Sutanuti. At the same time, the Company launched a naval offensive for the capture of Chittagong, located further east along the coast, in 1688. The directors had devised a scheme for constructing a fortified factory in Chittagong, which would be the headquarters of the Company in Bengal. Dacca (present-day Dhaka) in eastern Bengal, situated northwest of Chittagong, was the capital of the suba for most of the seventeenth century. The Company's scheme failed as the English were in no position to oppose the formidable Mughal war machine at this stage, definitely not on land. Eventually, they had to appeal to the Mughal authorities to allow them to continue with their commercial activities in Bengal, and, after negotiations with local officials, were granted permission in 1690 to resume their trade. Sutanuti became the Company's trading station for Bengal goods, primarily cotton textiles and raw silk, for the European market. The assignment of talluqdari rights for Sutanuti was negotiated by Job Charnock, who held charge of the EIC's establishments in Bengal. Charnock has been made famous as the 'founder of Calcutta' through a constant repetition of this assertion in later colonial writings, and continues to be regarded as such in popular writings. In fact, he had merely secured the assignment of revenue rights for Sutanuti. The acquisition of rights for Kalikata, and perhaps Govindapur, took place slightly later, after Charnock's death in 1693. The transfer of talluqdari rights to the Company by the Sabarna Choudhuries, who held the zamindari, or superior rights to the produce of the villages, was approved by the subedar of Bengal, Azim-us-Shan (grandson of Aurangzeb), in 1698. A judgement of the Calcutta High Court in the *Sabarna Roychowdhury Paribar … vs The State of West Bengal and Ors, 2003*, while accepting the report submitted to it by a committee constituted by the court comprising historians to examine the historical evidence relating to the 'founding' of Calcutta and the role of Charnock, noted that it would be difficult to recognize him as its founder, however important he might have been to its early history. The report stated that Charnock could not be called the founder of Calcutta since the emergence of the city was the outcome of a long historical process. Charnock was one among many individuals who had contributed to its genesis. As the city was the product of a historical process, it did not have a 'birthday' or a founder. Moreover, the beginnings of commercial activity in and around the three villages antedated the arrival of the English, which was precisely the reason why the Company's agents found the area suitable for their business.

It should be borne in mind that none of the political entities in the Indian subcontinent, in whose domains the Company had factories/agencies or settlements, had ceded sovereignty to the EIC over the strips of land where these were situated. Colonial historiography frequently obfuscated the details of the early histories of many of these settlements. All three principal English settlements—Madras, Bombay and Calcutta—established during the seventeenth century, stood on territory over which the EIC did not exercise sovereignty.

The beginnings of the Company's presence in Calcutta belong to the phase of its history when the VOC's fortunes were waning. Around the same time, another European company, the French East India Company (Compagnie Française des Indes Orientales), had emerged as the EIC's new rival. The Compagnie was founded in 1664. Within a decade, it had a trading post at Pondicherry (Puducherry) on the Coromandel Coast, a stone's throw away from Madras, and tapped into the same pool of producers in the countryside for cotton textiles as the EIC. Given the expansion of the European demand for cotton textiles produced in eastern India, the French company sent its agents to Bengal to explore the possibilities of trade with the region, and a location was identified on the banks of the Hooghly River for building a warehouse for the purpose. By 1688, permission had been obtained from the provincial Mughal authorities to trade in the region and establish a factory at the site of the warehouse. This was the nucleus of Chandernagore (Chandannagar), which became the chief French factory in Bengal. The Compagnie's trade was flourishing by the 1730s. It had become a profitable concern, carrying more silver to Asia than the EIC for the purchase of goods. Many of the varieties produced for the French company were superior to and more diverse than the types in the English list. Competition had reached a stage where any further breakthrough for either of the two was possible only at the cost of the other. This state of affairs has to be seen in the context of the international conflict between Britain and France over colonial possessions, and their European quarrels. From the early 1740s to the end of the 1750s, the two were engaged in a fierce struggle for supremacy in India. The main arena of the conflict was southern India. It is in the midst of the battles of the 1740s that we first hear of a Company employee, Robert Clive, who was to become notorious for the part he played in the conquest of Bengal.

II

THE ASCENDANCY OF CLIVE

The early career of Robert, Lord Clive, is quite typical of the eighteenth-century Company employees sent out in their teens as copying clerks to the various agencies, factories, and presidencies that the EIC had in the Indian subcontinent. The expansion of its activities necessitated a large workforce in India, for which boys usually aged sixteen to seventeen were recruited in England from among families with connections to the EIC's directors. A position as a 'writer', which was the official designation of these copying clerks—who spent all their working hours writing, producing copies of documents prepared by more senior personnel—could only be obtained through a recommendation by a director of the Company. Clive's father, Richard, belonged to the lesser gentry, a social class who were owners of small landed estates in the English countryside. Those belonging to this class took great pride in their ancestry, which linked them to illustrious nobles and aristocrats of previous centuries. Their conditions in the early eighteenth century were quite different—a circumstance to which the bigger landowners had contributed by gradually enlarging their estates at the cost of the lower strata of landowners, leaving the lesser gentry generally impoverished. Many of these families had meagre means, possessing ancestral country residences that they were unable to maintain.

The Clive family had its seat at Styche Hall in Shropshire. Styche Hall had been in the family's possession for nearly 300 years, and the Clives claimed to have an impressive genealogy linking them to, among others, George Clyve, chancellor of the exchequer for Ireland during Queen Elizabeth's reign. Richard

Clive had an income of about £500 from the rents he received on the estate he had inherited. His attempt to augment his income by practising law was not successful, nor was his foray into business. It was the family's hardship that impelled Robert's parents to send him when he was three years old to the house of his mother's sister. His aunt and uncle lived in Manchester. As he grew up, Robert was sent to a series of schools. The quality of education at these schools seems to have been below average, a reflection of the state of school education in England for children whose parents could not afford elite public schools. Later in life, Clive did not show much interest in learning. The last institution he attended taught him how to improve his handwriting (though his handwriting remained untidy) and book-keeping. This would have been in preparation for his writership, for which an application was made sometime in 1742, around the time Clive attained the age of seventeen. Reasonably decent handwriting and some basic knowledge of accountancy were the only two essential requirements for the job. Being in the legal profession, Richard had some direct or indirect connections with the EIC establishment in London. It was somewhat of a departure from contemporary convention for the eldest male child of the owner of an estate in the countryside—even if it did not yield an adequate income—to be pushed into such a career. As the eldest son, Robert would have succeeded to the estate. That he was sent out to India suggests that the family's financial condition was worrisome. At the same time, it indicates that choosing to serve the Company in India was, by the 1740s—when it was on the verge of large-scale territorial expansion—quite an attractive career option for young boys due to the solidity of the EIC's business, the steady income the job provided, and prospects of increase in earnings with promotion, combined with profits from private trade. A sum of £500 had to be deposited as security before the formalities for the appointment could be finalized.

Robert reached Madras in 1744 to take up his duties. The journey from England to the Coromandel Coast took more than a year, as the ship on which he was travelling strayed in the direction of Brazil, where it spent several months. Ships destined for the Cape could, if they ran into adverse weather conditions, be blown across the Atlantic to the South American coast. The detour made the trip arduous and extraordinarily lengthy, certainly not a pleasant experience for a teenager on his first trans-oceanic journey.

It was exactly a century since Clive's place of work, Fort St George, had been built. Madras had grown in size and attracted a large number of migrant weavers, artisans, and traders who resided in the 'Black Town', which had grown up adjacent to the fortified 'White Town' of the Europeans. About 3,00,000 inhabitants resided in the former, and 200 in the latter, in the closing years of the seventeenth century. Of the two hundred Europeans, thirty were EIC employees, whose number would have risen marginally by the time Clive joined. His arrival coincided with the outbreak of hostilities between the English and the French in India, engulfing large parts of southern India in the First Carnatic War (1746–48). England and France were also embroiled in a European conflict at the time—the War of Austrian Succession (1740–48)—in which the two sides backed different candidates for succession to the Habsburg throne. France declared war against England in 1744. The French and English companies had so far kept away from the European conflicts in which their respective states were involved. On this occasion, the war extended to Asia and the Indian Ocean. What is more, given the intensity of their business rivalry by the 1740s, the companies used this as an opportunity to inflict damage on each other's commercial, political, and military power in the region. Clive had barely settled down when Madras was captured by the French in 1746. The campaign against the EIC was led by Joseph François Dupleix, who had taken over as governor of the Compagnie's possessions in 1742, remaining in the position till 1754. He pursued a vigorous policy for expanding the operations of the French company in India by aggressively promoting trade through sustained political and military intervention.

In the second week of September 1746, Madras was bombarded by a French naval fleet commanded by Mahé de La Bourdonnais. Fort St George was unable to withstand the offensive, and French troops landed in the town, occupying the citadel and the Company's warehouses without much resistance. Having achieved his main objective, La Bourdonnais offered to evacuate Madras and release Company servants who had been held captive, in return for the payment of a sum equivalent to about £420,000, which was to be paid over three years. All the EIC's stores were to be confiscated. The Madras council had already, La Bourdonnais's colleagues learnt, given a fairly large sum of money to the French commander in his private capacity. It was alleged that this was the reason for imposing what were regarded as relatively reasonable conditions for ending the occupation of Madras. The offer was opposed by Dupleix, who intended to continue with the occupation as a prelude to driving the English out of southern India. He ordered the annulment of the agreement made by La Bourdonnais, which the latter was unwilling to do. While the two were trying to sort out their differences, the onset of the Northeast Monsoon on the Tamil Nadu coast in mid-October was catastrophic for the French naval operations. The fleet under La Bourdonnais had to abandon the coast, removing the challenge to Dupleix's authority.

The English were informed that the agreement made with La Bourdonnais was no longer valid. Madras would remain under French occupation. The captives were released on the condition that they promised not to take up arms against France, pending an exchange of prisoners of war. Following his release from detention in Madras, Clive proceeded to another of the Company's outposts on the Coromandel Coast—Fort St David near Cuddalore, about twenty-five kilometres south of Pondicherry. This was a fortified factory, subordinate to Madras, with the chief EIC official designated as deputy-governor of Coromandel settlements. The site on which Fort St David was built had been in the possession of the English since the end of the seventeenth century. The adjacent town of Cuddalore, where the Indian textile dealers resided, was the centre of the EIC's trade. Fort St David soon became the target of the French, who attacked it several times. Whereas the junior employees who had been attached to the Madras civilian establishment were put to work at Fort St David as writers, some of them offered to (or were asked to, as the routine tasks would have been disrupted by the French offensive) enlist temporarily as volunteer soldiers to supplement the small English force that constituted the local garrison. Clive, who was among the volunteers, was commissioned as an ensign in 1747. This was the lowest commissioned rank in the EIC's nascent land force and was the military equivalent of a civilian writer in the Company's rigid hierarchy.

Participation in the defence of Fort St David gave Clive his preliminary experience of warfare. For the English, the situation changed when Stringer Lawrence assumed command of the Company's troops in January 1748. Lawrence, who had retired from the royal army as a captain, was engaged by the EIC as commander of its troops in Madras with the rank of major. He played a key role in the early history of the EIC army, helping it develop as an efficient fighting force in which the soldiers were recruited from among Indians while the officers were European. The charters granted to the Company had, since the 1660s, authorized it to raise its own army in India. It was during the Anglo–French conflict that the army grew substantially in size, recruiting a large number of troops from the regional military market in South India as sipahis ('sepoys'). Nevertheless, the EIC had to frequently rely on the crown's European land forces at critical moments, as in its armed conflict with the French. This often created difficulties during military operations due to disagreements over the chain of command. Royal officers invariably tended to look down on the Company's officers whom they regarded as socially inferior and militarily inept. It took time for the Company to build its cadre of commissioned officers. In the meantime, its army had to make do with the available resources. The acute shortage of officer material and the prevailing military emergency were the reasons for the speed with which the Fort St David officials accepted Clive's application.

The British besieged Pondicherry in 1748, when the ships already stationed on the Coromandel Coast were reinforced by the arrival of a large naval fleet. The fleet was commanded by Edward Boscawen. The siege, lasting for forty days, was a disaster. Clive was present during the campaign. Boscawen had been given command over operations both on sea and land, and was not able to achieve success in either. With the failure of the siege, Boscawen withdrew to Fort St David. British losses amounted to nearly one-third of their men. The commander of the EIC's forces, Lawrence, was captured during the fighting. French success in the conflict (Madras was still in their possession) was a personal triumph for Dupleix, whose reputation as an outstanding military leader was greatly enhanced. While the offensive against Pondicherry was in progress, negotiations were taking place in Europe to put an end to the War of Austrian Succession and were concluding just as Boscawen retreated. It took a few months for news of the recently concluded peace to reach the Coromandel. The French and the British had agreed to restore many of each other's possessions, or mutually exchange territory occupied during the war. In 1749, Madras was handed back to the EIC.

In later years, legends about the valour and wisdom of Clive would fill the chronological gap between his entry into the army in 1747 and the lucky break he received at Plassey a decade later. The main source for most of the information about his daring exploits during these years is Clive himself. Biographies of Clive rely heavily on the published writings of Robert Orme, supplemented occasionally by Orme's unpublished papers. Orme was an employee of the EIC, posted initially in Bengal, who authored a history of British military campaigns during the formative phase of empire. The first volume of his *History of the Military Transactions of the British Nation in Indostan* was published in 1763. An early draft of the volume was available by 1753–54, when it was presented to, among others, the powerful Duke of Cumberland, William Augustus.[1] Orme hoped thereby to further his career. The Duke was the youngest son of the reigning monarch, George II (r. 1727–60). He commanded the main British force during the War of Austrian Succession. Cumberland took a keen interest in developments in India and kept himself well-informed about the EIC's struggle with the Compagnie. The draft might have brought Clive to his notice.

Clive had befriended Orme shortly after his arrival in Madras. Orme, who had been posted in Bengal since his arrival in India in 1742 at the age of fourteen, initially used Clive as the agent for his personal commercial dealings in Madras. The two became business partners, setting up a firm known as Robert Orme & Clive, which conducted private trade in goods between Bengal and the Coromandel. The two remained friends throughout the fifties and early sixties. This is the period when Orme was preparing the first volume of his *History* which, when published, brought him fame and critical appreciation. It became a bestseller in England, as it vividly narrated the story of the battles in southern India from circa 1744 to 1756, in a style which was lucid and straightforward. The narrative is incredibly detailed. To his readers, who had hitherto known little about events in India, Orme presented a thrilling spectacle in which English soldiers displayed their courage and bold spirit, winning battle after battle amidst great adversity. Among the outstanding heroes of the unfolding drama was Orme's friend and business associate, Clive, who had regularly communicated reports of campaigns in which he was a participant. His is the only version available for many of the events described in the *History*. The role played by Orme's 1763 book in portraying Clive as a larger-than-life figure can hardly be exaggerated. It

---

[1]This was a title conferred on Prince William Augustus. The line of the earls of Cumberland, to which George, Lord Cumberland, referred in Chapter 1, belonged, had become extinct in the mid-seventeenth century.

brought him instant renown in Britain. By the time the first volume of Orme's *History* was published, Clive's celebrity status had been further reinforced by the remarkable exploits he had undertaken in Bengal, which were regarded as extraordinary in Britain. These exploits were the subject of the second volume of the book, published in 1778, by which time Clive had been dead for four years. Thus, his initial fame was based on the wide circulation of Orme's account of the EIC's pre-Plassey military campaigns.

The limitations and biases of Orme's writings need to be borne in mind when we outline Clive's early military career in Madras, using them as a historical source. Orme and Clive travelled together to England aboard the same ship in 1753, intending to seek opportunities in England. Surely, the two would have discussed aspects of the historical work which Orme had undertaken to write. As we shall see, after being disappointed by not securing a seat in Parliament, Clive departed a second time for India in 1755. Orme had returned in 1754, now as a member of the Madras council. He had risen from the lowest rung of the Company's managerial hierarchy to a position at the topmost levels. Such rapid promotion may be attributed to the impression he made on London officialdom during his brief sojourn. Orme was regarded as being very knowledgeable about Indian affairs, for which reason he was consulted by senior bureaucrats, Company directors, and even high-ranking ministers: 'As a result of his expertise, Orme was deputed by Holderness [secretary of state for the southern department, the portfolio which dealt with matters pertaining to British interests in India] to prepare an outline for the prospective peace negotiations [with France]. For all his youth and relatively junior position, Orme's opinions seem to have been listened to at the highest levels.'[2] This should also be seen as a reflection of the scarcity in London of bureaucrats or military officials

---

[2] Sinharaja Tammita Delgoda, '"Nabob, Historian and Orientalist" Robert Orme: The Life and Career of an East India Company Servant (1728-1801)', *Journal of the Royal Asiatic Society*, Vol. 2, No. 3, 1992, p. 367.

having sufficient familiarity with political conditions in the Indian subcontinent. Policymakers in the government lacked the confidence at this stage to formulate policies vis-à-vis other European powers with stakes in India, and were willing to seek the advice of a novice like Orme.

∽

In 1749, the year in which Madras was restored to the English, Clive was promoted from ensign to lieutenant in the Company's army and, in that capacity, took part in fighting triggered by the EIC's territorial ambitions in the Coromandel. Following the cessation of hostilities with the French, the EIC attempted to use its augmented military strength to extend its sphere of influence in central Tamil Nadu, in the tract lying south of its Fort St David outpost. The factory had functioned as its headquarters while Madras was under French occupation. An opportunity for military intervention was provided by a quarrel in the kingdom of Tanjore (Thanjavur). The EIC's intervention was part of the low key confrontation between the English and French companies in the years after the war had formally ended in Europe. There was an intense struggle between them for the control of strategic locations on the Coromandel Coast to gain better access to centres of textile production in northern and central Tamil Nadu. In 1738, the Compagnie had managed to acquire rights over the coastal settlement of Karaikal, which lies a short distance north of Nagapattinam. The settlement was part of the territories of the Tanjore kingdom. The kingdom, with territories in central Tamil Nadu, was ruled by a Maratha dynasty of the Bhonsle clan. The founder of the dynasty, Venkoji (r. 1675–84), was closely related to Shivaji.

An ongoing dispute within the kingdom provided the EIC the pretext for interference. There had been a slight delay in giving possession of Karaikal to the French due to some differences over the terms on which the rights had been granted. In the meantime, the incumbent ruler with whom the Compagnie negotiated the deal for Karaikal, Shahuji II (r. 1738–

39), was deposed in 1739 and was succeeded by Pratap Singh (r. 1739–63). The dispute between Pratap Singh and Shahuji was revived a decade later, obviously with some encouragement from the EIC's Coromandel establishment. Shahuji had been offered protection by the English after he was ousted from Tanjore and dwelt for some time in Fort St David. Company officials might have hoped to destabilize the French presence in Karaikal by supporting Shahuji's claim to the throne. The first English offensive in April 1749, ostensibly on Shahuji's behalf, ended in a fiasco. A second campaign was launched a month later in which the Company's forces were led by Major Lawrence. The immediate objective of this invasion of the Tanjore kingdom was the capture of Devicottah (Tivukottai), on the coast south of Fort St David. Devicottah had an island fort situated at the mouth of the Kollidam River and could be used as a harbour for smaller ships. The English were successful in capturing the fort, where a minor garrison was established. The cause of Shahuji was forgotten; Pratap Singh formally handed over Devicottah to the EIC, bringing the petty war to a close. Clive was part of the invading force on both occasions. This relatively obscure episode of little political consequence usually finds a prominent place in accounts of his early military career. Today, it is not easy to locate Devicottah, the scene of Clive's actions, on a map.

By the end of 1749, Clive himself was no longer keen on staying on in the army. He wrote to his superiors that he wished to resign his military commission and revert to his civilian status. His application was accepted, and he was appointed steward in Fort St George. The department in which he was posted looked after supplies, including provisions for the garrison. The officially sanctioned or unsanctioned commissions he is likely to have received for giving contracts to favoured suppliers afforded him an additional source of income, some of which he would have invested in the private business he carried on in partnership with Orme. According to Orme's reckoning, Clive was able to earn five rupees on each soldier per month. The prospect of adding to his earnings improved further with Clive's promotion to the rank of junior merchant, the second highest level in the EIC's managerial hierarchy. Junior merchants had the option of legitimately engaging in private trade, which Company servants at lower levels could only conduct clandestinely.

His peacetime career as a steward, combined with commercial dealings, was disrupted when war once again reached the doorstep of Madras. Clive was deeply involved in business transactions at this point, having sent goods to Calcutta as well as to Cuddalore, and was awaiting word about the outcome of his most recent venture. Large parts of Tamil Nadu and the Deccan were already in turmoil. With their large military resources, the English and French companies had altered the political landscape of the region, wherein the struggle between the two was intertwined with local factional squabbles, which became increasingly intense and bloody due to European intervention. A large part of southern India was drawn into the new phase of the Anglo–French conflict, known as the Second Carnatic War (1749–54).

The Mughal empire by now encompassed portions of present-day Tamil Nadu and the Coromandel Coast. These were administratively part of the Karnatak Payanghat province.[3] Arcot (district Vellore, Tamil Nadu), situated west of Madras, was the seat of the subedar or governor of Karnatak Payanghat, who was directly answerable to the Mughal governor of the Deccan. The Arcot territories were a recent addition to the southern provinces of the Mughal empire. In the 1720s, Arcot had emerged as the nucleus of a virtually independent principality under the Mughal diwan of Karnatak Payanghat, Saadatullah Khan (d.1732), the founder of the Navaiyat dynasty which ruled over Arcot till 1744.

The Mughal subas, or provinces, of the Deccan collectively formed an autonomous political entity since the

---

[3]'Carnatic' is the anglicized form of Karnatak and in this context should not be confused with the present-day state of Karnataka.

early 1720s, when Nizam-ul-Mulk Chin Qilich Khan (Asaf Jah I), then the most powerful noble at the Mughal court, moved permanently to the Deccan to rule over the region independently. The capital of his state was at Aurangabad; it shifted to Hyderabad under his successors, who are more familiar as the nizams of Hyderabad.[4] Nizam-ul-Mulk did not repudiate his allegiance to the Mughal emperor, maintaining that the subas were still an integral part of the empire.

As for Arcot, Nizam-ul-Mulk exercised authority over it without any reference to Delhi. In 1743, he replaced the Navaiyats with his own appointee. The appointment of the new subedar of Arcot did not go uncontested. A Navaiyat claimant, Husain Dost Khan, better known as Chanda Sahib, appeared on the political scene in 1748 to challenge the incumbent subedar. Chanda Sahib had been held in captivity since 1741 when he was captured by the Marathas during an incursion in central Tamil Nadu. The Maratha expedition was led on this occasion by the prominent military chief, Raghoji Bhonsle. In a convoluted sequence of events, a Navaiyat faction, of which Chanda Sahib was the leader, had assumed independent control in the 1730s over Trichinopoly or Trichy (Thiruchirapalli), distancing himself from the Arcot Navaiyats. With Trichinopoly as his base, Chanda Sahib had attempted to expand into central and southern Tamil Nadu. He also intervened in the affairs of the neighbouring Maratha-ruled Tanjore kingdom and helped sort out some disagreements between the French and the Tanjore ruler over the terms for the acquisition of Karaikal, paving the way for an alliance with the Compagnie. The troubles of 1738–39 in Tanjore, to which reference has been made above, and the triangular conflict over Trichinopoly (involving the Arcot subedar, Chanda Sahib, and the Madurai nayaka lineage which had ruled over Trichinopoly), led to the despatch of a large army to the area by the Pune court under Raghoji for protecting

---

[4]For the sake of consistency we shall refer to the state created by Nizam-ul-Mulk as that of Hyderabad for the earlier period as well.

Pune's interests in this Maratha-ruled enclave in Tamil Nadu. Trichinopoly, with its formidable fort and strategic location is a short distance from Tanjore. Maratha territories were ruled by the peshwas since the end of the 1710s, who had their seat at Pune. The Madurai nayakas were once subservient to Vijayanagara. After a prolonged siege, Trichinopoly was occupied by the Marathas in 1741, and Chanda Sahib was taken away as a captive. The territories of the Madurai nayakas, which included Trichinopoly, were ruled from Pune until 1743, when Nizam-ul-Mulk launched an offensive to restore his authority over the Carnatic. Anwaruddin Khan was made subedar of Arcot in 1744, replacing the Navaiyats, and in this capacity he also had charge of Trichinopoly.

The return of Chanda Sahib upset the administrative arrangements of 1743–44. The situation was further complicated by the death of Nizam-ul-Mulk in 1748 and a dispute over succession. The English and the French rushed to support rival candidates to further their respective interests. The course of the tussle in Hyderabad need not detain us. It is hardly surprising that the EIC should have chosen to support Anwaruddin when Chanda Sahib, with whom the French were aligned, mobilized his forces to take over Arcot. The two European companies had a direct interest in Arcot as their settlements were located in the subedar's territories. Anwaruddin was killed while engaged in fighting during the Battle of Ambur (1749) in which he was pitted against the combined forces of Chanda Sahib, the French, and the French-supported nizam of Hyderabad. Chanda Sahib became the Arcot subedar. The English now lent support to one of Anwaruddin's sons, Muhammad Ali, in his contest with Chanda Sahib for the Arcot subedari. This marked the beginning of the Second Carnatic War. For the time being, Chanda Sahib was in a stronger position to enforce his claim as he could rely on Dupleix's assistance. After a series of clashes between the contenders, spread over nearly two years, Chanda Sahib's forces surrounded Trichinopoly where Muhammad Ali had taken refuge following a setback. Since the English did not have sufficient troops to render any meaningful help to Muhammad Ali in resisting Chanda Sahib, the Madras governor agreed to send some of his men to Arcot at the urging of Muhammad Ali, who hoped thereby to relieve the pressure on Trichinopoly through what was essentially a diversionary move. Chanda Sahib was forced to disengage a portion of his troops from Trichinopoly and send them for the protection of his capital, Arcot.

The English contingent was placed under Clive. He had just resumed his military duties in January 1751 following the renewed fighting, with the rank of captain (the decision to send troops to Arcot was taken in August). That a very junior officer, without much experience, should have been asked to lead the troops, indicates that the expedition was expected to be a minor affair. Trichinopoly was the main focus of the ongoing fight. Chanda Sahib had left his capital virtually unprotected, which, as Muhammad Ali had expected, soon made the defence of Arcot a major concern for him. The EIC's contingent was able to occupy the town and the citadel without much opposition. However, the force was soon surrounded and rendered ineffective. Reinforcements sent by Chanda Sahib confined the English contingent to the fort, besieging it for nearly two months from early September onwards. The situation for the English was critical by the beginning of November. The arrival of the Maratha military chief Murari Rao—whose base was the fort of Gooty, located nearly 400 kms away in present-day Andhra Pradesh—in the vicinity of Arcot during an unrelated expedition revived their hopes, as he was expected to aid the beleaguered force. Murari Rao had been the administrator of Trichinopoly when it was under the control of Pune in 1741–43, and was friendly with the British.

Murari Rao's troops had set up camp at some distance from Arcot. They were mobilized for an offensive only when Clive sent a desperate message appealing for help. Before Murari Rao could intervene, Chanda Sahib's force launched a ferocious attack on the fort on 14 November. Several hours of fierce fighting ended in a setback for the Arcot troops, who withdrew from the town, abandoning it to the English. Soon afterwards, English reinforcements arrived from Madras, to which was added the large contingent of Murari Rao. Together, this joint force marched towards neighbouring Kanchipuram. Clive then went on to Fort St David. Subsequently, he took part, or led small bodies of troops, in a few other engagements. It is doubtful that these can be regarded as noteworthy military confrontations. For instance, in February 1752, he successfully led a force of 1600 European and Indian men at the Battle of Kaveripak (Kaveripakkam in present-day Tamil Nadu). Kaveripak is a short distance from Arcot. The troops were marching from Madras to Arcot when they were fired upon at Kaveripak by Chanda Sahib's loyalists, who were stationed there along with French troops. The English were successful in this affray. Kaveripak was one among numerous similar minor encounters in the Carnatic War but has been depicted in hagiographical accounts as 'Clive's masterpiece as a commander in the field'.[5] Further, it was during the siege of Arcot that Clive is supposed to have revealed his military genius. In the period after Plassey, his part in it was blown out of all proportion. In the words of one of his biographers, Percival Spear, 'His achievement was overpraised at the time because of the gloom from which the [British] had been rescued; it has been overpraised since because historical crystal-gazers have seen in it the genesis of a great empire-builder'.[6] We would do well to remember that historians are dependent on Orme's account for most of the details about Clive's role at Arcot, and Orme's main source was Clive himself.

The campaigns of the Second Carnatic War came to an end in June 1752 with the surrender of Chanda Sahib, along with the French force stationed at Trichinopoly. The French troops were

---

[5] A. Mervyn Davies, *Clive of Plassey: A Biography*, London: Nicholson and Watson, 1939, p. 91.
[6] Percival Spear, *Master of Bengal: Clive and His India*, London: Thames and Hudson, 1975, p. 54.

commanded by Jean Law. Chanda Sahib was betrayed and put to death even though he had been assured that his life would be spared. Lawrence led the EIC's troops in this final offensive for the capture of Trichinopoly and has been blamed for not ensuring the safety of Chanda Sahib. Yet another incident, which occurred in the course of consultations regarding terms for the surrender of the French force under Law, demonstrates the callousness with which Indians who had submitted were treated and does not show Clive in a good light. Law had insisted that Indian officers (native officers commanding units of sipahis) serving in the Compagnie's army ought to be regarded as French officers and sent to Pondicherry like the European officers. The Indian officers in question included the person who was responsible for the killing of Anwaruddin on the battlefield at Ambur. The terms were not accepted. Law later alleged that Clive had taken Lawrence aside during the consultations and dissuaded him from acceding to the terms. Whereas it is difficult to assess the extent to which Clive influenced Lawrence in refusing these terms, the accusation points towards a hard-heartedness at a very young age which was to remain a marked feature of his character in public life.

Just as he was beginning to get noticed, Clive decided to return home. He had accumulated sufficient savings through the private trade he conducted in partnership with Orme, in addition to the commissions he received for arranging provisions in his capacity as steward, and his share of war booty. He could now contemplate a fresh career in Britain. It is estimated that he had about £40,000 at his disposal when he sailed for Britain in 1753. This was a fairly large fortune for a boy of twenty-eight, who was almost destitute at the time of his arrival and had spent less than a decade in India, most of this time as a lowly clerk in the EIC's establishment. The military campaigns of the EIC had provided opportunities for plunder which substantially augmented the 'legitimate' earnings of employees such as Clive.

Shortly before he departed for England, he married seventeen-year-old Margaret Maskelyne in Madras. Clive had formed a close association with Edmund Maskelyne, one of Margaret's elder brothers. Edmund was also an employee of the EIC. Clive and Edmund had been together during the French siege of Madras in 1746, and had together trekked from Madras to Fort St David when Company servants, who had been made captive, were allowed to depart from the town. The bond between the two was strengthened with Clive's marriage to Margaret, and they remained friends throughout their not-very-long lives. Both were almost of the same age. Edmund died in 1775, a year after Clive's death. Margaret had travelled to India in 1752 with, it would appear, the aim of finding a suitable husband, which was not unusual at this time for young women of landed families living in genteel poverty and having some link with the EIC's service. She had more or less the same social background as that of Clive. Robert's marriage would give him access to important political and social networks of which the Maskelynes were a part in later years. These connections played a role in the appointment of Nevil, another of Margaret's elder brothers, as astronomer royal, chief astronomer of the Greenwich Observatory, a position he held for nearly half a century (1765–1811). Nevil's scholarship and expertise as an astronomer and mathematician alone would not have sufficed for the appointment. When Clive set out to pursue a political career in Britain, the extended Maskelyne family provided him with much-needed support. Margaret outlived her husband by forty-seven years, dying at the age of eighty-two when the empire was poised for massive territorial expansion at the end of the Napoleonic Wars. Her husband's eminence as the founder of that empire was fully established by that time.

Clive's initial foray into politics was quite brief. He was elected to the House of Commons in 1754, disqualified in 1755, and then returned to India in the same year, having spent about eighteen months in England. He rejoined the EIC's service on a five-year contract. Clive was made deputy governor of Madras, which simultaneously made him governor of Fort St David. It was understood that when the tenure of George Pigot, the newly appointed governor of Madras, ended, Clive would become governor of the presidency. He assumed office in the middle of 1756, his arrival coinciding with a serious crisis in the Company's Bengal operations. These had come to a standstill due to a conflict with the provincial authorities. The conflict culminated in the Battle of Plassey, the outcome of which (rather than the military encounter itself) would make Clive a household name in Britain. The outcome, as is well known, was the acquisition of a vast expanse of territory in eastern India, the Mughal subas of Bengal, Bihar, and a small part of Orissa.

∽

While Bengal was formally still a part of the Mughal empire in the mid-eighteenth century, it had become virtually autonomous since the time of Murshid Quli Khan (d. 1727), a prominent noble of the Aurangzeb era. Murshid Quli Khan was the diwan of the suba at the turn of the century. The capital of the suba or province had been moved from Dacca (Dhaka), then named Jahangirnagar, in eastern Bengal, to Murshidabad in the first decade of the century. Murshid Quli Khan and his immediate successors, now hereditary governors, acknowledged the suzerainty of the Mughal emperor. They regularly sent a share of the revenues of the province as tribute, or peshkash, to the emperor, though the quantum of the tribute dwindled over a period of time. In 1740, Alivardi Khan, who had emerged in the preceding years as the principal official of the suba, replaced Murshid Quli Khan's descendant, Sarfaraz Khan, as the governor of Bengal. The domain of the governor or nāzim of Bengal included Bihar and (nominally at least) Orissa. Alivardi Khan had held several leading positions at the provincial level, including charge of Bihar, before he unseated the incumbent nāzim or nawab, Sarfaraz Khan (we shall henceforth be using the more familiar appellation, nawab). Alivardi Khan's rule ushered in an era of political stability. He passed away in 1756 and was succeeded by his grandson Siraj-ud-Daula. Mounting tensions between the EIC and nawab Siraj-ud-Daula set in motion events that culminated in the Battle of Plassey. The blatant misuse by the Company of commercial concessions granted to it by Mughal authorities and, more importantly, their misuse by its employees who were engaged in private trade, resulted in serious problems for the economy, which the nawab tried to resolve by drastically curbing the activities of the English. Seeking to discipline the Company and its servants, Siraj-ud-Daula drove the English out of Calcutta in June 1756, when they refused to comply with instructions not to strengthen the defences of Fort William. The action at Calcutta was preceded by the seizure of the fortified Cossimbazar factory, which had a small garrison mainly comprising Dutch mercenaries and Creole Indo-Portuguese soldiers. The garrison surrendered, and the Company's European employees, including Warren Hastings, an official stationed by the EIC at Cossimbazar on whom more later, were taken to Murshidabad as prisoners.

Cossimbazar (Kasimbazar) was located close to Murshidabad, which was the seat of the Mughal governor of Bengal. Unlike Calcutta, Murshidabad was a major urban centre, being the commercial hub of the region. Till the end of the seventeenth century, the EIC's main factory in Bengal was situated in Cossimbazar. Its proximity to Murshidabad, of which it was a suburb, made the Cossimbazar establishment politically important. The head of the Cossimbazar factory, William Watts, would play a key role in the conspiracy that led to the colonial conquest of Bengal. Incidentally, his daughter Amelia was the mother of Lord Liverpool, the British prime minister from 1812 to 1827, about whom we shall have more to say later. Watts himself retired to England with a large fortune acquired in the wake of the Battle of Plassey, after a brief stint as governor of Fort William.

These were months during which the Company was faced with the possibility of being permanently expelled from Bengal. Fort William had been evacuated and abandoned to its fate by senior functionaries in Calcutta. A few Company employees continued to reside within the fort even after its evacuation. Of these, some, mainly soldiers, were imprisoned after Siraj's troops occupied the fort, apparently as punishment for unruly behaviour. It is likely that a small number of prisoners perished in the cell in which they had been confined. The number has remained at the centre of the controversy over the so-called 'black hole' incident in colonial narratives about the capture of Fort William. The principal EIC official who was present in Calcutta at the time of the alleged incident, J.Z. Holwell, later claimed that of the 146 prisoners incarcerated in the 'black hole', only twenty-three survived. Almost all accounts of the incident may be traced back to Holwell, who is the only source for what transpired following the occupation of the fort by the nawab's army.

The Company's Calcutta officials had moved their base downstream along the river to a place called Fulta (or Falta), which was a small VOC outpost about 50 km south of Calcutta. At this remote location, they had no direct access to information about developments in Murshidabad. One important episode, while the officials were at Fulta, was the elimination of a rival contender for the subedari of Bengal in a brief armed encounter at the beginning of October. Siraj-ud-Daula could now concentrate on dealing with the recalcitrant English company, though Maratha incursions too were a cause for great concern. The Maratha chief Raghoji Bhonsle (d. 1755), Chanda Sahib's captor, had acquired a large part of Orissa and became its de facto ruler in the early 1750s. The river Subarnarekha marked the boundary between Bengal and Maratha-ruled Orissa. The dynasty of Raghoji Bhonsle continued to rule over Orissa till 1803. Another cause for concern were the invasions of the Durrani ruler, Ahmad Shah Durrani (also known as Ahmad Shah Abadali), in northern India and Punjab, which led to widespread dislocation in the Mughal territories. However, for the nawab of Bengal, the immediate problem was the EIC, which was trying to undermine the authority of the provincial government.

As the situation in Fulta became desperate for the EIC and its hangers-on, the hopes of the refugees were revived by news that reinforcements were being sent from Madras. A naval fleet commanded by Charles Watson, recently arrived on the Coromandel Coast from England, reached Fulta in the first week of December. Land troops, both of the Company (including a large number of Indian soldiers, sipahis) and the royal army were transported aboard the fleet. They had been placed under Clive's command as a compromise formula, whereby Watson commanded the naval force, Clive the land army, and the Calcutta council retained vaguely defined overall authority. The compromise was a solution to the vexed problem of finding a suitable officer with military experience to lead the expedition—a problem that seemed to defy solution, as there were several well-qualified candidates. The problem was compounded by the antagonism between royal officers (officers with king's commissions) and Company officers. These tensions between EIC officers and royal army officers would persist down to the end of Company rule. Watson, for example, insisted that he was answerable only to London and not to Company authorities in India. Further, Clive would assert during the campaign that in an emergency, he could act without seeking the approval of the Calcutta council. This was highly irregular in terms of EIC policy, which gave overriding powers to its senior civilian personnel. It may be mentioned that Clive had by now obtained a royal commission as a lieutenant colonel, valid in areas of the Company's operations in the Indian subcontinent.

The force was transported upriver along the Hooghly and managed to recapture Calcutta on 2 January 1757. Fort William was occupied by troops under the command of Eyre Coote, a young officer in the royal army. Coote was a captain in the 39th infantry regiment (39th Regiment of Foot) which had been sent out for duty in the Company's territories in 1754, the first royal regiment to be deployed in India. The regiment was stationed in India, at the EIC's request, amidst tensions between England and France on the eve of the Seven Years'

War (1756–63). It had been transported aboard the fleet led by Watson and was under the overall command of Colonel John Adlercron. Adlercron did not accompany his troops to Bengal. Coote commanded one of the three companies of the 39th Foot, which was despatched to Bengal along with the Company's contingent. Whereas Watson had instructed Coote to assume charge of Fort William upon its recapture, Clive questioned the admiral's authority, appointing himself commander of the fort. This caused a serious quarrel between Watson and Clive. To retrieve his prestige, Clive then stated that he would hand over the keys of the garrison to Watson if he came ashore, which the latter agreed to do. Coote became a bitter opponent of Clive due to this incident.

Siraj-ud-Daula reacted to the reoccupation of Fort William by mobilizing his army for an attack on Calcutta. There was a brief military encounter in which the English received a setback, suffering heavy losses. Somewhat inexplicably, Siraj withdrew his army from Calcutta immediately afterwards. There were then several days of hectic negotiations, in which Warren Hastings acted as one of the emissaries. The EIC was keen to resume its commercial activities in Bengal, and the negotiations focussed on conditions relating to trade. An agreement was concluded between the nawab and the Company on 9 February 1757, whereby the concessions granted to the Company by the emperor through a farman of 1717 were restored, and permission was given for the construction of defences at Fort William. The EIC's Cossimbazar premises could now be reopened. Watts was sent to resume his responsibilities as head of the factory, with Hastings as his deputy. The day-to-day functioning of the factory was entrusted to Hastings, while Watts was asked to handle communications with the nawab's court at Murshidabad, gather intelligence about factional manoeuvres, and report on activities of the French official Jean Law, who was posted in Bengal at this time. Since England and France had been at war from 1756 onwards, the two companies regarded the settlements of each other as legitimate targets.

The large English force assembled for the recapture of Calcutta could now easily be used against the French, especially as its main objective had been achieved. Chandernagore, further upstream from Calcutta and not too distant, was occupied by the end of March. This precipitated a crisis, as such a military action undermined the nawab's authority. Moreover, Siraj had a cordial relationship with the French. His hostility towards the English intensified as a result of this act. Meanwhile, some of the EIC officials, of whom Clive was the most active, were conspiring to oust Siraj-ud-Daula by engineering a coup. Two prominent courtiers, Mir Jafar and Rai Durlabh, were drawn into the plot. Mir Jafar was a brother-in-law of Alivardi Khan and commanded some of the contingents of the army; Rai Durlabh held charge of the diwani, or revenue department. The EIC had already forged an alliance with the two officials, as well as with the powerful banking firm of the Jagat Seths.[7] Mir Jafar, Rai Durlabh, and their associates were assured of military assistance by the Company for ousting Siraj and promised to make large payments to the EIC and its servants in their personal capacity, in return for the support they would receive to install a nawab of their choice. It was decided, after consultations with the English, that Mir Jafar would replace Siraj, although Clive himself had never met him. The affair was so murky that Clive double-crossed the principal go-between in these negotiations, a merchant by the name of Amirchand (Amichand/Omichund).

---

[7]The banking firm of the Jagat Seths, the leading financial concern of Bengal in the era of Alivardi Khan, rose to prominence under Murshid Quli Khan. The family of the Jagat Seths, Oswals from Rajasthan, had migrated to Bihar, and gradually their operations extended to Dacca and Delhi. The firm's founder, Manikchand, was involved in high finance, providing credit to Mughal provincial functionaries and arranging for the transfer of imperial revenues from Bengal to Delhi. Manikchand's successor, Fatehchand, enlarged the firm's financial empire by establishing a grip over the revenues of Bengal through his proximity to Alivardi Khan. In the early 1720s, emperor Muhammad Shah (r. 1719–48) bestowed on Fatehchand the title 'Jagat Seth'. Fatehchand and his successors are better known by the ceremonial title of Jagat Seth, as is their firm.

Amirchand was the Company's chief broker for the supply of Bengal goods. Their relationship went back to the beginning of the century. Amirchand also had an excellent rapport with the adherents of Siraj, which gave him access to key functionaries at Murshidabad. Much of the communication between Watts, the go-between on the Company's side, and Mir Jafar was carried out through Amirchand. The conspiracy for the coup (euphemistically referred to in colonial narratives as a 'revolution') became murkier as the details of the bargain were negotiated and finalized. Clive is known to have forged the signature of Watson on a document related to the plot when he realized that the admiral was reluctant to back all his shady deals. It is important to note that Watson was not a functionary of the Company and, as an officer of the crown, need not have been involved in every move made by the EIC's servants to further their employer's interests. The forgery would later become a major charge against Clive when proceedings were initiated against him in the British Parliament. Once the plot was in place, Watts secretly departed from Murshidabad on 12 June. The following day the combined English force began its march north from Chandernagore, where Clive was based, in the direction of Murshidabad. Clive assured the Murshidabad authorities that he was only marching up to Cossimbazar to seek the mediation of influential people there to sort out differences with the nawab.

It would appear that even on the eve of Plassey, the Company's officials were not sure about the extent to which Mir Jafar and his co-conspirators would actively assist in the overthrow of Siraj. The march towards Murshidabad, it was hoped, would compel Mir Jafar to commit himself to the coup more firmly than he was willing to at this stage. Clive's letter of 19 June, four days before the battle, to Mir Jafar is revealing. 'It gives me great concern,' he wrote, 'that in an affair of so great consequence to yourself in particular that you do not exert yourself more. So long as I have been on my march, you have not yet given me that least information what measures it is necessary for me to take'.[8]

There was still no clarity on the 21st when a council of war was held to consider whether an offensive should be launched immediately or whether any action should be deferred. According to Coote's account of the meeting, which was attended by twenty-one officers and over which Clive presided, the overwhelming majority (including Clive himself) voted against immediate action. Coote was in favour of immediate action, while three other officers of the 39th Foot voted with the majority. The officers had been informed by Clive at the outset that they 'could not depend on Meer Jaffier [Mir Jafar] for anything more than his standing neuter in case we came to an action with the Nabob; that Monsieur Law, with a body of French', was then within three days' march of joining the Nabob, whose army (by the best intelligence he could get) consisted of about 50,000 men;' and according to Coote, 'he called us together to desire our opinions, whether in those circumstances it would be prudent to come to immediate action with the Nabob, or fortify ourselves where we were and remain till the monsoon was over …'.[9] Sushil Chaudhury has pointed out that at this date, 'Mir Jafar and his allies were only half-hearted in their approach,' and that 'even a few days before Plassey, Clive was thinking of an alliance with the Marathas to overthrow Siraj-ud- Daula, clearly indicating that the coup was essentially a British project which they were anxious to carry out with the help of any indigenous power and not necessarily with the assistance of disgruntled elements in Murshidabad'.[10]

The council of war had barely concluded when Clive overturned its decision and reversed his own opinion. Coote was intimated that the army would march the very next day. Siraj-ud-Daula's army confronted the British at Plassey (Palashi),

[8]Sushil Chaudhury, 'The Road to Plassey: A Reappraisal of the British Conquest of Bengal, 1757', *Proceedings of the Indian History Congress*, Session 59, 1998, p. 737.
[9]H. C. Wylly, *A Life of Lieutenant-General Sir Eyre Coote*, Oxford: Clarendon Press, 1922, p. 39.
[10]Chaudhury, 'The Road to Plassey', pp. 737–38.

located about fifty kilometres south of his capital. A military engagement took place on 23 June, in which the Company's forces were able to overwhelm their opponent. The greater part of the Bengal army did not participate in the fighting on the instructions of Mir Jafar and Rai Durlabh. Clive reached Murshidabad on the 29th. Mir Jafar was acknowledged as the new nawab. This marked the beginning of British rule over Bengal, Bihar, and parts of Orissa, though it took some time for the EIC to consolidate its position as the de facto ruler of eastern India. Siraj was assassinated on 2 July by Mir Jafar's son, Mir Miran.

∽

The events in Bengal overlapped with the Seven Years' War in Europe which was, in many ways, a continuation of the War of Austrian Succession. With the fresh confrontation between England and France, the two companies were once again ranged on opposite sides. Southern India was the main arena of the conflict between the two, and the conflict in this theatre is more specifically known as the Third Carnatic War (1757–63). Events in southern India were soon overtaken by the coup in Bengal, which completely altered the balance of forces in the subcontinent. A senior French military officer, Thomas Arthur de Lally-Tollendal, had arrived in India in April 1758 as commander-general of French colonies in the East Indies, with instructions to immobilize the English. Dupleix had already been recalled in 1754 at the end of the Second Carnatic War. At the beginning of the Third Carnatic War, and soon after the fall of Chandernagore, the French had taken over English factories on the Orissa coast and annexed a large stretch of territory in the area between Ganjam (in present-day Orissa) and Masulipatam. However, the French campaigns against the English led by de Lally were not successful. The failure to capture Madras, which was besieged by the French for a few weeks, between December 1758 and February 1759, followed by the decisive defeat inflicted on the force commanded by de

Lally at Wandiwash (Vandavasi, in Tiruvannamalai district of present-day Tamil Nadu) in January 1760, were major setbacks for the French. The English were led by Coote at Wandiwash. Pondicherry was seized from the severely demoralized French company in 1761 and remained under the English till the end of the Seven Years' War. It was restored to the French under the provisions of the Treaty of Paris (1763). Henceforth, the territorial possessions of the French East India Company were confined to Pondicherry and four other outposts: namely Karaikal; Yanam, on a branch of the Godavari River; Chandernagore; and Mahé, south of Cannanore (Kannur) in Kerala. Besides, the king of France agreed to give up claims to territorial gains made on the Coromandel and Orissa coasts 'from the start of 1749'. This marked the end of attempts by the French East India Company to create an empire in the subcontinent.

As for the situation in Bengal, the transformation of the Company's status had been so rapid that orders from the directors were, for nearly two years since the eviction of its servants from Calcutta in the summer of 1756, often no longer applicable by the time they arrived. Clive took full advantage of the interval between the receipt of one set of instructions and their supersession by another set of instructions—and the resultant muddle—to entrench himself. The directors learnt of the capture of Fort William by Siraj as late as the first week of June 1757; news of the restoration of the EIC's commercial concessions by Siraj in February 1757 reached them somewhat faster. The directors assumed that the status quo had been restored in Bengal. They would have been ignorant of the manoeuvres of Clive and his associates in Bengal from the first week of January onwards. This is not to suggest that they would have disowned the actions of their servants; they simply did not have information about the conspiracy that was being hatched in Bengal and the key role being played by Clive in it. Had he obeyed the original directive from London, Clive would have been back in Madras after the immediate objective of the military expedition to Bengal had been achieved. The EIC had already acquired Bengal long before the directors learnt that their orders had been disobeyed.

From the point of view of the directors, once apprised of the momentous changes, what required immediate attention were the organizational arrangements of their Bengal establishment due to problems created by the prolonged instability at Calcutta. They began by reconstituting the Council of Fort William. The letter of the Court of Directors conveying this decision is dated 11 November 1757 and was delivered in June 1758, a full year after Plassey. According to orders contained in the despatch, the council was to consist of ten members, of whom the four most senior would constitute a select committee to deal with political and diplomatic matters, especially those related to relations with the nawab's government. The four senior members would also preside over the council by rotation, each for three months. Given the EIC's deep involvement in the politics of Bengal, it had been felt necessary, even before the accession of Siraj-ud-Daula, to form a separate body to handle political and diplomatic affairs. Orders were issued in February 1756 to constitute a select committee from among members of the Council of Fort William 'for the transaction of affairs with the Country Government and neighbouring powers, also with the French, Dutch and other Europeans, and for other duties connected with the rights of the Company'.[11] This arrangement, whereby a select committee undertook the important political and diplomatic aspects of the Company's functioning, particularly those requiring secrecy, continued after the Company's ascendancy in the post-Plassey period.

Some of the biographers of Clive have suggested that he was greatly dismayed, in view of the key role he had played in the overthrow of Siraj, that his name was omitted in the November 1757 despatch, which provided for a rotating presidency. They

---

[11]Walter K. Firminger (ed.), *Proceedings of the Select Committee at Fort William in Bengal, 1758, Bengal Historical Records*, Calcutta: Bengal Secretariat Record Room, 1914, p. ii.

go on to point out that what he 'did not realize was that the directors were not aware that he was in Bengal' (because Clive was supposed to have returned to Madras after the restoration of Fort William) and was needlessly upset with the directors.[12] For it seems that he was indeed upset with them and defied the November orders. Surely, Clive would have known that this was a letter from November 1757 and was drafted before news about the coup had been relayed to London. The report about Plassey and its sensational aftermath was received in London in February 1758. The orders contained in the November 1757 despatch were thereupon superseded by another letter, dated 8 March 1758, which acknowledged the part played by Clive in the acquisition of Bengal for the Company. In recognition of his role, he was now appointed 'President and Governor of Fort William "in consideration of his eminent and repeated services to the Company, and in particular for the share he had in bringing about the late glorious and advantageous revolution in Bengal, and to be the chief and constant presiding member of the Select Committee appointed by the Court's letter of 11th November [1757]."'[13]

Much before the orders of 8 March reached Calcutta, Clive and his friends had already devised their own scheme for placing the colonel at the head of the select committee. The committee members, who included Watts, had offered the chair to Clive, who promptly accepted. The arrangement was regularized by the March 1758 letter from the directors, which was received in November of that year. All this while, Clive had been steadily consolidating his hold over Bengal.

Clive was the head of the EIC's establishment in Bengal officially from the end of 1758 to February 1760, when he departed for England. He had been planning to return home before Plassey. Once he became part of the conspiracy to engineer the coup, it was difficult to withdraw till the aim of

---

[12]Nirad C. Chaudhuri, *Clive of India: A Political and Psychological Essay*, London: Barrie & Jenkins, p. 262.
[13]Firminger, *Select Committee Proceedings, 1758*, p. i.

installing a new nawab in Murshidabad had been achieved. Success opened up further possibilities. The overthrow of Siraj made Clive and other leading officials of the EIC immensely powerful. More importantly, they acquired vast personal fortunes. Clive decided to stay on for some time to use his position as governor to accumulate more wealth. There can be little doubt that he had no long-term interest in Bengal or Bihar and intended to use his ill-gotten wealth to further his political ambitions in England. He went back an extremely rich man—the main beneficiary of Plassey.

Upon his return, he began lobbying for a peerage. He aspired to an honour that would elevate his social standing and allow him to claim the status of a British aristocrat. He was partially successful in this, being bestowed an Irish title at the level of a baron, which is at the bottom of the hierarchy in the peerage. What is more, he was given an Irish peerage, which was considered quite inferior to being ennobled as a peer of Great Britain. Many of the Irish peerages were of relatively recent, eighteenth-century origin. Clive was rather disappointed that he had to opt for the less prestigious honour. The decision by the government to make him an Irish peer was informally conveyed towards the end of 1761. Having agreed to this, he proposed that he might be known as 'Robert, Lord Clive, Baron Plassey in the Kingdom of Ireland'. In anticipation of the title, Clive had invested a portion of his Bengal fortune in the purchase of landed property in Ireland—over thirty thousand Irish pounds.[14] This was not, as has at times been assumed, an essential precondition for an Irish title, or for him to be known as Baron of Plassey, i.e., being bestowed a title incorporating the name of a place in Ireland called Plassey (Clive renamed his estate as 'Plassey'). Yet he was aware that as the owner of a substantial estate in Ireland, he would be able to reinforce his status as an Irish peer, making sure

---

[14]John Logan, 'Robert Clive's Irish Peerage and Estate, 1761-1842', *North Munster Antiquarian Journal*, Vol. 43, 2003, p. 3.

that this would not be an empty title. With the help of one of his former military colleagues from India, Caleb Powell, he bought an estate measuring about 14,000 acres, situated mainly in Clare County in the southwestern part of Ireland. A portion of the estate was located in the neighbouring county of Limerick.[15] The property, together with some land in the small town of Ballykilty, or Ballykelty, comprised 'an incredibly disjointed estate and ran into several thousand acres'.[16] On the other hand, in his study of the history of Irish peerages of the eighteenth and nineteenth centuries, Anthony Malcomson suggests that Clive was the baron of an 'imaginary Plassey' in Clare County, and that the statement in several writings about Clive's ownership of the Plassey estate (in County Limerick) is incorrect.[17] John Logan has meticulously examined local records relating to Clive's properties and identified the location of his estate. From his evidence, it would appear that Clive did invest in land in Ireland and that his estate was named 'Plassey, otherwise Ballykilty'.

Powell and Clive had become acquainted in 1755 when the two were posted in Fort St David—the former as an officer in the 39th Regiment and the latter as head of the outpost. Powell joined the Company's army after Plassey and returned home at the same time as Clive. Logan has pointed out that a few other EIC employees, some of them contemporaries of Clive, had invested in landed property in the area upon their return from India. At least two of them, apart from Powell, had been present at Plassey.[18] Unlike an English peer, an Irish peer did not become a member of the House of Lords (of Britain). Irish peers sat in the Irish House of Lords in Dublin, which

---

[15]The following details regarding Clive's relationship with Caleb Powell are based on Logan, 'Robert Clive's Irish Peerage and Estate'.

[16]Kevin Hannan, 'How Plassey Got its Name', *Old Limerick Journal*, Vol. 1, 1978, p. 8.

[17]A. P. W. Malcomson, 'The Irish Peerage and the Act of Union, 1800-1971', *Transactions of the Royal Historical Society*, Vol. 10, 2000, p. 304n53.

[18]Logan, 'Robert Clive's Irish Peerage and Estate', pp. 12 and 15.

existed until 1800. We shall later discuss Cornwallis's role in the historical process that led to the abolition of the house.

Clive did not engage in Irish politics or local affairs as a prominent landed aristocrat. It seems unlikely that he ever stayed on his estate or attended any session of the Irish House of Lords. His ambitions lay elsewhere. Clive became a member of the British House of Commons in 1761. This was possible for an Irish peer, unlike a British peer. He had also secured a seat for his father, Richard, before he left India. Following his return, he managed to get a few more relatives elected to Parliament. Soon, however, he found himself embroiled in a bitter conflict with a section of the EIC's directors. This dispute consumed much of his time over the next three years before he left for yet another sojourn in Bengal.

The growing involvement in parliamentary politics was partly linked to Clive's efforts to counter the mounting criticism of his misdeeds in Bengal. The immediate manifestation of this public criticism was the accusation that he had received personal favours from the new regime at Murshidabad in return for the assistance that the Company had rendered in overthrowing Siraj-ud-Daula. Apart from the astronomical amount of money he had received, there were costly presents in the form of jewels and other valuable articles of luxury. News about the huge sums (and jewels) he had transmitted to England had been circulating, along with reports about the political shifts in Bengal. The two were inseparable and, as we shall see, led to parliamentary enquiries about the conduct, before and immediately after Plassey, of Clive and his associates. What his critics highlighted most prominently was the assignment of revenues derived from a jagir that had been bestowed on him by the Mughal imperial court on the recommendation of the nawab of Bengal. Strictly speaking, a jagir was the grant of the state's share of the produce from land assigned to a jagirdar or holder of a jagir. The revenue assessed on the assigned land was payable to the jagirdar, in lieu of the salary due to him for services rendered to the state. While the bureaucratic and military apparatus was still functional till the late seventeenth century, all imperial mansabdars received emoluments in accordance with their rank or mansab in the hierarchy of the Mughal state. The system began facing problems in the latter half of the seventeenth century, and it collapsed by the turn of the century.

During the eighteenth century, the assignment of a jagir became one of the means whereby the Mughal emperor indicated his appreciation of services rendered to him personally or to the state. This was a device that several powerful nobles who governed parts of the empire almost independently, yet owed nominal allegiance to the emperor, also found useful for rewarding their adherents. Mansab and jagir went hand in hand in the Mughal system, as the jagir, or state's share of the produce, was equivalent, in theory, to the salary of the holder of a mansab (mansabdar). It may be mentioned that when the system was evolving in Akbar's reign (1556–1605), a substantial proportion of mansabdars received their salaries in cash. Under the successors of Akbar, the proportion of mansabdars who were given jagirs in lieu of cash salary began to increase, and this tendency intensified towards the end of the seventeenth century. Moreover, jagirs tended to become hereditary towards the end of the century.

Officials of European companies trying to embed themselves in Indian society were attentive to the symbolic value attached to Mughal titles and therefore eagerly sought these for themselves. These titles gave them greater acceptability among elites. Clive had a Mughal title before the Plassey skirmish: 'Sabut Jung Bahadur' ('experienced in war; experienced warrior'), which he had obtained for his role in the Carnatic Wars. This was the name by which he was known to Indians with whom he had official dealings, and it was used by him to sign formal documents. Then, in April 1758 he received a communication that he had been made a mansabdar of the rank of '6000', the highest rank then available to mansabdars who did not belong to the imperial family or were not prominent nobles, along with other, more high-sounding titles than Sabut Jung Bahadur. Clive had canvassed for the new titles, nudging the Jagat Seths to use their influence in Delhi. He was certainly more interested in the jagir than the title. The jagir, according to Mughal practice, had to be assigned to him as a mansabdar to uphold the fiction that he was an imperial functionary with an obligation to maintain a cavalry contingent of 5,000 horses, a notional figure corresponding to his mansab. The jagir was not immediately forthcoming, and once again, he had to rely on the Jagat Seths to pursue the matter with the relevant officials. The imperial court had not entirely lost its relevance.

Eventually, the royal document sanctioning the jagir was received in the middle of 1759. An intricate formula was worked out, tying the Company to the jagir. The jagir was located in Bengal, which in itself was unusual since the imperial secretariat even in the heyday of Mughal power avoided allotting jagirs in the suba. Moreover, the jagir was the same revenue unit (24-Parganas, adjacent to Calcutta) for which the zamindari rights were assigned to the EIC by Mir Jafar as a reward for assisting him in the coup. The zamindari rights gave to the Company a superior share in the produce, namely, ten per cent (or more) of the sum collected as revenue on behalf of the state, claims arising out of proprietary right, and a few other traditional perquisites. With the assignment of 24-Parganas to Clive as his jagir, the revenue now became payable to him as jagirdar, instead of to the state. In other words, the EIC's local establishment was to collect the revenue and hand it over to Clive or his representatives rather than to the state, after deducting the zamindari share of ten per cent. There was nothing devious about this arrangement; it was intended to guarantee that the revenue was collected regularly—something that the Company was in a position to do—and that Clive received his share on time. The revenue (state's share) of the estate was assessed at a sum between £27,000 and £30,000 annually, and the EIC's personnel would have been ruthless in realizing the full demand. As the jagir was retained by Clive upon his return, he was guaranteed an ample income for the rest of his life. It is not surprising that Clive's adversaries in England should have targeted the jagir in such a focused manner when they launched their offensive against him.

The offensive against Clive was intertwined with an intense struggle for control over the Company's affairs. The directors had, overnight, become mighty rulers. The emergence of the EIC as a major territorial power resulted in tensions among senior executives, who tried to strengthen their respective factions by aligning with prominent political figures. From the point of view of the latter, it made sense to intervene in the struggle for supremacy within the Court of Directors to be able to use the Company's resources—lately augmented to an unbelievable extent—to further their political interests. These tensions reached a high point in 1762–64, when a bitter feud broke out between the group led by Clive and that headed by Laurence Sulivan, a prominent director of the Company. Sulivan (1713–86) had served in India in the first half of the eighteenth century. He was elected to the Court of Directors several times between 1757 and 1785 and was chairman on four occasions. Since the early sixties, the Court of Directors had been divided into two mutually hostile groups: the 'Bombay squad' led by Sulivan (who had been posted in the Bombay Presidency), and the 'Bengal squad' comprising wealthy officials who had become prosperous through plunder in the wake of Plassey. Clive, though not a member of the court himself, became the leader of the 'Bengal squad'. He indirectly controlled a large number of votes in the Court of Proprietors, or General Court, comprising owners of EIC stock. The dispute became very acrimonious by the 1760s and led to the campaign which culminated in the public denunciation of Clive and parliamentary proceedings against him.

In the annual election of 1763 for the Court of Directors, the Sulivan faction, which had governed since 1758, trounced Clive's group. The Court of Proprietors elected twenty-four directors annually. Clive's associates had challenged the dominance of the Bombay squad in this election. The newly elected court instantly issued instructions according to which Clive's share of the revenue from the Bengal jagir was henceforth to be paid to the Company. This was a blow to the former governor's prestige as well as to his financial standing. The proceeds from the jagir were essential for allowing him to maintain the kind of lifestyle that, in his perception, accorded with his status. The peerage, albeit an inferior one, and membership of the House of Commons were all status symbols for him. He needed ready money to realize his social ambitions (a large proportion of the wealth he had amassed was tied up in landed property). The transmission, on a recurring basis, of approximately £30,000 annually on account of Clive's jagir, and the zamindari share payable to the EIC, must be added to estimates for the overall transfer of resources from Bengal to Britain in the post-Plassey period when calculating the 'drain of wealth' under colonial rule.

The defeat of the Clive faction in the 1763 election coincided with problems in Bengal, which threatened to put an end to the EIC's sway over eastern India. Shortly after Clive left for Britain, Company officials in Bengal engineered the ouster of Mir Jafar, mainly due to his inability to arrange for the huge sums of money that had been promised in return for support in installing him as the nawab. Towards the end of 1760, he was substituted with his son-in-law, Mir Qasim, who, contrary to the Company's expectations, set about restoring the authority of the Murshidabad government. For this, it was necessary to make the province financially stable, which, in turn was the precondition for strengthening the army. Mir Qasim realized that a military showdown with the English was inevitable if he were to assert his independence. He had the support of an influential section of the regional aristocracy, which had not reconciled to the Company's usurpation of authority in Bengal.

Mir Qasim moved rapidly to strengthen his hold over finances and reorganize the army, thereby annoying the Company. He transferred the nawab's court from Murshidabad to Munger in Bihar, east of Patna. This reduced the EIC's interference in the administration. With Mir Qasim's capital located at Munger, Bihar became the main zone of conflict. By the middle of 1763, the EIC managed to bring about another realignment whereby Mir Jafar was once again recognized as nawab by the pro-Company faction in Murshidabad. War was declared against Mir Qasim in July 1763. Soon, a wider conflict developed as Mir Qasim forged an alliance with the recently installed Mughal emperor Shah Alam (r. 1759–1806), and with Shuja-ud-Daula, Mughal subedar of Awadh (1754–75). The conflict culminated in the Battle of Buxar (Baksar) in October 1764, fought between the English and the combined forces of Mir Qasim and Shuja-ud-Daula on behalf of the emperor, who himself had no army. The Company's army managed to gain the upper hand in the military encounter. This marked the end of Mir Qasim's political career. Mir Jafar was once again recognized as the nawab of Bengal (and Bihar).

Disturbing news about the turbulent political situation in Bengal, before the confrontation at Buxar, reached London in February 1764. Anxious shareholders of the Company immediately requisitioned a special meeting of the General Court, which took place on 12 March. This was a crucial meeting from the point of view of Clive's future. Against the backdrop of the factional tussle among the directors, Clive's supporters had been mobilizing support for him and had lobbied with the prime minister, George Grenville, to intervene in the Company's affairs. Grenville had assumed office in April 1763. He was persuaded to back Clive, and the ground was thus prepared for his return to Bengal to handle the crisis created by Mir Qasim. The General Court agreed to a proposal for appointing Clive as governor of Fort William. He sailed from England at the beginning of June, reaching Calcutta a year later, in May 1765. His ship had a difficult journey, being blown in the direction of Brazil as had happened on his outward journey more than twenty years earlier. It had to spend several weeks at Rio de Janeiro. In other words, during the months immediately preceding and following Buxar, he was in transit, and the issue that required urgent attention had already been settled by the time he took up his post. The question of the jagir, too, had been resolved for the time being, with the General Court allowing him to retain its income for ten years. The General Court's resolution sanctioning Clive's share of the revenue from the jagir for a limited duration was passed with much difficulty—583 members voted in favour, while 396 voted against.

Within a few weeks of his arrival in Calcutta, Clive 'journeyed to Ilahabad, where he had the honor to pay his respects to the Emperor', Shah Alam, whose court was based in the city at this time.[19] With the assistance of Shuja-ud-Daula, who was also the imperial vazir, Clive convinced the emperor that 'the Company should be invested with the Divan-ship [charge of the revenue establishment] of three provinces of Bengal, Bahar and Ooressa', 'of which office he requested the proper Patents from the Vezir and the Emperor'.[20] The farman granting the diwani of Bengal, Bihar, and Orissa to the EIC was received by Clive at a formal darbar held by the emperor at Allahabad on 12 August 1765. Standard protocol was scrupulously followed on the occasion, to which Clive willingly adhered. A major stipulation of the farman was that the Company was to ensure the payment into the imperial treasury of a sum of twenty-six lakh rupees annually, out of the revenues of the three provinces. This sum represented peshkash or tribute for the emperor, an acknowledgement of his de jure sovereignty over the territories that had come under the Company's control after Plassey. Mir Jafar had died in early 1765 while these arrangements were being finalized. He was succeeded by his son Najm-ud-Daula as the subedar of the eastern provinces of the Mughal empire. Najm-ud-Daula had already been officially recognized as the subedar by Shah Alam through a parwana despatched from the imperial court a few

---

[19]Seid Gholam Hossain Khan, *The Seir Mutaqherin*, Nota Manus (tr.), Vol. 3, New Delhi: Inter-India Publications, 1986, p. 9. This is the English translation of Ghulam Hussain Tabatabai's *Siyar al-Mutakhhirin*.
[20]Ibid., p. 9.

months before the diwani farman was issued to the Company. The EIC's officials were aware that the validity of the diwani was dependent upon compliance with imperial procedures. The commitment made by the EIC in 1765 for the payment of ₹26,00,000 was to remain an important cause of friction between the Company and the emperors for several decades— indeed right until the time of the revolt—due to the irregular payment of the peshkash after the 1770s and its eventual termination.

With the EIC now taking over the functions of the diwan, a Byzantine system was devised for governing Bengal and Bihar. Whereas the Company held charge of the revenue establishment, all other aspects of the administration were supposedly the responsibility of the nawab (the subedar/nazim of Bengal). This was the origin of the infamous 'dual' system of government, whereby the functions of the diwani (revenue and related matters) were directly the Company's concern, while the nizamat (law and order, defence, justice, and residual matters) was to be looked after by the nawab. In practice, there was no clear-cut distinction. By the end of the 1760s, the nawab had no troops left, except for ceremonial purposes, so that defence and maintenance of internal law and order, too, were taken over by the Company. Insofar as the judicial machinery was concerned, most civil matters (excluding disputes in the area of personal law) were under the diwani. Criminal justice, though under the jurisdiction of the nizamat, also began to be monitored by European officials from the mid-seventies. Thus, the nizamat's tasks were progressively curtailed.

The two wings of the state apparatus, nizamat and diwani, were unified in the person of Saiyid Muhammad Reza Khan. In 1765, Reza Khan was appointed naib nazim or deputy to Nawab Najm-ud-Daula. He was a nominee of Clive. Born in Shiraz, Khan belonged to an Iranian family that migrated to India at the beginning of the eighteenth century. His father was a physician who moved to Murshidabad, where he was given a position at the court of Alivardi Khan. Reza Khan married into the family of Alivardi Khan, which made him a member of the Bengal aristocracy, giving him access to political power. He seems to have played an important role in behind-the-scenes manoeuvres during the critical period preceding the Company's break with Mir Qasim. He aligned himself closely with the British who, by the middle of the 1760s, had come to recognize him as a key figure in Bengal. However, he was marginalized by the early 1770s and eventually dispensed with altogether.

There might have been some hope among sections of the regional elite in eastern India, even in the late 1760s and early 1770s, that all was not lost after Plassey and Buxar and that some elements of the pre-Buxar dispensation could be retrieved to reconstitute the regime in a manner that would allow the provincial ruling class to exercise limited power, notwithstanding the ascendancy of the English. To describe all top-level Indian functionaries of the state after 1765 as outright collaborators would be inaccurate. Summing up the attitudes of Reza Khan and his arch-rival Nandakumar (we shall have more to say about their rivalry), Abdul Majed Khan, in his study of the early years of transition notes that, '[whereas] Nandakumar was quite ready to help deprive Reza Khan of the Nizamat powers ... he was no more ready than the Khan to see Mughal sovereignty pass to the Company'.[21] The two are representative of that section of important Mughal provincial functionaries who made themselves useful to the EIC and continued to wield some power after the 1757 coup, while not entirely giving up their allegiance to the emperor.

It took the Company several years to replace these functionaries with its own personnel. Although the EIC tried to regulate appointments for senior positions in the 'dual' government, it was not always successful. The complicated administrative system introduced following the acquisition of diwani, and the presence of officials who had served under

---

[21]Abdul Majed Khan, *The Transition in Bengal, 1756-1775: A Study of Sayid Muhammad Reza Khan*, Cambridge: Cambridge University Press, 1969, p. 344.

Alivardi Khan or under Siraj-ud-Daula, left some room for manoeuvre until almost the mid-1770s. The marginalization by 1775 of Reza Khan—the most important Indian administrator of the new regime—marked the end of the relevance of nawabi elements at the upper levels of the government.

Clive's second governorship, too, was quite brief. He was on his way back by January 1767. In September of that year, shortly after his return, the General Court extended his possession of the jagir for another ten years, i.e., till 1784, ten years beyond the first extension. Whereas the jagir issue was resolved for the moment, ensuring a regular flow of ready money amounting to the substantial sum of about thirty thousand pounds annually, the closing years of Clive's relatively short life were spent dealing with a parliamentary investigation into offenses committed by him while he was posted in eastern India. He had to devote all his energy to refuting charges—of which he was certainly guilty—of rapaciousness in his dealings with Indian beneficiaries of the coup which led to the Company's ascendancy in Bengal. He was accused of amassing a huge private fortune from the vast amounts he had extracted from individuals, as well as the money he had appropriated from the Murshidabad treasury after Plassey. These sums were in addition to the lavish presents received by him as 'Master of Bengal'—presents which were often given involuntarily. The accusations pertained to his second stint in Bengal as well.

Clive's short-lived political influence in England had diminished by the end of the 1760s, especially with the demise of Grenville, who passed away in 1770. Lord North, prime minister from 1770 onwards, was not particularly fond of Clive. The conduct of the EIC's servants in India began to be scrutinized under North's government. The EIC's activities in India became the subject of parliamentary scrutiny in Britain as a consequence of the public articulation of a critique of its monopoly, as well as of the private fortunes amassed by its servants. The social and political implications for Britain of the 'new money' brought back by corrupt officials such as

Clive were major issues in this critique. Such officials came to be labelled pejoratively by contemporaries as 'nabobs' (literally, the anglicized form of 'nawab'). These nabobs had ostentatious lifestyles reflecting the tastes of social upstarts. They constructed expensive houses, often of flashy and bizarre architectural design. One of the better-known examples, though of a slightly later period, 'Sezincote' in Gloucestershire, is a typical example of such buildings. Sezincote was the residence of Charles Cockerell, who was posted for several years in India and returned with a large fortune. The building was constructed at the beginning of the nineteenth century (Cockerell went to India in 1775). Designed like a pleasure pavilion topped by a bulbous dome, it features minarets at its four corners, and is set in a 'Mughal' garden. Such structures must have evoked both envy and resentment. The loud display of 'new' money by nabobs was not appreciated either by the old aristocracy or the less affluent sections of society. A more serious issue was the potential for nabobs to undermine democratic institutions. Advocates of electoral reform attacked the blatant manner in which they used their wealth to purchase access to Parliament.

In 1772, Parliament initiated an enquiry into Clive's activities in India. Two committees were constituted for the purpose: a select parliamentary committee with thirty-one members and a secret parliamentary committee comprising thirteen members. Although Clive was eventually exonerated in 1773 and was even thanked for the services he had rendered to Britain, the massive loot indulged in by the Company's servants was exposed during the enquiry. The remarkably detailed reports compiled by these committees documented the greed and violence with which the Company and its servants had plundered the resources of its Indian territories since 1757. Moreover, Parliament officially recorded that Clive had personally received, at the very least, £234,000 from Mir Jafar and those who had sponsored him.

Clive had barely a year and a half to enjoy his retirement undisturbed after the House of Commons concluded the debate over allegations against him. In November 1774, he committed suicide by slashing his throat with a sharp instrument, perhaps a penknife. Among the reasons for his reluctance to stay on in Calcutta in 1767 had been a debilitating medical condition triggered by a nervous disorder with which he had been afflicted for several years. His condition had deteriorated in the mid-1760s, and had become a major physical problem. He suffered a serious breakdown towards the end of 1766. The episodes had become more frequent and more painful. To alleviate the symptoms, Clive had begun ingesting large doses of opium. The quantities consumed by him had increased progressively (apparently, there were intervals when he desisted from consuming the drug entirely), and opium consumption became an underlying factor responsible for his suicide. His family and close friends never admitted publicly that he had killed himself and instead spread a story of accidental death due to an overdose of laudanum (a medical preparation containing opium). Significantly, he was buried in an unmarked grave, which would confirm that he had taken his life and was thus denied burial on consecrated ground.

III

THE RISE AND FALL OF
WARREN HASTINGS

Warren Hastings was a near-contemporary of Clive. He was seven years younger than his predecessor as the principal colonial official presiding over the EIC's territories in India. He was born in 1732, into a poor family which had possessed land several generations earlier. Warren's grandfather was an Anglican priest, barely surviving on the tiny remuneration he received as the local rector of Daylesford village. Daylesford (then in Worcestershire County; now in Gloucestershire) is about forty kilometres from Oxford. The old Hastings mansion at Daylesford with its former estate was to absorb much of Warren Hastings's leisure time after he returned from India and settled down to a retired life. We shall have more to say about the estate below.

The rector's younger son, Warren's father, too, became a priest. Much later in life Warren summed up his father's career with the terse remark that, 'There was not much in my father's history that would be worth repeating except that, when he became old enough, he entered into holy orders, and went to one of the West India Islands [Barbados], where he died'.[1] The father quickly abandoned his family, leaving his son and a daughter named Anne—who was born two years before Warren—orphans. His wife had died within a few days of Warren's birth. Nevertheless, as a family settled in the countryside for long, which had been part of the lesser gentry a few generations

---

[1]G. R. Gleig, *Memoirs: The Life of the Right Hon. Warren Hastings*, Vol. 1, London: Richard Bentley, 1841, p. 6.

earlier, the Hastings had connections that gave them access to prestigious institutions of learning. Warren's grandfather and father were both educated at Oxford. Warren himself, after some preliminary schooling in the village, and at a preparatory school near London, was sent to Westminster School. This was an institution founded in the mid-sixteenth century, its roots going back to an earlier period, and was attached to Westminster Abbey. Clive's brother-in-law, the astronomer Nevil Maskelyne, exactly the same age as Hastings, also studied at Westminster School, and they might have been acquainted with each other. They certainly completed their school education in the same year, 1749. The future astronomer royal went on to study at Cambridge, as did another schoolmate, Elijah Impey, who, as the first chief justice of the Calcutta Supreme Court, would play an important role in Hastings's career in India. Impey's term as chief justice coincided with that of Hastings as governor-general. The two got to know each other well at school. Hastings himself had to give up the prospect of higher education, even though he had shown his scholarly talent by being placed at the top of the merit list in 1747 for the prestigious King's Scholarships awarded to students of Westminster. The scholarship would have facilitated his entry into Cambridge or Oxford. However, at this crucial juncture, the death in February 1749 of his uncle, his father's brother, under whose care Warren had received his school education, seems to have put an end to any academic ambitions he might have possessed.[2]

Following the death of his uncle, a distant relative by the name of Joseph Creswicke, most probably at his own initiative, placed Warren in an institution for undertaking (as mentioned in the certificate submitted to the EIC), a 'regular course of Merchants' Accounts' and writing (penmanship).[3] This enabled

---

[2]Though some biographies mention 1748 as the year of death of Hastings's uncle, I have gone by the date mentioned in Keith Feiling, *Warren Hastings*, London: Macmillan, 1966, p. 8.
[3]Charles Lawson, *The Private Life of Warren Hastings*, London: Swan Sonnenschein & Co., 1895, pp. 31–32.

him to apply for a writership in the EIC's service. We can see that employment in the Company's establishment in India was already, even before the territorial acquisitions of 1757, considered a suitable career option for a young boy of Hastings's social class. With a little support, Hastings could have managed to study at a good university in England, given his above-average academic performance at Westminster. In fact the headmaster of the school, whom Warren always remembered very fondly, had offered to arrange for financial assistance so that he could continue with his education. That was not to be. The decision had been taken for Warren, perhaps with his reluctant acceptance of it. Creswicke might have been associated with the Company in some capacity, which enabled him to secure a recommendation from a director for his ward's appointment. He was employed in the Custom House in London, as was Warren's deceased uncle, which might explain how Creswicke came to be the guardian of the young Hastings and executor of the will of Warren's uncle. The candidate fulfilled the main requirements for recruitment as a writer: he was aged 'sixteen years and upwards', and had been 'bred up to Writing and Accounts'; his 'humble petition' was accepted in 1750 and he was inducted as a writer, about eight years junior to Clive in the service.

Warren was posted in the Bengal establishment of the EIC. Sailing from England, he initially disembarked at Fort St David, and a few weeks later, the East Indiaman *London*, which had brought him from London to the Coromandel, took him to Calcutta where he was to take up his station. After spending over two years in Calcutta, Hastings was transferred to Cossimbazar.

While stationed in Cossimbazar, Warren was sent out to silk-producing villages in the vicinity to supervise the purchase of raw silk. During the first half of the eighteenth century, raw silk had become a valuable component of the Company's exports from Bengal. The Cossimbazar area was a major supplier of the varieties of silk that were in demand in the English market. Several decades of experience had shown that the superfine silk for which the area was famous was not suitable for the silk weavers of England, who preferred to work with the coarser types of Cossimbazar silk. It was necessary to supervise the process of reeling or winding the filament with a lot of attention to detail to ensure that the varieties suitable for the English market were supplied to the Company. In the 1750s, the EIC had taken the initiative to introduce machinery for winding silk according to the desired specifications, and some of the processing was done in on its own premises. The Cossimbazar factory usually relied on petty brokers (pykars) for making advances to silk rearers in the villages, from whom the material was collected after minute inspection by Company servants well-versed in the essentials of the trade. Warren spent over three years in rural north Bengal acquiring this experience.

When Siraj-ud-Daula seized the Cossimbazar factory in 1756, Hastings was taken to Murshidabad as a prisoner along with other EIC employees. He was not, it seems, placed in strict confinement, mainly due to the local connections he had managed to establish during his stay in Cossimbazar. Besides, he had a good rapport with George Vernet, head of the Dutch factory, and eventually secured his release from captivity through his mediation. Subsequently, as an expression of his gratitude to Vernet, Hastings privately supported his widow with a pension, which he continued to provide till her death in 1793. After his release, Hastings became the Company's principal representative for dealing with the provincial authorities and for gathering intelligence that might have been useful for the Calcutta officials.

Hastings departed from Cossimbazar in the second week of October (1756) and proceeded to Fulta via the Dutch settlement of Chinsura located north of Calcutta. The English refugees at Fulta included some women who had sought shelter in this outpost when Fort William was evacuated. During the few weeks that Warren was at Fulta, he married one of these evacuees, Mary Elliott. Mary had recently lost her husband, Captain John Buchanan, a British soldier whom she had married in 1753. John died while in captivity when the fort in Calcutta was occupied by Siraj. Mary passed away in 1759 and was buried at Cossimbazar, where her grave may still be seen. The inscription on the gravestone of this simple tomb, placed by Warren, seems to have been erased over a period of time, and a century later was replaced by the British Indian government. A daughter born to the couple in 1759, who died when she was just a few days old, is also buried at the same place. Another child, a son who was born shortly after their marriage (the first born), was sent to England for his education but died when he was still very young. Warren thus had no surviving children of his own after the death of his son—even from his second marriage, which took place several years later. He did, however, have stepchildren from his first marriage, two daughters of Mary and John who were infants when their mother married for a second time. He would also have stepchildren from his second marriage.

In the EIC's campaign in Bengal that led to the recapturing of Calcutta in 1757, Hastings participated as a volunteer. As we have seen in the previous chapter, he was one of the emissaries during the negotiations between Siraj-ud-Daula and the Company after the latter's reoccupation of Fort William. When the Cossimbazar factory reopened following the February 1757 agreement with the nawab, Hastings was sent as Watts's assistant.

Following the overthrow of Siraj-ud-Daula, Hastings was given charge of the Cossimbazar establishment, formally as Watts's deputy. As Watts was frequently away in Calcutta, where he now had a bigger role having played a prominent part in the coup, Hastings was for all practical purposes the head of the factory. There is nothing to suggest that he was directly involved in the plot to overthrow Siraj, though he might have been taken into confidence by his immediate superior, and was certainly helpful as a source of news and gossip. Considering that the trading activities of the EIC had been disrupted for over a year, it is likely that his duties were mostly related to the commercial aspects of the large Cossimbazar factory with its several warehouses. Hastings's business skills would have been valuable to his employer for this purpose. In October, he was made head of the Cossimbazar factory. As the political and commercial functions of the Company's officials were so closely interlinked, Hastings could not have worked in a purely commercial capacity and must have been occasionally assigned political or diplomatic duties too. Thus, in August 1758, he was appointed as resident at the court of the nawab, which was essentially a political–diplomatic assignment at a very critical moment.

∽

When, at the beginning of 1765, Clive's ship was on its way from Rio de Janeiro to Madras—having been compelled by unfavourable winds to make a long detour through the Atlantic—Hastings had embarked on his homeward journey, with no intention of going back to India. He was in England during the brief period when Clive was governor of Fort William, between 1765 and 1767, and was still there when Clive finally returned home.

Hastings had been made a member of the council of Fort William in 1761, necessitating his shift from Cossimbazar to Calcutta. Sharp differences within the council amidst the tumult caused by the conflict with Mir Qasim eventually led to his resignation, and his decision to leave Bengal. He might have left earlier had it not been for the events which preceded the Battle of Buxar, and the military confrontation itself.

The battle took place in the last week of October 1764; Hastings resigned at the end of December. He was moderately well-off and had spent nearly fifteen years in India in the service of the EIC, without once going home on furlough. The earnings from his private trade were modest compared to the riches accumulated by Clive. According to one estimate, it amounted to £30,000—the equivalent of Clive's annual income from his jagir. Hastings had made profits from trade in commodities such as salt, opium, and carpets, benefiting, like other EIC employees, from the politically advantageous position in which the English were placed after Plassey. For his commercial dealings, he had used the services and local connections of Krishna Kanta Nandy, or Cantoo Baboo as he was then known to the English. Cantoo Baboo had been Hastings's business manager ('banian') since 1754. Hastings perhaps came to know Cantoo Baboo through one of his colleagues in Cossimbazar, Francis Sykes. Sykes was posted at Cossimbazar as a writer a little before Hastings. Sykes and Hastings became firm friends, the former finally returning home in 1769 with a fortune 'reckoned by his contemporaries to be one of the largest to come out of India'.[4]

Sykes was away in England between 1761 and 1764 to recuperate and returned to Bengal when Clive became governor of Fort William for a second term. Clive appointed him head of the Cossimbazar establishment of the Company and resident at the Murshidabad court. He was also a member of the Calcutta Council, and a prominent trader.

Cantoo Baboo played a pivotal role in the expansion of his private business. The commodities they bought and sold included salt, tobacco, saltpetre, silk, and betel nut. Cantoo Baboo himself had started his career as a dealer in raw silk, which would have been the basis of the relationship between him and Hastings in the first place. Hastings, it will be remembered, supervised the purchase of raw silk at Cossimbazar in the early fifties.

Cantoo invested his profits in land, especially in orchards and fruit gardens. He prospered through his association with Sykes and later under Hastings's regime. Land management was his forte, and he used the political influence he derived from his intimate connection with these two powerful EIC functionaries in Bengal to create a vast landed estate, the Cossimbazar Raj. At the beginning of the nineteenth century, the total annual income from the estate was estimated at over fourteen lakh rupees.

---

[4]John Sykes, 'The Indian Seal of Sir Francis Sykes: A Tale of Two Families', Margot Finn and Kate Smith (eds.), *East India Company at Home, 1757-1857*, London: UCL Press, 2018, p. 423.

Before his departure, Hastings had invested a substantial part of his savings in Bengal. Most of these investments were wiped out due to losses, leaving him with no option but to seek a job again. He applied to the Company for re-employment within a year of his arrival in England.

At this stage, the EIC did not provide any pensions to its employees. Initially, the request was turned down, mainly because Hastings was aligned with—or perceived to be close to—the anti-Clive faction of Sulivan. It may be recalled that Clive's faction had been defeated in the 1763 elections for the court. The situation had changed by 1764. Sulivan and his group received a setback when Clive succeeded in getting one of his adherents elected as chairman of the Company. This facilitated Clive's appointment as governor of Fort William on his own terms. The Clive faction gained strength during his absence, and Sulivan himself was further marginalized. Sulivan would stage a comeback in 1769, by which time Clive's adversaries had multiplied. The challenge these opponents posed to him was formidable.

Yet between 1766, when Hastings learnt of his financial ruin, and April 1769, when Sulivan was once again elected a director after a gap of five years, the Company was controlled by Clive's supporters. They could not be expected to be sympathetic to Hastings. The directors were especially unwilling to reappoint Hastings in view of his proximity to Henry Vansittart, governor of Fort William from 1760 to 1764. Hastings had backed Vansittart's views while the two were members of the Calcutta council. Vansittart had returned to England at the end of his tenure in 1764, and had gravitated towards the Sulivan camp in EIC politics.

Vansittart was appointed governor of Fort William after Clive departed from Bengal in early 1760 and had to deal with the fallout of the break with Mir Qasim. The criticism of his policies, especially by Clive's supporters, was among the factors that made him an ally of Sulivan. Clive disliked him intensely. It is not surprising that Hastings's application was rejected. Subsequently, with the intervention of Sykes—who had the almost unique distinction of being close to both Clive and Hastings—the request was granted. However, Clive recommended that Hastings be sent to Madras rather than to Bengal. He rejoined the Company's service as a member of the Madras Council, second in the order of seniority. This entitled him to succeed the incumbent governor when the latter's term ended.

Hastings embarked for Madras in March 1769. Aboard the ship, he became friendly with Anna Maria and her husband, Baron Carl von Imhoff. Anna Maria, née Chapusetin, better known as Marian, would later divorce the baron and marry Hastings. A warm relationship between Marian and Warren developed while the two were on their way to India. At the time they got to know each other, Marian was about twenty-two years old, so that there was a considerable age gap between her and Hastings. Imhoff was travelling to Madras with his family to join the EIC's army as a junior officer. He subsequently had a modestly successful career as a painter. During the years that Hastings was posted in Madras, the relationship between him and Marian acquired romantic overtones, marking the beginning of a lifelong bond. They married in 1777. Marian outlived her second husband by nearly twenty years.

At Madras, Hastings's main responsibility was the purchase of goods for the Company's business. He was expected to ensure that the goods were procured at the lowest possible rates, efficiently utilizing the EIC's 'investment', which referred to the resources provided by the EIC in the form of precious metal, the inflow of which had drastically come down with the acquisition of territories in eastern India. The directors were pleased with his competence in managing the Company's commercial enterprise in the Coromandel, and in 1771, he was appointed governor of Fort William, replacing John Cartier (governor from 1769 to 1772).

The decision of the Court of Directors appointing Hastings as governor was preceded by factional manoeuvres in which

Hastings's friend Sykes played a key role. Hastings left for Calcutta in February 1772. He assumed office in April. This coincided with the relocation of the Mughal court from Allahabad to Delhi. Simultaneously, the Bengal tribute amounting to ₹26 lakh per annum—initially withheld temporarily—was suspended indefinitely. The remittance of the tribute had become irregular by the end of the 1760s, but had not been entirely withheld.

However, in a letter addressed to the Court of Directors shortly before he formally took over, Hastings declared that, 'I think I may promise that no more payment will be made... nor, if I can prevent it, ever more'.[5] The terrible Bengal famine of 1770, caused by the Company's avariciousness, provided an excuse for not remitting the tribute. Shah Alam was initially assured that 'with the advent of better times he [Hastings] will be able to resume to His Majesty the Bengal tribute'.[6]

In 1775, the directors endorsed Hastings's decision 'to suspend payment of tribute to His Majesty Shaw Allum', instructing the Bengal officials not to resume it again without the permission of the Court of Directors.

Hastings began his tenure as governor of Bengal (Fort William) on 13 April 1772. A few days after he had assumed charge, the naib (deputy to the nawab), Muhammad Reza Khan, was arrested. This was done on the orders of the directors. In 1772, the EIC had directly taken over the diwani instead of operating through Indian deputies. It is likely that the action against Reza Khan was intended to discredit him so that the Company's decision to 'stand forth as Dewan' (as the directive of the Court of Directors put it) could be justified publicly. Further, Hastings had been enjoined to exploit the contradictions between Nandakumar and Reza Khan to prepare the ground for ejecting the incumbent naib:[7]

[5] K. K. Datta, *Shah Alam II and the East India Company*, Calcutta: World Press, 1965, p. 62.
[6] Ibid., p. 63.
[7] Khan, *Transition in Bengal, 1756-1775*, p. 302.

We... cannot forbear recommending to you to avail yourself of the intelligence which Nundcomar may be able to give respecting the Naib's [Reza Khan's] administration; and while the envy, which Nundcomar is supposed to bear this minister may prompt him to a ready communication of all proceedings which have come to his knowledge, we are persuaded that no scrupulous part of the Naib's conduct can have escaped the watchful eye of his jealous and penetrating rival.

Nandakumar Ray was one of the principal Indian officials of the new regime. He had been the faujdar of Hugli before the Battle of Plassey and had close links with the family of Mir Jafar. The current head of the Jagat Seth banking firm was Nandakumar's son-in-law. By the late 1760s, he had become the focal point of opposition to Reza Khan in the nawab's establishment. Hastings had a strong dislike for him, the reasons for which are not entirely clear. Clive and his adherents, however, had a cordial relationship with him. Hastings was not particularly enthusiastic about prosecuting Reza Khan or encouraging Nandakumar in this matter. Reza Khan was acquitted in 1774.

On the other hand, Nandakumar had become a liability for some of the Company's officials. The possibility that he might have information about their shady deals made them wary of him. Hastings certainly felt that he was a threat and could undermine his position just when he was engaged in a power struggle with many of his senior colleagues in India. We shall have more to say about this tussle. In March 1775, Nandakumar accused Hastings of having taken large sums of money from the widow of Mir Jafar as a bribe for giving her control over the nawab's household. Hastings had to admit that he had taken the money although he refused to accept that this amounted to a bribe, claiming that it was a customary allowance for the governor.

Nandakumar had shown himself to be a dangerous enemy who knew too many dark secrets. He had to be eliminated. It was suddenly discovered that a case had been pending against him for several years, relating to a charge of forgery. He was tried by the recently established Supreme Court of Calcutta (Supreme Court of Judicature at Fort William), though it is not certain that the court had jurisdiction over Indians. The court had been set up to handle cases relating to those British subjects over whom the EIC, which had its own judicial mechanism, did not have jurisdiction. Nandakumar was found guilty and condemned to death. He was executed in August 1775. Elijah Impey, whom Hastings had gotten to know well when both were studying at Westminster School, was the chief justice of the Supreme Court. He presided over the bench that conducted the trial of Nandakumar. Impey's intervention is believed to have been responsible for the hasty conviction and swift execution.

Many of Impey's contemporaries, such as the prominent political thinker and parliamentarian Edmund Burke, condemned the chief justice and Hastings for the hanging of Nandakumar. Burke regarded it as an act of judicial murder.

Hastings's promotion as governor (and, from 1774 onwards, as the EIC's governor-general in India) provided him with ever-greater opportunities for conducting his business ventures profitably. He was also able to recover some of the losses he had suffered on his Indian investments when he returned to England in 1765.

According to figures calculated by P.J. Marshall, who estimated the private fortune of Hastings, he was able to remit £218,000 to Britain over a period of thirteen years, from 1772 to 1785—an annual average of £17,000. Between April 1772 and January 1776 alone, he sent home £122,000 through various means. The salary and allowances received by him as governor-general, for a period of ten years, amounted to £30,000 annually: 'To maintain this rate of remittances, he must either have saved well over half his salary or received money from other sources.'[8] He was a substantial dealer in diamonds, using them regularly for transferring earnings to England.

Hastings spent quite extravagantly on the construction and maintenance of well-appointed residences in Calcutta and neighbouring Alipur, on entertainment, food and wine, a large retinue of personal servants, and supporting Marian's ostentatious lifestyle after their marriage.

ↄ

As Hastings settled down to govern Bengal and Bihar as the de facto ruler (the nawab, formally subservient to the Mughal emperor, was still the nominal ruler), the campaign within the British Parliament for disciplining the EIC's servants in India was being revived after a brief lull following the collapse of the proceedings against Clive. By the early 1770s, political opinion was strongly in favour of some measure of government control over the Company's Indian possessions.

At this time, imperial policies began to be seriously questioned against the backdrop of problems Britain was facing in holding on to its colonies in America. The 'Boston Tea Party', the prelude to the War of American Independence, belongs to the same year as the passage of the Regulating Act (1773), the first major piece of legislation for the 'Better Management of the Affairs of the East India Company'.

The Regulating Act provided the basic framework for colonial governance in India and, at the same time modified certain aspects of the Company's organizational structure. It confirmed the primacy of the presidency of Fort William in Bengal. The governor of Fort William was now designated governor-general and was to be assisted by a council comprising four members. The act specifically named the first governor-general, Warren Hastings, as well as the four initial members of the council: John Clavering, George Monson, Richard Barwell,

---

[8]P. J. Marshall, 'The Personal Fortune of Warren Hastings', *Economic History Review*, Vol. 17, No. 2, 1964, p. 292.

and Philip Francis. Each was appointed for a five-year term. The presidencies of Madras and Bombay were placed under the overall supervision of Fort William (Bengal). Copies of the Company's correspondence relating to India were henceforth to be submitted regularly to the British government so that it could keep an eye on how the Indian territories were being administered.

The numerical composition of the council (four members in addition to the governor-general) rendered the governor-general vulnerable in case three of the members combined to oppose him. Moreover, by packing the council with members who were already hostile to Hastings, Parliament created a difficult situation for the governor-general.

Of the four newly appointed members, three—Philip Francis, George Monson, and John Clavering—regularly voted against Hastings on virtually every major issue. Before they left for Calcutta, Francis and Clavering had been in close touch with Clive, who was very critical of how Bengal was being governed, especially the changes initiated by Hastings.

The differences between Hastings (who soon had the support of Barwell) on the one hand, and Francis, Clavering and Monson on the other, were also a reflection of serious differences over policies to be pursued by the Company for preserving and extending its authority in India.

Francis, Clavering, and Monson travelled to India together. Barwell was already in Calcutta. Francis emerged as the leader of the anti-Hastings faction in the council. Opposition by the Francis group made it difficult for the governor-general to function, at least until 1776 when Monson died. Luckily for Hastings, Clavering died the following year, and Francis departed for England in 1780 after being wounded in a duel with Hastings.

In England, Francis joined the campaign against Hastings, which had now become vociferous, publishing several pamphlets (anonymously) to expose him. He became a member of Parliament in 1784 and later actively assisted with the trial against Hastings.

Among the issues on which Francis had a sharp difference of opinion with Hastings in the council, an important one was that of land revenue policy. Francis proposed a plan for a permanent land revenue settlement, which later provided the inspiration for the 'Permanent Settlement' introduced under Charles Cornwallis. Hastings, however, would have preferred to gather more information about the produce of the land, and determine the revenue demand on the basis of more comprehensive information before implementing any scheme. Such information was not easily forthcoming. Besides, he was not inclined to introduce a settlement that was permanent, benefitting the zamindars, or holders of superior rights in land, or reinforcing their authority. Temporary settlements were more suitable for the time being.

On the question of withholding the remittance of the Bengal peshkash to Shah Alam, too, there was a fundamental disagreement. Francis was strongly opposed to stopping the remittance and underlined that 'The treaty concluded by Lord Clive in August 1765 [Treaty of Allahabad, formalizing the grant of diwani] not only acknowledges him as King of Bengal, but ... by particular agreement between him and the Company of the same date, they engaged themselves to be security for the payment of 26 lacs a year out of the territorial revenue in consideration of His Majesty's having been graciously pleased to grant them the Diwani of Bengal'.[9]

This was quite consistent with his understanding that it was necessary to respect 'ancient' rights in order to strengthen British rule. Francis, it should be noted, 'used the word "ancient" repeatedly, always to mean Mughal precedence'.[10] Thus, for him, the emperor was a stabilizing factor, respect for whose status would in turn help the EIC to consolidate its gains.

---

[9]Sophia Weitzman, *Warren Hastings and Philip Francis*, Manchester: Manchester University Press, 1929, p. 85.

[10]Tirthankar Roy, 'The Permanent Settlement and the Emergence of a British State in Late-eighteenth-century India', *Economic History Working Papers*, London School of Economics, No. 355, 2023, p. 7.

By the time Francis and his colleagues reached Calcutta in October 1774, Hastings had undone some of the key features of the post-Buxar arrangements. These arrangements had mainly been put in place during Clive's tenure. Besides the suspension of the peshkash, Hastings divested the Mughal emperor of his share of revenues from tracts in Awadh which were reserved for the maintenance of the royal court. The Treaty of Allahabad (1765) had a provision under which Allahabad and the adjacent tract of Kora, both part of Awadh, were to be set aside for Shah Alam's expenses as his 'royal demesne'. Hastings encouraged Awadh to take over Allahabad and Kora in 1773, extracting fifty lakh rupees for agreeing to the transfer. These revenue units, as indeed Awadh itself, were nominally part of the emperor's dominions. This status had all along been acknowledged by the Company. The transfer formed the prelude to military operations against the Rohillas—the so-called Rohilla War.

Lineages of Afghan descent, which had settled during the eighteenth century in a compact region extending north and east from the left bank of the Ganga to the Himalayan foothills and the Tarai, were referred to in this period as 'Rohillas'. The entire region in which they settled came to be known as Rohilkhand, in the upper Doab.

In the upheavals of the mid-eighteenth-century, following the incursions of Ahmad Shah Durrani and the Third Battle of Panipat (1761), several Rohilla chiefs had carved out petty principalities in the Rohilkhand region. Once the Marathas had recovered from the setback of Panipat, their intrusion into the region threatened the existence of these recently formed principalities. This also created a dangerous situation in the frontier areas of Awadh.

The boundaries demarcating the Rohilla chiefdoms from Awadh had remained fluid since the emergence of these political entities. In 1773, Hastings readily agreed to assist Shuja-ud-Daula, who negotiated with him to enlist the Company's support in his endeavour to check Maratha inroads while at the same time subordinating the Rohilla chiefs to his authority.

This joint military venture, the Rohilla War of 1774, ended with the dissolution of most of the Rohilla principalities. The transfer of Allahabad and Kora to Awadh was part of the deal worked out between Hastings and Shuja-ud-Daula on the eve of the war.

Awadh itself became an easy target for the EIC after the death of Shuja-ud-Daula in 1775. Hastings's intervention in the suba on several occasions steadily undermined the position of the subedar (nawab) of Awadh, setting in motion the process that culminated in the formal annexation of Awadh several decades later.

The roots of the problems that the province was to face in the early nineteenth century may be traced to the Company's policies in the Hastings era. The occupation of the Banaras area, adjoining Company-ruled Bihar, foreshadowed the subsequent annexation of large chunks of Awadh on the pretext of financing the EIC military force stationed in the suba, until eventually, it was left with only a truncated portion of its territories at the beginning of the nineteenth century.

In 1773, the Company had forced Awadh to accept the notorious 'subsidiary' alliance conceived by its policymakers to minimize military costs. The so-called 'subsidiary' alliance obliged Awadh to pay for an EIC force stationed in its territory supposedly for its own 'protection'. The transfer of Banaras, amounting to a cession, was linked to the appropriation of resources, ostensibly for the maintenance of the Company's contingents stationed in Awadh.

In the latter half of the eighteenth century, Banaras had emerged as a semi-autonomous petty-chieftaincy, encompassing some of the eastern and central districts of present-day Uttar Pradesh. The landholder or zamindar of Banaras acknowledged the nominal overlordship of the subedar of Awadh.

Upon the accession of Shuja's son, Asaf-ud-Daula, as the nawab of Awadh in 1775, Hastings exerted pressure on him to transfer to the Company his authority over the Banaras region (a major opium-producing tract—an important consideration for the EIC). The Banaras zamindar continued to administer the region as formerly but was henceforth subject to the authority of Fort William.

As part of the 1775 arrangement, the Company imposed a large tribute on the Banaras chief, amounting to over twenty lakh rupees annually. The zamindar was clearly not in a position to pay this sum. Further, over the next five years, Hastings continuously demanded additional payments on behalf of the English from the incumbent chief, Chait Singh (1770–81). Finding it impossible to withstand such unrelenting pressure, Chait Singh agreed to give a bribe of two lakh rupees to Hastings so that he might be left in peace. The bribe was accepted, but this did not put an end to the Company's coercion. Chait Singh then resolved to resist the EIC's demands by force. In the resulting showdown, Hastings entered Banaras with a military contingent in 1781 and placed the chief under detention. This was met with resistance. In the ensuing armed clash, several of the Company's soldiers, including Europeans, were killed by the retainers of Chait Singh.

After a brief military campaign, the British re-established control over the Banaras region. Chait Singh was stripped of his title. Mahip Narayan Singh, a nephew of Chait Singh, who happened to be a minor, was acknowledged as the new zamindar of Banaras and the tribute due from the state was enhanced to forty lakh rupees. The Company would later take over the administration of Banaras, reducing the zamindar to a titular position.

Another incident in which Hastings was involved was the extortion of money from the 'begums of Oudh'—Asaf-ud-Daula's mother and grandmother. A few years after he succeeded Shuja-ud-Daula as the nawab, Asaf-ud-Daula resorted to forcibly seizing some of the private treasure belonging to the two senior women of the family in order to comply with the Company's persistent demands for money to meet the costs of the subsidiary force. A large part of the treasure in the possession of the begums had been inherited by them from

Shuja-ud-Daula. Asaf-ud-Daula was encouraged by Hastings to confiscate the entire bequest.

When the nawab showed some reluctance in using force against his mother and grandmother, the governor-general ordered troops to be sent to Faizabad, where the begums resided, for the purpose of seizing the treasure. Faizabad was then the seat of the subedar (Asaf-ud-Daula later shifted the capital to Lucknow). The harassment of the begums, the cruelty with which their personal retinue was treated, and the seizure of their fortune were to figure prominently among the main charges in the trial of Hastings.

Whereas the Calcutta authorities did not have much control at this stage over the Bombay establishment, they did try to intervene in Maratha affairs, which were in disarray after the disaster at Panipat in 1761. The death in 1772 of peshwa Madhav Rao (1761–72) had resulted in a prolonged dispute over succession, in which one of the contenders, Raghunath Rao, solicited the aid of the EIC, promising to hand over to it Salsette, Bassein, and some islands in the vicinity of Bombay, in return for assistance. An agreement to this effect, signed by the Bombay Council in 1775, was repudiated by the governor-general.

On the other hand, it was endorsed by the Court of Directors revealing serious differences among colonial policymakers over tactics to be adopted for undermining Maratha power. Bombay was asked by the directors to intervene on behalf of Raghunath Rao, which in turn led to an indecisive military conflict known as the First Anglo–Maratha War. The conflict ended with the Treaty of Salbai (1782). Under the terms of the treaty, Pune formally relinquished control over Salsette, the only territorial gain for the Company at the end of the war. More importantly, the Company obtained a toehold in Maratha polity.

∽

The expansion of the administrative functions of the Company's establishment in eastern and in southern India (it had few possessions in western India at this stage) meant that a sizeable proportion of its personnel hired for commercial work was saddled with administrative and judicial tasks. This required that its servants be imparted some knowledge about India, especially about the regions under Company rule. Senior functionaries such as Francis, as well as a few relatively junior officials posted in districts, attempted to familiarize themselves with aspects of society, history, law, and revenue systems. A few of them tried to learn Persian or Sanskrit, or languages of the regions where they worked. Hastings and some of his colleagues showed an awareness of the urgency of acquiring knowledge about the society over which they ruled.

Towards the end of his tenure, Hastings, through official patronage, helped in giving shape to a programme for institutionally generating knowledge about India by systematically utilizing the intellectual resources that had become available in the process of governing Bengal and the other presidencies. The establishment of the Asiatic Society (of Bengal) in 1784 was one notable outcome of this endeavour. William Jones, a judge of the Calcutta Supreme Court who arrived in India in 1783, was the moving spirit of the venture, and was the first president of the Asiatic Society. He would soon make a name for himself as a philologist, renowned for his knowledge of several languages, including Arabic, Persian, and Sanskrit. The organization itself could be launched because of the presence of several Company officials in Bengal who, during the preceding decade, had taken an interest in learning languages which might give them access to 'oriental' texts.

There was already a group of Company employees, both civilian and military, who were engaged in producing translations of historical and religious writings. One such text was the *Tarikh* of Muhammad Qasim Firishta (1560–1620). This historical account in Persian was translated, with the assistance of an Indian munshi, or scribe-interpreter-tutor, by Alexander Dow, a Scottish officer in the EIC army. It was published in three volumes between 1768 and 1772. Dow's translation, along with the writings of some of his contemporaries—such as Holwell (whom we have referred to in the context of the colonial narrative about the 'Black Hole') and another veteran EIC employee, Quintin Craufurd—marked the beginnings of 'Indological studies', which, as Ranajit Guha notes, 'with all its curious mixture of the erudite and the polemical, must be recognized as being among the first intellectual attempts in modern times to explore the East'.[11]

The last quarter of the eighteenth century and the first quarter of the nineteenth century saw the emergence of a distinct tradition of British Orientalist learning, with the active support of the Hastings administration. Hastings took a personal interest in promoting the study of Persian, Sanskrit, Hindustani, and Bengali. He was actively involved in the establishment of the Calcutta Madrasa in 1781 for imparting classical learning to Indians. These initiatives brought together British scholars and learned Indians. Their interaction, while not on equal terms, played a vital role in the production of colonial knowledge about India's past, its institutions, social organization, and religious beliefs.

One of the most important initiatives of Hastings, soon after he had become governor of the Fort William presidency, was the compilation of a so-called 'code' of 'Gentoo' laws—the *Gentoo Code* (1776). 'Gentoo' is an archaic word for 'Hindu', which soon replaced it. The codification project was preceded by the formation of a roving committee (Committee of Circuit), headed by Hastings, for touring districts in Bengal and Bihar to gather information about the people, their customs, modes of settling disputes, and general economic conditions.

---

[11]Ranajit Guha, *A Rule of Property for Bengal: An Essay on the Idea of Permanent Settlement*, Hyderabad and Ranikhet: Orient BlackSwan and Permanent Black, 2016, p. 22. Quintin Craufurd was in the Company's service for several decades before he returned to Europe and published a two-volume work entitled *Sketches Chiefly Relating to the History, Religion, Learning, and Manners, of the Hindoos...* etc. (London, 1790).

The committee undertook its work against the backdrop of the famine of 1770 in the region, in which over one-third of the population perished. The effects of the famine continued to be felt for a long time; in fact, Bengal did not recover from this calamity for over three decades. In its report, the committee expressed concern over the breakdown of the administrative machinery, and emphasized the need for a well-organized system of justice for enforcing the Company's authority.

EIC personnel who had to deal with judicial matters lacked the competence to do so both because they had no legal training and because they did not know much about the laws of the various communities in eastern India over whom they exercised power. Revenue work itself involved attending to numerous legal matters. Senior officials were aware that a basic understanding of law and jurisprudence, in the Indian context, was essential for judicial work and for governing territories conquered by the Company.

As for the laws to be applied in Company courts (as distinct from the king's courts, in which English laws were applicable), the consensus was that they would have to be those which had traditionally operated in India. This meant that, in civil matters, Hindus and Muslims would be governed by their respective laws. The separation of criminal and civil courts itself was a colonial innovation. Hastings and his associates assumed that these laws were enshrined in sacred scripture. Therefore, they would have to put together a team of scholars well-versed in scripture to compile and translate the relevant laws.

According to a plan finalized in 1772, 'In all suits regarding inheritance, marriage and caste and other religious usages and institutions, the laws of the Koran with respect to Mahomedans and those of the Shaster [Shastra] with respect to Gentoos shall be invariably adhered to. On all such occasions, the Molavies and Brahmins shall respectively attend to and expound the law...'.[12]

---

[12]George C. Rankin, 'The Personal Law in British India', *Journal of the Royal*

An act passed by the British Parliament in 1781 further stated that, 'Inheritance and succession to lands, rents and goods, and all matters of contract and dealing between party and party, shall be determined in the case of Mahomedans by the laws and usages of Mahomedans, and in the case of Gentoos, by the laws and usages of Gentoos; and where only one of the parties shall be a Mahomedan or Gentoo by the law and usages of the defendant'.[13]

Although the colonial state claimed that, in dispensing justice, it was adhering to the laws of the Muslims and the Hindus—who came to be seen as two internally undifferentiated and homogenous pan-Indian communities—the laws were assembled and codified in accordance with the perceptions of senior officials about definite texts as sources. In the process, these texts came to be regarded as authoritative. Customary rules and diverse local practices of communities were ignored as the British imposed their interpretations, thereby modifying law and jurisprudence.

For the Muslims, they identified an influential work on Islamic jurisprudence—the *Hidaya* of Burhan al-Din al-Marghinani—as the key legal text. The dominant school of jurisprudence (fiqh) among the Sunnis in India is the Hanafi School, and this was an important text for Hanafi jurists and scholars. An English translation of *Hidaya* was published in 1791. Charles Hamilton, who translated the work, was an employee of the EIC. He had joined the Company's army and begun his career during Hastings's tenure. Hamilton was encouraged by the governor-general to undertake the translation, for which purpose he was allowed to go to England for five years.

The translated version, entitled *The Hedaya, or Guide*, was published in four volumes, and on its title page acknowledged the inspiration of Hastings (who had returned home by this

Society of Arts, Vol. 89, No. 4588 (1941), pp. 431–32. Rankin was chief justice of Calcutta High Court from 1926 to 1934.
[13]Ibid., p. 432.

time): 'Published by Order of the Governor-General and Council of Bengal'. The statement made this an authoritative text bearing the stamp of the state.

In his introduction to the translation, Hamilton states that soon after the 'Gentoo' code had been published, 'a number of the principal Mohammedan professors in Bengal were employed in translating from the Arabic into the Persian tongue a commentary upon the Mussulman law, called the *Hedaya*, or *Guide*, a work held in high estimation among the people of that persuasion'. Hamilton had translated the Persian version into English.[14] Several colonial officials by now had competence in written Farsi.

The collection of laws which were assembled to produce a code for Hindus was first translated from Sanskrit to Persian. The Persian version was then translated into English by a Company official, Nathaniel Halhed who had acquired considerable proficiency in the language. He was yet another young official working under Hastings, who became part of the larger translation project due to his language skills. Halhed would go on to produce *A Grammar of the Bengal Language* (1778), which was made possible by his command over Bengali. According to his biographer, Rosane Rocher, 'Halhed was apparently first [among Company servants] to acquire it in a superior manner'.[15]

Halhed's *Grammar of the Bengal Language* laid the foundations of Bengali printing.[16] The typeface was designed by his colleague Charles Wilkins, with the assistance of Panchanana (Karmakara), who was also the punchcutter. Wilkins subsequently earned renown for his English translation

---

[14]Charles Hamilton, *The Hedaya, or Guide*, London, Vol. I, 1791, p. vii.
[15]Rosane Rocher, *Orientalism, Poetry, and the Millennium: The Checkered Life of Nathaniel Brassey Halhed, 1751-1830*, New Delhi: Motilal Banarsidass Publications, 1983, p. 73.
[16]The Portuguese missionary Manoel da Assumpçam (Assumpção), had prepared a grammar of the language (*Vocabulario em Idioma Bengalla, e Portuguez*) which was published in 1743, and is regarded as the first Bengali grammar. However, the grammar used the Roman script for Bengali.

of the Bhagavad Gita (*The Bhagvat-Geeta, or Dialogues of Kreeshna and Arjoon*) published in 1785.

At the time the *Gentoo Code* was commissioned, no employee of the EIC knew Sanskrit. Therefore, the translation from Sanskrit to Persian was a rather complicated process. A team comprising eleven pandits, or Brahmin scholars well-versed in scripture, was constituted by Hastings for producing the compendium.

Once the pandits had finished their work on the compendium (which was entitled *Vivadarnavasetu*, 'the bridge across the ocean of disputes'), one of the members of the team, Gaurikanta Tarkasiddhanta, verbally explained each portion in Bengali to the Persian translator, Zain ud-Din Ali Rasai. Thereupon Zain ud-Din translated the Bengali version into Persian based on notes made by him.

Although some contemporaries, of whom Jones was the most knowledgeable, were of the opinion that the Persian version was not a very reliable translation of the Sanskrit text, we still do not have a comprehensive scholarly evaluation of Zain ud-Din's translation based on a comparison with the Sanskrit original text.

We would do well to remember that there was a rich tradition of translating sacred texts from Sanskrit to Persian at the Mughal court. It is not clear why the Hastings group did not tap into the intellectual resources of this tradition to facilitate the translation of the Sanskrit compilation. Part of the reason was colonial stereotyping, which equated the Mughals exclusively with the Persian language, and with Islam. Recent research has shown that the intelligentsia in Bengal was quite aware of the existence of a large body of Mughal-era manuscripts which were Persian translations of Sanskrit texts. Some scribes and translators were proficient in both Sanskrit and Persian and often served EIC officials as tutors or secretaries. Many of them were from Kayastha families of Bengal. Ramram Basu is representative of this type of scribe–translator. He was employed as a Persian tutor to one of the judges of the Supreme Court, and served the Serampore-based missionary William Carey as translator/interpreter for Bengali and Sanskrit. Serampore (Srirampur), not far from Calcutta, was a Danish colonial enclave.

Given the immense scale of the endeavour, there is every possibility that Sanskrit–Persian experts were asked to lend their support to it. The entire project was completed by February 1775, and the English translation of *Vivadarnavasetu* was published from London in 1776 with the title, *A Code of Gentoo Laws, or, Ordinations of the Pundits.*

The code was not intended for public circulation. The title was misleading, for it suggested that the 'ordinations' represented a code, and that the Dharmashastras from which they were compiled were actually law books of the Hindus. The Dharmashastras are normative texts which deal with a wide range of subjects that together constitute the science or teaching of righteousness. As Nandini Bhattacharyya-Panda has pointed out, 'Extant pre-colonial evidence of the Dharmaśāstra tradition suggests that it evolved as a tradition of intellectual and philosophical knowledge rather than one integral to administration'.[17]

The codification-cum-translation project continued after Hastings's retirement in 1785, with Jones playing an important role in identifying relevant texts and translating them. He proposed the compilation of a new code or digest incorporating both Hindu and Muslim laws, sponsored by the Company's government. The proposal was accepted, and two scholarly Indians—a pandit and a maulvi—were appointed to assist with the project. The digest was to be an improvement over the *Gentoo Code.*

Meanwhile, he was learning Sanskrit and began translating literary compositions. His English translation of Kalidasa's Śakuntalā was published in 1789. Work on the digest was still

---

[17]Nandini Bhattacharyya-Panda, *Appropriation and Invention of Tradition: The East India Company and Hindu Law in Early Colonial Bengal*, New Delhi: Oxford University Press, 2008, p. 23.

in progress when Jones passed away in 1794. He did, however, finish his English translation of the *Manusmriti*, published with the title *Institutes of Hindu Law; or The Ordinances of Menu* (1794). Jones declared that the *Manusmriti* was the basis of all Hindu law, and this became the standard colonial understanding of the text.

Meanwhile, work on the new version of the 'code' continued and was completed after Jones's death. The original Sanskrit digest emerging from this venture, bearing the title *Vivadabhangarnava*, was compiled by the pandit employed in the project, Jagannatha Tercapanchanana (Tarkapanchanana). The translation of the digest into English was undertaken by H.T. Colebrooke, who belonged to a younger generation of EIC officials well-versed in Sanskrit. The first volume was published in 1797 as *A Digest of Hindu Law on Contracts and Successions*, with two more volumes following in 1798. A multi-volume English translation of Shia law, which had been prepared under Jones's direction, was published in 1805.

∽

Very soon after he had become governor-general, Hastings was being talked about among influential political circles in England as an example of the worst excesses of the Company. The campaign against him carried forward the larger political agendas of the parliamentary enquiry relating to Clive—agendas that had to be temporarily shelved due to the setback of Clive's exoneration.

The most serious charges against Hastings pertained to the crimes committed by him against the raja of Banaras, and the begums of Awadh. Hastings had departed from India in February 1785, and reached England in June. For nearly three years before his return, the British Parliament had been considering reports about the several unsavoury doings of his administration, leading to a House of Commons resolution in 1782 for his recall. The move had to be abandoned for the time being, as it did not get the approval of the EIC's Court of Proprietors. The General Court still had the authority to veto decisions of the Court of Directors.

However, parliamentary censure and the lack of support from the Court of Directors made it difficult for Hastings to stay on. He resigned reluctantly and handed over charge to John Macpherson, who was the seniormost member of the Bengal council at the time. Macpherson remained acting governor-general till 1786, when Cornwallis took over.

Within a year of Hastings's arrival, while he was settling down and negotiating the purchase of his ancestral house in Daylesford, the House of Commons voted for his impeachment on the Chait Singh issue. He was charged with having harassed the zamindar of Banaras and extorted large sums of money from him. The prime minister, William Pitt, personally intervened in the debate, speaking in support of the motion for impeaching the former governor-general. The motion was passed in June 1786, with 118 members voting in favour and 79 against. This was the beginning of the impeachment proceedings and trial, of Hastings, which continued till April 1795. The huge amount of paperwork the trial generated, spread over nearly a decade, has provided readymade material for historians and biographers who have written extensively about it— many of whom have laboured to exonerate Hastings. Many of these writings date back to the latter half of the nineteenth century and generally denounce Burke, who spearheaded the campaign, for his crusade against Hastings.

The next charge which came up for discussion in Parliament was the ill-treatment of the begums of Awadh by Hastings. One of Burke's key associates in Parliament who helped him with the investigation, the playwright John Sheridan, made an impassioned speech in the House of Commons lasting nearly six hours, in which he exposed Hastings's wrongdoings in this affair. The motion for impeachment on this charge was passed in February 1787, with 175 votes in favour and 86 against. This paved the way for a trial before the High Court of Parliament.

The British Parliament had criminal jurisdiction in certain cases of a special nature. For this purpose, 'The House of Lords is a court of justice in which peers [members of the aristocracy] may be tried for any offence, and commoners for any offence not being treason or felony ... upon an accusation or impeachment by the House of Commons, which is the grand jury of the whole nation'.[18] Once the House of Commons had pronounced that the charges brought against Hastings were impeachable, the evidence was referred to a select committee for framing the articles of impeachment. Burke was the leading member of this committee. When the charges had been framed, the House of Lords was given intimation, as was required by the procedure, of the impeachment of Hastings by the House of Commons. Thereupon, he was taken into custody and delivered to the 'gentleman usher of the black rod' (the chief official traditionally responsible for maintaining order in the premises of the upper house), and then granted bail. The trial was to commence in February 1788.

A committee of twenty members from the Commons was constituted to prosecute Hastings. They acted as the managers of the prosecution at the trial and were assisted by two solicitors. On 13 February, the opening day of trial, members of the House of Lords, after assembling briefly in the House, adjourned to Westminster Hall. A few minutes' walk from the House, Westminster Hall was the venue of the trial for its entire duration. A contemporary account of the proceedings contains a detailed description of the elaborate seating arrangements for the trial. It is worth mentioning that the hall was also the venue of the trial of Charles I (1649), at the end of which he was sentenced to beheading.

The preparation for the trial involved searching for precedents to confirm the procedure. Whatever information was available about the arrangements for the trial of Charles I in Westminster

---

[18]James Fitzjames Stephen, *A History of the Criminal Law of England*, Vol. 1, London: Macmillan, 1883, pp. 146 and 161.

Hall was useful for designing the setting for the court, in a sense recreating the layout of 1649. Upon his appearance before the tribunal at the beginning of the proceedings, Hastings was required to kneel before it in keeping with established protocol. He was then allowed to rise, and, as a courtesy, provided with a chair. He was accompanied by his three-member legal defence team, headed by Edward Law, who later on became Lord Chief Justice. Law's son, Lord Ellenborough, was governor-general of India from 1842 to 1844.

The trial went on for over seven years, to which may be added two more years of the impeachment process in the Commons. The extraordinary length of the trial is not surprising, given that the members of Parliament also had to attend to other work while the proceedings were in progress. The court had 148 sittings during these seven years. Yet, only six of the twenty articles of impeachment could be taken up systematically in these sittings. A vast quantity of evidence collected from India was produced during the trial, and, along with the material assembled for the Clive enquiry, reveals the enormity of the Company's crimes in the years after Plassey. Before the conclusion of the trial, Lord Cornwallis was summoned as a witness for the defendant. He was back in England after his seven-year tenure as governor-general. His testimony was favourable to Hastings, who, according to Cornwallis, was much respected in India. Here was one empire builder defending another empire builder. This kind of endorsement, coming from someone whose views were regarded as authoritative by the tribunal, certainly weakened the prosecution's case.

The judgement of the Lords, delivered in April 1795, pronounced Hastings to be not guilty, and he was acquitted. James Mill, author of *The History of British India* (1817), remarks in his work that, 'Had Mr. Hastings ... really submitted himself to scrutiny; instead of using, to defend himself ... every effort which the artifice of lawyers could invent, and every subterfuge which the imperfections of the law could afford, he might have left his rectitude, if real, without a suspicion;

whereas now, if his accusers could not prove his guilt, it is still more certain that he has not proved his innocence'.[19]

Burke's famous speech at the beginning of the trial, even while focussing on Hastings's tenure, in fact, highlighted the systematic plunder carried out by the Company's servants in Bengal, as well as in other parts of the Indian empire since Plassey. Hastings, Burke's main target, was accused of having 'wasted the country, ruined the landed interest, cruelly harassed the peasants, burnt their houses, seized their crops, tortured and degraded their persons, and destroyed the honor of the whole female race of that country'.[20] Nevertheless, his speech was a denunciation not of empire per se, but of how the empire had been acquired and was being managed. His interventions, most prominently his overall leadership in the trial, made the Company's conquests a matter of national concern. We would be mistaken to suppose that Burke's critique was not a reflection of his serious concern about the misery that the conquests of the Company had inflicted on the people of Bengal. He consistently condemned the conduct of the EIC's senior officials and their sponsors in England, both within and outside the Company, in callously destroying Indian society.

In his important study on liberal attitudes towards the Indian empire, Uday Mehta has highlighted the uncompromising position of Burke on the iniquities of territorial expansion in India. He was almost unique in upholding the rights of the people subjugated by the Company:

> No other statesman or thinker expresses the depth of pathos, the pained embarrassment, the capacious compassion, and the sustained moral revulsion for the cruelty, torture, deprivation and injustice that the company

---

[19]James Mill, *The History of British India*, Fifth Edition, Vol. 5, London: James Madden, 1858, p.126. Hastings was still living when the book was published.
[20]Edmund Burke, 'Speeches in the Impeachment of Warren Hastings', *The Writings and Speeches of Edmund Burke*, Vol. 10, New York: Oxford University Press, 1887, p. 141.

was perpetrating. Burke is virtually alone [in contemporary Britain] in owning up to this as an indictment of Britain's moral and political rectitude.[21]

During the course of the lengthy trial, Burke launched a full-scale attack on all those who were complicit in the ruthless acquisition of empire and the evil consequences for Britain flowing from the immoral actions of the Company:

> There is scarcely a page in the thousands that Burke wrote and uttered during the Hastings trial ... in which a simple but piercing concern with brutality, exploitation, humiliation of women, the avarice of the company and its parliamentary patrons, the corresponding effect of destitution, and the arbitrary use of unjust power is not an illuminated feature of the background that he is aware of, and the implications of which he is at pains to convey to his audience'.[22]

Nicholas Dirks, in *The Scandal of Empire* has examined the sordid history of the formation of empire, its predatory character, and how the relationship between the EIC as a commercial body and Britain was transformed in the 1780s. It might be worthwhile to quote at some length his assessment of Burke's critique of the Company and its servants:[23]

> Edmund Burke was an eloquent and powerful critic of empire. Few orators, then or now, have captured the excesses and abuses of imperial power in such ringing rhetorical registers. His speeches and writings were embarrassing to later generations of British imperialists for whom the history of empire had to be glorious in its beginnings as it was in its present and future, and for

---

[21]Uday Singh Mehta, *Liberalism and Empire: India in British Liberal Thought*, New Delhi: Oxford University Press, 1999, p. 156.
[22]Ibid.
[23]Nicholas B. Dirks, *The Scandal of Empire: India and the Creation of Imperial Britain*, Ranikhet: Permanent Black, 2006, pp. 313–14.

whom Hastings increasingly became a key icon of imperial greatness. Yet despite the force of Burke's critique and the years spent prosecuting the East India Company, he neither condemned empire altogether, nor held the East India Company responsible for the manifold abuses of its imperial conduct. In the end, Burke's real legacy was the transformation of Company rule into British imperium.

The impeachment proceedings cannot be seen in isolation; they were closely linked to the programme for exercising more effective control over the Company. The parliamentary investigation relating to Clive, and the Regulating Act of 1773, had been part of the programme. The 1773 Act had several anomalies that were sought to be rectified through a subsequent legislative measure enacted in 1784. As we have seen, the numerical composition of the council (four members in addition to the governor-general) constituted under the 1773 Act rendered the governor-general vulnerable in case three of the members combined to oppose him. The new legislation relating to India, which came to be known as the India Act of 1784, was passed immediately after the general election of 1784, in which William Pitt (Pitt the Younger) won a large majority in the House of Commons. Pitt was to remain prime minister for the next two decades. The election had been necessitated by the dissolution of the House, which, in turn was the outcome of serious disagreements over, among other issues, the manner in which the Indian empire was to be governed. Further, Britain had lost its American colonies by now, resulting in widespread criticism of colonial policies.

British reverses in the War of American Independence, especially the military debacle at Yorktown in October 1781, in which troops led by Cornwallis had to surrender, led to a serious political crisis (see Chapter IV). The Tory ministry of Lord North, which had been in office for twelve years since 1770, had to resign on the American question when it was defeated in a vote on a no-confidence motion in Parliament in 1782.

In March 1782, North was succeeded by Lord Rockingham as prime minister, who set in motion the process culminating in peace with an independent America (1783). Rockingham was the leader of a relatively more radical section of the Whigs, which included Burke. He had briefly been prime minister in 1765–66. (Burke was the private secretary of Rockingham during his first tenure as prime minister, and later emerged as a prominent ideologue of the Rockinghamites.)

Throughout the period that North was in power, Rockingham and his adherents had consistently criticized the policies of the Tory government. North had the backing of the reigning monarch, George III (r. 1760–1820); the Rockingham Whigs were strongly opposed to royal interference in politics.

Rockingham passed away in July 1782. His death led to further complications. A new Whig ministry was formed under Lord Shelburne, despite the objections of George III. Nevertheless, some of the leading Rockingham Whigs, such as Charles Fox, were not prepared to accept Shelburne's leadership. In a dramatic political swing, Fox joined hands with North—whom he and his colleagues had opposed all the while that North had been prime minister. The Fox–North coalition ministry (April–December 1783) was formally headed by the Duke of Portland (father of William Bentinck, governor-general of India, 1828–35). George III detested Fox, not least because there was a 'whiff of republicanism' about him.

In the latter half of 1783, the Whig-led coalition government introduced a bill that proposed to place the Company's territories in India directly under the British government. Burke played a major role in drafting the bill. In his speech on the bill in the House of Commons, Burke stated that the legislation 'was intended to form the *Magna Charta* of Hindostan'. Whereas the House of Commons passed the bill, it was defeated in the House of Lords, leading to the dismissal of the ministry.

George III used his influence to have the bill rejected by the House of Lords as its provisions were seen as an attack on private property and the special privileges of the EIC. The

Company's possessions and the profits of its shareholders were considered sacrosanct. The EIC deployed the wealth of its officials and shareholders, derived from the plunder of India, to mobilize opinion against the bill. These funds also ensured Pitt's enormous success in the election of 1784.

Parliament had been dissolved in March 1784, and Pitt's victory in the general elections that followed was seen more as a vote in favour of George III than for Pitt himself. The India bill of the previous government was discarded and a new bill (which became the India Act) was drafted. Pitt, barely twenty-four years old at this time, would have been guided by experienced 'India hands' while finalizing the proposals relating to India. The person who was instrumental in formulating the British government's policies relating to India in the Pitt era was the Scottish lawyer Henry Dundas (d. 1811). In 1782–83, he devised a scheme for putting the EIC's structure of colonial governance on a firm footing. This scheme became the basis of Pitt's India bill.

The most important feature of the 1784 Act was the introduction of a permanent mechanism to monitor the administration of the Indian empire on behalf of Parliament. A body consisting of six members, who were designated as 'commissioners for the affairs of India', was constituted for the purpose. This body, generally known as the Board of Control, became the main instrument until 1858 for parliamentary supervision over, and government direction of, the Indian empire. The Board of Control included two high-ranking ministers. Dundas was a member of the board for eighteen years, right from its inception till 1801. He was formally the president of the board from 1793 onwards. Throughout this period, 'the Board of Control for India meant Dundas, or at most, Dundas and Pitt'.[24]

Dundas was a well-known lawyer and prominent parliamentarian. He became the solicitor-general of Scotland

---

[24]Holden Furber, *Henry Dundas, First Viscount Melville, 1742-1811: Political Manager of Scotland, Statesman, Administrator of India*, London: Oxford University Press, 1931, p. 30.

in 1766, held several other positions in Scotland, and was elected a member of the House of Commons in 1774. He was a member of the house continuously for the next three decades. Initially, Dundas was a follower of Lord North. He gradually moved closer to Pitt when the troubles in America destabilized North's government. Dundas consolidated his position after Pitt became prime minister and came to be recognized as his right-hand man. His political sway over Scotland was unchallenged and his views determined the policy regarding India.

The immense power that Dundas wielded under the Pitt regime was reinforced by the patronage he could extend as the key political functionary monitoring the EIC's management of the Indian empire on behalf of the Parliament. The extensive recruitment of young men from Scotland into the Company's service through his patronage brought about what has been called the 'Scotticization of India', though some scholars would date this phenomenon to an earlier period.

The union of Scotland with England (and Wales) in 1707 had caused widespread resentment among the Scots, providing an opportunity for the Stuart heir, Charles Edward, to foment rebellion and attempt restoration of the dynasty with Scottish support. The Stuart line—successors to the Tudors—had ended in 1688 when James II (r. 1685–88, second surviving son of Charles I) was ousted in the Glorious Revolution.[25] A series of Jacobite (pro-Stuart) uprisings and invasions, spread over nearly three decades after the union resulted in turmoil in Scotland as well as in England. These uprisings were violently suppressed, and the Jacobite opposition had effectively ended by 1745–46.

Scottish sympathy for the Stuart venture and the turbulence in Scotland in the years after the union reinforced English prejudice against the supposedly backward and unreliable Scots. For the Scots, whereas union opened up new avenues for employment and commerce in England, these prospects were still relatively limited in the latter half of the eighteenth century.

---

[25]The last Tudor monarch, Elizabeth I, died childless, in 1603.

The real breakthrough came with the expansion of the empire in Asia. Young men from Scotland were attracted in large numbers to newly acquired territories in India. Their energies could be channelled into empire building. The empire made it possible to contain Scottish discontent and speed up assimilation.

Linda Colley, in her study of the making of British—as distinct from English—identity in the period between the 1707 Act of Union and the accession of Victoria in 1837, has argued that there was a marked increase in the proportion of the EIC's Scottish employees in India during Hastings's governor-generalship. This predated the Scotticization of India under Dundas. 'It was India, though,' she writes, 'that the Scots made their own, long before the reign of ... Henry Dundas. More than a quarter of the East India Company's army officers were Scotsmen; so, by mid-century, were a good proportion of its civilian officers in Madras and Bengal—the Scottish bankers and stockholders who had a strong grip on the Company made sure of that. Yet, paradoxically, it seems to have been an Englishman, Warren Hastings ... who converted this stream of Caledonians [inhabitants of Scotland] into positions of influence in the East into a torrent'.[26]

One of the charges brought against Hastings at his trial was that he had appointed far too many Scots, had given them contracts and generous allowances, and thereby encouraged corruption. Colley then poses the question, in the context of the allegations about the Scots: 'Were these accusations against Hastings anything more than just another expression of English ... envy and resentment at the increased scope for Scottish ambition?'[27]

As a member of Parliament, Dundas had begun taking a keen interest in Indian affairs. It was North who first assigned to him some work in 1781 concerning the Company's officials in India. Within a short time, he had become an expert on the

---

[26]Linda Colley, *Britons: Forging the Nation, 1707-1837*, London: Pimlico, 1992, p. 128.
[27]Ibid., p. 130.

subject. Holden Furber, in his biography of Dundas, observes that 'he positively enjoyed wading through the masses of Indian documents, and he probably spent more of his time on Indian affairs than on anything else in his long public career'.[28]

In a plan drafted in 1782, Dundas had envisaged the creation of a new portfolio in the cabinet—a secretary of state (full-fledged cabinet minister) for 'India and Plantations'. The office of the President of the Board of Control, or India Minister, would evolve into that of the secretary of state for India in 1858, when the government took over all the functions of the Court of Directors.

Whereas Burke did not succeed in having Hastings convicted, the high-profile trial that dragged on for nearly a decade kept the Company's affairs in the public limelight. There was growing opposition by this time, to its monopoly over commerce with India and China. Private traders were keen to share in the profits of this commerce and resented their exclusion. The Company's interests were at variance with those of the Lancashire cotton-textile manufacturers, pioneers of the Industrial Revolution.

Towards the end of the eighteenth century, the EIC's business was increasingly focused on the import of Chinese tea and silk. The Indian empire was vital for procuring these commodities. The so-called 'trade triangle' devised by the Company involved the supply of opium and raw cotton from India to China. Tea was procured with the profits of opium. Lancashire cotton textiles, obviously, had no place in this scheme of things.

Of course, by now the EIC's earnings were no longer confined to its commercial profits. It had access to the resources of its territories in India. What is more, the greatly enlarged scope of the Company's activities—political, administrative, military, commercial, and technical—necessitated the cooperation of several sections of British society.

By the beginning of the nineteenth century, the Indian empire was no longer the concern of just a handful of merchant

---

[28]Furber, *Henry Dundas*, p. 11.

capitalists based in London. With 'free trade' becoming the dominant economic doctrine in Britain in the first half of the nineteenth century, it was even more difficult for the government to resist demands for the termination of the Company's monopoly.

The EIC nevertheless fiercely contested the proposal to abolish its Indian monopoly when its charter came up for renewal in 1813. It mobilized many of its senior functionaries living in retirement in England—the aged Warren Hastings, for example—to oppose the proposal. Parliament, on the other hand, was unconvinced by the Company's arguments, and the Charter Act of 1813 put an end to its monopoly over India.

∽

Following his acquittal, Hastings retreated to Daylesford. He had managed to buy the house in 1788, as well as extensive grounds and gardens around it, to which more land was added subsequently. For the next twenty-three years, until he died in 1818, he lived here in seclusion with Marian and his stepson, Charles Imhoff. The main building, with its unusual architecture that incorporated some Indian elements, was designed by Samuel Pepys Cockerell, who later became surveyor to the EIC. Samuel Pepys was the elder brother of Charles Cockerell, the owner of Sezincote. Charles had joined the Company's service as a writer a few years after Hastings became governor-general. That connection might have influenced the choice of the architect for Daylesford. In turn, working and interacting with Hastings would have been a useful experience for Samuel Pepys when he later designed Sezincote.

Hastings spent considerable time—and much of what remained of his fortune after meeting the expenses of the trial—developing the lawns, landscaping the grounds and decorating the house. The Daylesford house was sumptuously furnished and contained priceless art objects from India including furniture made of ivory—footstools, armchairs, tables, couches, and a cot; paintings; and two chairs of buffalo horn, 'most delicately formed'.[29] Some of the more opulent ivory furniture had been gifted by members of the Awadh nawab's family. The former governor-general, for his part, had presented an ivory state bed to the queen.

Hastings came out of his retirement for a brief moment in 1806, hoping that some political opportunity might come his way when the Whigs won the election that year. The death of Pitt in 1806 was a setback for the Tories, bringing the Whigs to power. He quickly realized that there was no place for him in the world of English politics, and went back to his quiet life in Daylesford. Marian passed away in 1837 at the age of ninety, and the estate was sold to another owner after the death of Hastings's stepson Charles in 1853.

---

[29]Lindsay Boynton, 'The Furniture of Warren Hastings', *Burlington Magazine*, Vol. 112, No. 809, 1970, p. 511.

IV

IMPERIAL AMBITIONS

In colonial historiography, the Cornwallis era is invariably portrayed as one that ushered in the golden age of British rule. Vincent Smith, amateur historian and colonial civil servant, in his widely used textbook *The Oxford History of India*, first published in 1919, states that, 'It is refreshing for the historian to escape from the turbid politics of the time of Hastings and Macpherson and to pass into the more wholesome atmosphere of the Cornwallis regime'.[1]

The Oxford scholar P.E. Roberts, author of another popular—and perhaps the most compact—textbook of the early twentieth century on the subject, *History of British India*, initially published in 1921, writes: 'Few [governors-general] were destined to do more permanent work than Lord Charles Cornwallis, especially in the department of internal affairs ... In internal affairs his governor-generalship is one of the most notable, and his achievements in order of importance are the reform of the covenanted service, the permanent settlement of the land revenues of Bengal, and the reorganization of the Bengal courts of law'.[2]

Cornwallis's social origins were very different from those of his predecessors. His family belonged to the upper levels of British aristocracy. Barring a few exceptions, the trend henceforth was to pick a member of the aristocracy as governor-general rather than a servant of the Company who had risen

---

[1] Vincent A. Smith, *The Oxford History of India, from the Earliest Times to the End of 1911*, Oxford: Clarendon Press, 1919, p. 556.
[2] P. E. Roberts, *History of British India Under the Company and the Crown*, London: Oxford University Press, 1945, p. 225.

to the top through successive promotions from the position of writer. The last time a Company employee became governor-general was soon after the revolt of 1857, when John Lawrence was appointed in 1864.

With his high status in British society, Cornwallis could command deference that neither Clive nor Hastings could have expected. He corresponded directly with the prime minister, and Pitt often wrote to him about the political situation in Europe when Cornwallis was in India.

The decade of the 1780s was one of instability in Europe. On the eve of the French Revolution (1789), a crisis erupted in the Netherlands. A struggle for limiting the authority of the chief executive of the Netherlands, who bore the title of stadtholder (the Netherlands, it may be recalled was a republic for nearly two centuries, c.1580s–1790s), led to a civil war, culminating in Prussian military intervention in 1787. France and England were both keen to protect their interests in the Dutch Republic, and it was against this backdrop that Pitt wrote to Cornwallis confidentially from time to time, conveying his assessment of the state of affairs in Europe and British strategy for dealing with disputes:

> From the instructions which have been sent to Paris and to the Hague, as well as to Berlin and Vienna, much of our uncertainty must be cleared up in a very short time. Our great object is to prevent France from taking steps to carry her point in Holland by force. In doing this, we wish to avoid as much as possible the risk of a rupture; and if there is a fair opening to terminate the disputes in the Republic safely and honourably by a joint mediation, we shall eagerly embrace it.[3]

Moreover, Cornwallis was a renowned military commander and, notwithstanding his failure in America, his reputation was

---

[3]Charles Ross, *Correspondence of Charles, First Marquis Cornwallis*, Vol. 1, London: John Murray, 1859, p. 336.

untarnished mainly due to his proximity to the royal court. In later historical assessments, Cornwallis was seen as someone who had been partially responsible for the loss of British colonies in one part of the world, and then, as recompense, strengthened the empire in another. He was already a well-known imperial figure when he assumed office in Calcutta. He could lecture his subordinates, override the decisions of military officials of the EIC, and push through changes in colonial policy without much opposition.

Pitt had a high opinion of his abilities as governor-general. The Company's territories were safe in his hands. 'The sentiment of security and confidence,' he wrote at the beginning of Cornwallis's tenure, 'which I have long felt from the interests of this country in India being under your Lordship's direction, is a source of peculiar satisfaction at this moment'.[4]

Nevertheless, a handful of veteran Company officials refused to be overawed by the governor-general's aristocratic status. Foremost among them was Macpherson, who asserted that Cornwallis had usurped the office. He and his friends claimed that Macpherson's appointment in 1785, when he succeeded Hastings, was for a term of five years under the provisions of the Regulating Act and 'that Lord Cornwallis was aware that *every act he had performed was illegal*' (emphasis in the original).[5] The claim was not taken seriously by London.

Charles Cornwallis was the eldest son of the first Earl of Cornwallis (earl being the third-highest rank of the formal aristocratic hierarchy, or peerage, in Britain). The family had held peerages for several generations, since the 1660s. The first earl had been elevated to the rank of earl in 1753. Cornwallis's mother, too, came from an aristocratic family, and his maternal grandmother was closely related to the Duke of Newcastle (duke is the highest and most exclusive rank).

---

[4]Ibid.
[5]Ibid., p. 338.

Cornwallis's father held several important positions at the royal court. He was constable of the Tower of London (the head of the military establishment that guarded the main fortress of London), and a member of the privy council. Charles, too, was constable of the Tower for fourteen years, until 1784. His paternal uncle was Archbishop of Canterbury from 1768 to 1783.

At the very young age of twenty-two, Cornwallis became a member of the House of Commons for the constituency of Eye (Suffolk), in 1760. Eye is located in the eastern part of England, not far from what was then the seat of the Cornwallis family, the leading landowners in the area. It was a pocket borough, i.e., a constituency dominated by the family, with about two hundred voters. He vacated the seat in 1762 when, upon the death of his father, he inherited his titles, which gave him a place in the House of Lords.

What is more relevant is that he had embarked on a military career in 1756, was a captain by 1759, and lieutenant-colonel at the time of his father's demise. Soon after he had obtained his officer's commission, Cornwallis joined the Royal Military Academy in Turin, the capital of the Duchy of Savoy in Italy. This was the first of the modern military academies set up in Europe, and had been established in the last quarter of the seventeenth century, providing the model for other academies. It had recently introduced a special training course for young officers, open to candidates from outside Savoy. Cornwallis perhaps belonged to the first batch of the officer-trainees of the Turin academy. He then took part in some of the campaigns of the Seven Years' War, mainly in German theatres of war, and was present at the crucial Battle of Minden (1759) in Prussia, in which the opposing French army was defeated.

Cornwallis's parliamentary career was to remain a secondary interest for him. In any case, he was abroad for long periods, returning only intermittently, so that he was frequently not physically present to participate in parliamentary proceedings. Yet he did occasionally take a strong position as a member of the House of Lords. For instance, he was one of the five members of the House who voted against the Declaratory Act of 1766, by which the British Parliament declared that it had the right to legislate for the American colonies in all matters, including taxation. This was to become a contentious issue and a factor in the conflict between Britain and the American colonists. His opposition to this measure assumes significance in the context of his subsequent role as one of the leading English commanders in America in the military contest with the colonists struggling for independence.

With his aristocratic connections and his family's links with the royal court, Cornwallis gained rapid promotions after the Seven Years' War. In 1765, he was made aide-de-camp and personal attendant (lord of the bedchamber) to the king, and was then posted in Ireland for a year as joint vice-treasurer. The vice-treasurer at that time supervised the day-to-day business of the treasury in Ireland. Cornwallis became a member of the privy council in 1770.

The English cabinet, in its origins, was a smaller version of the privy council and had no independent constitutional status. The privy council may be regarded as an extended cabinet, with its members mainly having an advisory role as counsellors of the monarch in this period. In the latter half of the eighteenth century, most of the former executive functions of the privy council were concentrated in the hands of the cabinet. Nevertheless, membership of the council carried great prestige.

Although Cornwallis does not appear to have been a controversial figure at this stage, some actions or views of his did lead to public criticism of his politics. The precise reasons for the criticism are unclear. A political commentator writing under the pseudonym 'Junius' (who has often been identified with Philip Francis—an identification that has not been confirmed) bracketed him together with four other contemporary politicians who were described as:

'[A] set of men who, upon almost every action of their lives, are insulted with the pity both of their enemies and their friends. They seem to have discovered the art of doing whatever is base or detestable, without forfeiting their claim to the public compassion. ... They still preserve their natural mediocrity of character, and have as little chance of being honoured with the detestation as with the esteem of their country.'

He was specifically accused of having switched his political allegiance, of deserting the Whigs and moving closer to the Tories, presumably having 'shifted his company as well as his opinions'.[6]

As the crisis of the American colonies deepened, Cornwallis became a supporter of the government's policy of crushing resistance militarily. Fighting had broken out between the rebels and British troops in 1775. In April that year, the colonists defeated a British force at Lexington, near Boston. This marked the beginning of the Revolutionary War, which ended in 1781 with the surrender of the British army at Yorktown. Cornwallis was one of the military officers dispatched to America to deal with the rebels.

Cornwallis had been promoted to major-general in 1775, and subsequently made lieutenant-general (his local rank in America) before proceeding to America in early 1776. He sailed with reinforcements initially destined for the southern front of the war. The British had to abandon their position in the south and decided to move northwards, where they attempted to capture New York. In this, they were successful. The battle for New York was their major victory in this phase of the war.

Representatives of the American colonies had already issued the famous Declaration of Independence (4 July 1776), which implied a complete rupture with the metropole. Cornwallis, who had participated in the operations that culminated in the capture was subsequently sent by the commander-in-chief,

---

[6]John Wade (ed.), *The Letters of Junius*, Vol. 2, London: George Bell, 1894, p. 295.

William Howe, into neighbouring New Jersey to pursue troops commanded by George Washington. Here, the British suffered a setback at Princeton in January 1777, when the forces under Washington managed to outwit Cornwallis. The failure to corner Washington, which had been a possibility, had a demoralizing effect on the British.

In the operations carried out later that year, Cornwallis achieved some success, notably the occupation of the provisional capital, Philadelphia. However, following a decisive victory of the Americans at Saratoga in October 1777, the British increasingly concentrated their military strength in the south. A British force, led by John Burgoyne, which had marched southwards from Canada for a rendezvous with Howe's contingents to launch a major offensive against the Americans, was defeated at Saratoga, about three hundred kilometres north of New York. The disaster at Saratoga tilted the balance in favour of the colonists. Moreover, it led to direct French support for the American struggle for independence, which was to prove very useful for the colonists.

Cornwallis, who had gone on leave in December 1777, returned in the middle of the following year. In the meantime, Howe had been replaced by Henry Clinton as the supreme commander of the British forces in America. Cornwallis was to be second-in-command. The two did not get along well.

Cornwallis was back again in England in 1779 to be with his ailing wife, Jemima, to whom he had been married for over a decade. Jemima died in February. Cornwallis returned to America later in the year. The situation was now so unfavourable for the British forces that Clinton requested the government to allow him to resign his command and hand over charge to Cornwallis.

As we have noted, the British had shifted their focus to the south after the Saratoga debacle. The main British success in the south in the concluding phase of the war was the capture, in May 1780, of Charleston in South Carolina. Charleston was the main port of the American South. This was followed by another, and bigger, victory at Camden (South Carolina) in August, in which the British troops were led by Cornwallis.

Clinton had moved to New York, leaving Cornwallis in command of operations in the south. In the final stages of the campaign in the south, the British army attempted to extinguish American resistance in Virginia in the hope that this would put an end to the struggle for independence.

Cornwallis's invasion of the colony ended when his force was besieged in Yorktown (Virginia), and had to surrender in October 1781. He was taken prisoner. Clinton later published a series of pamphlets in Britain in which he blamed Cornwallis for the surrender at Yorktown as well as for marching troops into Virginia without consulting him. Contemporary observers considered Cornwallis's campaign in Virginia of 'doubtful prudence', and there were many in England who agreed with Clinton's censure of Cornwallis's actions. On the whole, however, Cornwallis escaped denunciation for the outcome of the war. To a large extent, this may be attributed to political opinion in Britain being reconciled to the loss of the colonies by the latter half of 1781.

Cornwallis arrived in England in January 1782. He remained a prisoner on parole till preliminary peace agreements were signed on 20 January 1783, following which there was a mutual exchange of prisoners. According to Charles Ross, whose father was aide-de-camp of Cornwallis in America and later served as his military secretary in India, 'It is certain, at least, that early in that month [January 1783], Lord Cornwallis still considered himself a prisoner on parole.'[7] The negotiations for his release had been going on ever since his return to England. The British had been given to understand that Cornwallis might be released in exchange for a leading American rebel leader, Henry Laurens.

Laurens was taken captive by the British while travelling to the Netherlands to seek support for the independence struggle.

---

[7]Ross, *Correspondence ... Cornwallis*, p. 142.

He was charged with high treason and imprisoned in the Tower of London. He thus had a status different from that of other prisoners of war, in so far as Britain was concerned. Laurens was eventually released in May 1782. Washington denied that any assurance had been given by the American side that Cornwallis would be released in exchange for Laurens. In fact, he sent a letter on behalf of the American Congress ordering Cornwallis 'to return to America according to his parole', since the negotiations were inconclusive.[8]

When Cornwallis was first offered the post of governor-general in India—i.e., governor-general of the EIC's territories in India—shortly after the conclusion of the American campaign, he declined on the grounds that he was still on parole and could therefore not accept any appointment. The offer was made following informal consultations regarding Hastings's successor in the context of the move to recall the incumbent governor-general and coincided with fresh proposals for parliamentary control over the EIC's territories in India.

The offer was repeated at the beginning of 1784. This time Cornwallis was willing to give it serious thought, as he was no longer a prisoner of war. Before giving his formal consent, he conferred with the relevant ministers and with his friends about the powers he would have in India.

Pitt's government was primarily interested in sending a capable military commander to deal with the situation in southern India, where the Company was locked in a fierce conflict with the kingdom of Mysore ruled by Haider Ali and his successor Tipu. The Company was almost on the verge of losing Madras in the First Anglo–Mysore War of 1767–69, the first of four bloody wars fought between Mysore and the British. It was forced to sue for peace when the Mysore army appeared at the gates of Madras.

The Second Anglo–Mysore War of 1780–84, during the course of which Haidar Ali passed away in 1782 and was

---

[8]Ibid.

succeeded by Tipu, concluded with the signing of the Treaty of Mangalore (March 1784) which, by and large, restored the pre-war territorial status of the region. It was clear that the conflict would be resumed, despite the treaty, as Tipu was unwilling to allow the EIC to expand its territories in the region.

In April 1784, Cornwallis had learnt from the Home Secretary (Home Minister) Lord Sydney that 'Government had determined to send a Lieut.-General immediately to Madras, but that whoever went was to be taught to expect a Commander-in-Chief soon after him'.[9] News of the ceasefire, and the signing of the treaty, would not yet have reached London.

The government sounded him out on his willingness to accept the command in India, to which he responded by 'laying particular stress on the circumscribed power of the Military command without the Civil'.[10] Pitt was inclined to make him both commander-in-chief and governor-general, but Cornwallis hesitated when he was informed that, in his military capacity, he could not extend any patronage and that he would have limited powers. The matter was discussed with him by the prime minister at the beginning of 1785 after some delay. Cornwallis complained that Pitt brought up the issue 'after having lost sight of my going for six months'.[11]

Cornwallis was still undecided, and his preliminary response was to decline the offer due to some of the provisions of the India Act that were not to his liking. By now, Hastings was on his way home. The decision on a successor was a matter of some urgency. Another name had also been proposed for the governor-generalship when Cornwallis expressed his reservations about accepting the offer. Dundas had suggested the name of Lord Macartney, the outgoing governor of the Madras presidency. As head of the Company's establishment in southern India, Lord Macartney had to deal directly with the complications of

---

[9]Ibid., p. 174. Cornwallis had been promoted to the rank of lieutenant-general in 1777. His earlier promotion was valid only in America.
[10]Ibid., p. 175.
[11]Ibid., p. 191.

the war with Mysore. He left India in 1785. When he found out, before leaving, that his name was being considered for the governor-generalship, he declined the offer to register his protest over the support that Hastings received from authorities in London when differences had surfaced between him and the governor-general over an issue related to the finances of the Madras presidency.

The prime minister was insistent that Cornwallis be appointed, upon which the offer to him was renewed. Some further consultations followed, during which the government agreed to simultaneously appoint him the commander-in-chief 'of all the forces'—both Company and Crown troops. Once the arrangement was finalized—necessitating an act of Parliament (Amending Act of 1786) under which the governor-general was concurrently the head of the army, Cornwallis departed England in May 1786. He reached Calcutta in September.

The ruling elite of Britain had strongly asserted their right to share political power in the Company's territories in India. The EIC's acquisitions could compensate for the loss of the American colonies. The appointment of the head of the colonial government henceforth came within the purview of the British cabinet. In the process, senior Company officials were sidelined: they could no longer, after Hastings, aspire to the top post. If we leave aside the brief interludes when a senior member of the council would be the acting governor-general until such time that a full-time appointment was made, a governor-general was selected from among EIC servants only twice after Warren Hastings—John Shore in 1793 and John Lawrence in 1864.

∽

The main obstacle to the Company's expansionist drive in southern India was the kingdom of Mysore. For Cornwallis, success in an operation to check Tipu's power might salvage his military reputation, which had been seriously damaged due to the failure in America. Ever since the signing of the Treaty of Mangalore—the terms of which had not at all been satisfactory for the British—the EIC had been looking for an opportunity to undo the outcome of the Second Anglo–Mysore War. The British would seize any chance to unleash another war. Cornwallis, in his correspondence between 1786 and 1790, repeatedly urges the officers posted in the south to be alert to even the slightest transgression by Mysore. This would justify the resumption of hostilities. Tipu's dispute with the kingdom of Travancore in southern Kerala provided the pretext.

In the mid-1760s, Haidar Ali had absorbed northern and central Kerala (Malabar), with their numerous petty-chieftaincies into the kingdom of Mysore. Besides, the small but strategically located principality of Cochin had agreed to render an annual tribute to the kingdom. With these acquisitions, Mysore had also gained access to the sea.

During the Second Anglo–Mysore War, the EIC had endeavoured to prevent Mysore from acquiring a dominant position in Kerala. It had actively supported its ally, the ruler of Travancore, in resisting Tipu's inroads into the kingdom.

The involvement of Mysore in the military conflicts of Kerala had a long history, which was largely the outcome of upheavals within Kerala triggered by attempts of regional powers, such as Calicut, to expand their territories. For instance, the incursions of Calicut into the chiefdom of Palakkad (Palghat) had prompted the ruler of Palakkad to appeal to Mysore for assistance in resisting these inroads in 1732 and again in 1735. Relations between Mysore and Palakkad deteriorated in the 1740s, with frequent raids by Mysore into Palakkad. The situation altered in the late 1750s, when the Calicut army invaded the chiefdom. Palakkad sustained heavy casualties in the fighting, and the ruler again appealed to Mysore.

The dalavai (hereditary commander-in-chief) of Mysore deputed Haidar Ali, then the military commander of Dindigul (in present-day Tamil Nadu), to deal with the invading Calicut army. The dalavai, was the de facto ruler of the Mysore kingdom. He was subsequently ejected by Haidar Ali, who became de facto ruler of Mysore in 1761. In 1757, Haidar Ali intervened in the fight between Palakkad and Calicut, on the side of the Palakkad chief. The Calicut army was forced to retreat. This intervention marked the beginning of his involvement in the politics of Malabar, culminating in 1766 in the annexation of northern Kerala. The rulers of Palakkad and Kannur (Cannanore) were his main allies during the 1766 campaign.

In the wake of Haidar Ali's offensive, many of the dispossessed chiefs of the region, along with their retinues, sought refuge in Travancore. Travancore itself had emerged as a powerful regional kingdom quite recently. The shelter provided by Travancore to these displaced ruling families became a factor in the Second and Third Anglo–Mysore Wars. Travancore was inescapably drawn into a conflict with Mysore.

Travancore and the EIC had together striven in several ways to undermine the control of Mysore over Malabar since the late 1760s. Cornwallis now decided to force the issue so that the British could subjugate Malabar and enhance their influence over Travancore.

There was one other major cause of friction between Mysore and Travancore which contributed to the breakdown in their relations after the Second Anglo–Mysore War. This was a dispute over fortifications on the northern borders of Travancore. The extension of these fortifications by the ruler of the kingdom was strongly opposed by Mysore.

On the Travancore frontier, there was a line of fortifications called nedumkotta in Malayalam, which had been constructed over several years from the mid-1760s onwards to strengthen the defences of the northern border. The construction of the nedumkotta lines had been linked to a perceived threat from Mysore, though the plan for their construction was conceived much earlier. The enlargement of the fortifications by extending them into Cochin was objected to by Tipu. This resulted in a military confrontation lasting for several months, from the end of 1789 to May 1790.

This was the prelude to the Third Anglo–Mysore War (1789–92), and provided the excuse Cornwallis had been looking for. It is obvious that many of the actions of the Travancore ruler, at the behest of the EIC, were intended to escalate tensions.

In the ensuing war, the Marathas and the nizam of Hyderabad were allies of the Company. Tipu had to fight simultaneously on several fronts: the Marathas and the nizam in the north, the British in the east, and a hostile Travancore in the rear. At one point, he was successful in cornering Cornwallis on the outskirts of his capital Seringapatam (Srirangapatna) in May 1791. Cornwallis had led his troops from Bangalore to the outskirts of Seringapatam with the aim of capturing Tipu's capital. Bangalore had been taken from Mysore a few months earlier. The expedition was a failure, and Cornwallis was forced to order his troops to retreat. Much of the heavy equipment carried by the British had to be destroyed before the retreat commenced.

The news was received in Britain with much derision, the more so as it confirmed the low regard that the public in Britain had for the military abilities of the commander who surrendered at Yorktown. At least two popular satirical prints mocking Cornwallis's retreat were published in 1791, one of them by the famous political cartoonist James Gillray, which bore the title 'The Coming-On of the Monsoons; or, the Retreat from Seringapatam', and the other 'How to gain a compleat victory, and say, you got safe out of the enemy's reach' by the Scottish caricaturist Isaac Cruikshank.[12] Gillray's brutal cartoon depicts Tipu standing behind the battlements of his fortress and urinating with all his might on British soldiers in flight, while Cornwallis flees on a mule.

British troops reappeared outside Seringapatam eight months later, along with their friends: Hyderabad and the Marathas.

---

[12]'James Gillray: The Suppressed Plates', Collections.vam.ac.uk, available at https://collections.vam.ac.uk/item/O1301907/james-gillray--the-suppressed-print-james-gillray/.

Mysore was unable to withstand the combined offensive of the joint force. Tipu eventually made a peace offer, leading to the signing of the Treaty of Seringapatam by which Mysore had to cede nearly half its territory to the British, the nizam, and the Marathas. The Company's acquisitions included Salem, Dindigul, and Malabar; and the kingdom of Coorg came under British 'protection'. A massive indemnity, amounting to 3.30 crore rupees (almost equal to the annual revenue of Bengal, Bihar, and Orissa) was imposed on the kingdom. Further, 'Two of Tippoo Sultan's three eldest sons [were] to be given as hostages for a due performance of the treaty'.

The handing over of two of Tipu's sons—the ten-year-old Abdul Khaliq and the eight-year-old Muiz-ud-din, to the governor-general became a familiar theme in colonial commemorative art at the close of the century. Fourteen years later, Muiz-ud-din, now in his early twenties and living in confinement in Vellore, to which the slain Tipu's family had been exiled, was among those who provided 'direct encouragement' for a major mutiny in the EIC's army in 1806.

Tipu was killed in 1799 while fighting in the Fourth Anglo–Mysore War. Following the suppression of the mutiny, Muiz-ud-din was incarcerated in Calcutta jail, while other members of the family were transported to a village on the outskirts of Calcutta. Muiz-ud-din remained in prison for several years. The story of his long captivity is little known. The popular perception in Seringapatam today is that Tipu's sons 'were taken away and secretly killed. They all became martyrs'. Discussing this tragedy, Partha Chatterjee remarks that, 'exile a thousand miles away was, after all, little else but death'.[13]

The hostages figure prominently in contemporary art, reflecting an obsession with Tipu Sultan in popular British imagination, which was to continue for a long time. The Tipu theme begins to appear in artworks from the early 1790s.

---

[13]Partha Chatterjee, *The Black Hole of Empire: History of a Global Practice of Power*, Ranikhet: Permanent Black, 2012, p. 103.

Among the earliest representations of the encounter between Tipu and the British is a depiction on the pedestal of a Cornwallis statue—one of the first objects created to publicly honour the governor-general. The statue was commissioned in the latter half of 1792 in commemoration of the signing of the Treaty of Seringapatam, 'at the joint expence of the principal [European] inhabitants of Madras, and of the civil and military servants of the East India Company belonging to the Presidency of Fort St George'.

The marble statue, now in the museum of Fort St George in Chennai, stands on an elaborately carved pedestal. This pedestal has a bas-relief depicting the arrival of the two sons of Tipu as hostages in the English camp.

The Royal Academy (formed in 1768) was approached by representatives of British residents of Madras for nominating an artist to create the statue. For the Royal Academy, this became, as Sarah Burnage in her study of the project has pointed out, 'a vehicle for disseminating its own aesthetic ambitions for a British school of sculpture'.[14] In acting as 'the arbiter of taste for a public commission', the academy attempted to 'hijack' the project. After all, this was to be the first public sculpture in India honouring an imperial figure. However, when it was announced that the sculptor would be chosen through a competition among invited artists, the only entry that the Royal Academy received was that of Thomas Banks, one of the most eminent British artists of that era. Other artists perhaps felt that they would be surrendering their autonomy to the Royal Academy if they were to undertake the project under its direction. The statue was unveiled in 1800.

The Banks statue, with the bas-relief on the plinth below it, would, Burnage notes, have 'helped to distract ... [viewers] from the brutal reality of British conquest: promoting instead a highly idealized vision of British rule in the region'.[15]

---

[14]Sarah Burnage, 'Commemorating Cornwallis: Sculpture in India 1792–1813', *Visual Culture in Britain*, Vol. 11, No. 2, 2010, pp. 174–75.
[15]Ibid., p. 178.

The bas-relief was based on illustrations of the scene that began to flood the British art market, most of which were inspired by Robert Home's 1792 painting, *The Reception of the Mysorean Hostage Princes by Marquis Cornwallis*. Home had arrived in India in 1791 and obtained permission to accompany the British force on the Mysore campaign, even though he did not have the EIC's mandatory official sanction to reside in India—a requirement for all British subjects in those days. There is a self-portrait of the artist in the painting. The painter portrayed himself observing the transfer of the princes as an eyewitness to the event, which he indeed was.

A series of paintings produced by Home against the backdrop of the Mysore invasion marked the beginning of his Indian career. He settled down permanently in North India, and passed away at Kanpur in 1834. Another painter, Arthur Devis, who came to Madras a year after the Seringapatam offensive of 1792 and did not himself witness the delivery of the princes, made use of the Home painting and available official reports to offer his own interpretation of the scene. Other artists who produced works on this theme in England had no personal familiarity with India and created romanticized versions which bore little resemblance to what actually transpired.

Banks found the Devis version, rather than the Home version, more suitable for depicting the event in his marble bas-relief. Home's representation has an element of authenticity, as he was an eyewitness to the episode. The Devis painting places a benevolent Cornwallis at the centre of the scene and shows one of the children extending his arms towards him, as if desirous of his affection.

The extensive visual record, primarily meant for an English audience, was intended to highlight the magnanimity of the governor-general and of the British in India, in their hour of triumph. A written account of the handing over of the princes, authored by Alexander Dirom, an officer in the royal army who participated in the invasion of Mysore, describes Cornwallis's treatment with cloying sentiment: 'Lord Cornwallis, who had received the boys as if they had been his own sons, anxiously assured the vakeel [Tipu's emissary] and the young Princes themselves that every attention possible would be shewn to them, and the greatest care taken of their persons. Their little faces brightened up; ... and not only their attendants, but all the spectators were delighted to see that any fears they might have harboured were removed, and that they would soon be reconciled to their change of situation and to their new friends'.[16] In Dirom's rendering, 'the menacing abuse of children as hostages, such as one might expect of a ruthless tyrant, was recast as an act of paternal kindness'.[17]

The hostages were released in 1794. Tipu remained a formidable foe, and another fiercely fought war would be necessary to annihilate the kingdom of Mysore. That task was completed by Lord Wellesley. The Third Anglo–Mysore War partially restored Cornwallis's standing as an army commander. Only on one more occasion did he subsequently lead an army in the field—as commander of British troops in Ireland—though the campaign was more in the nature of counter-insurgency operations.

In textbook histories of the colonial bureaucracy, Cornwallis is usually referred to as 'the father of the civil service in India'. Such a cliché reflects an inadequate understanding of the long historical process through which the civil services came into being in British India. It was not until the latter half of the 1850s—three years before Company rule came to an end—that recruitment for higher positions in the bureaucracy began to be made based on an open examination conducted in Britain. Britain itself did not have a modern bureaucracy recruited in this manner at this time. The notion that suitable personnel for the civil services ought to be recruited on the basis of merit

---

[16]Major Dirom, *A Narrative of the Campaign in India, Which Terminated the War with Tippoo Sultan, in 1792*, London: W. Bulmer, 1793, p. 229.
[17]Giles Tillotson, Giles Tillotson (ed.), '"Dropped from the Clouds": Tipu Sultan in History Painting and the British Imagination', *Tipu Sultan: Image and Distance*, New Delhi: DAG, 2022, p. 46.

determined through a public examination was still unacceptable for their own country to the elites of the metropole as late as the last quarter of the nineteenth century. Therefore, it is anachronistic to suggest that Cornwallis already had a vision of such a bureaucracy a century earlier.

Civil servants posted in districts and in presidency headquarters (Calcutta, Madras, Bombay) were drawn from the managerial hierarchy of the EIC for governing its territories. The district was the basic administrative unit of the colonial state and was controlled by colonial administrators. These civil servants would be the factors, junior merchants, or senior merchants within the Company's organizational structure. Leading functionaries in the district were entirely European.

As we have noted, 'writers' or copying clerks were located at the lowest rung of the organizational ladder. Once they had gained some experience and familiarity with the commercial work of the EIC, they would be promoted to the position of factor. Senior merchants stood at the top of the hierarchy, and the key administrative, revenue, and judicial posts were given to them. What Cornwallis did was to streamline the system and reduce the ad hocism that had been inherent in it so far. P. J. Marshall has pointed out that 'In the years after 1765, the functions of a late Mughal provincial state, as the British understood them, were engrafted onto the organization of a trading company'.[18]

Cornwallis's measures were necessitated by the vastly expanded scope of the administrative and judicial functions of the EIC by the time he assumed office. Several changes were introduced in 1793. Promotions were henceforth to be only based on seniority, i.e. the number of years that an employee had served in India, with corresponding fixed pay scales for each level. Salaries were enhanced. These provisions were exclusively applicable to employees recruited by the Company in England

---

[18]P. J. Marshall, *Bengal: The British Bridgehead: Eastern India 1740–1828*, Cambridge: Cambridge University Press, 1988, p. 100.

for vacancies in its establishments in India. The recruitment in Britain was through recommendations made by EIC directors. This system of recruitment continued till the Charter Act of 1853.

Cornwallis's term as governor-general is most prominently associated with the new system of land revenue imposed on Bengal and Bihar: the Permanent Settlement of 1793. This was to have an adverse impact on the agrarian economy of eastern India, with disastrous consequences for the peasantry. Land revenue was the foremost source of revenue for the state in this period and, therefore, of great concern to the Company. It was a major source of the wealth that was regularly transferred to the metropole.

Permanent Settlement was the product of ideas which had been circulating among policymakers since the 1770s. The central objective of the plan, first articulated by Philip Francis in 1776, was to stabilize revenue by recognizing a class of landed proprietors, making them answerable for the payment of revenue, and fixing the state's demand in perpetuity. The demand under the Cornwallis Settlement of 1793 was fixed at 89 per cent of the rent payable on the land, with the remaining 11 per cent as the share of the landowner.

Colonial officials identified holders of superior rights on land, zamindars and talluqdars—landed magnates who traditionally had the authority to collect land revenue from villages in their estates—as the class which could most suitably be recognized as landowners. There was enormous diversity among the zamindars and talluqdars in terms of their rights and the extent of the land over which they exercised control. Following the settlement, they were reduced to a homogeneous class of proprietors along the lines of English landowners, their status affirmed by a deed, and had the responsibility for collecting revenue from their estates. The zamindars were left to make their own arrangements with their tenants. These arrangements were invariably unfavourable to the tenants, the sub-tenants, and those below them. Cornwallis's tenure as governor-general cast a long shadow over the countryside. It was never the same again.

In 1792, following the successful conclusion of the Third Anglo–Mysore War, Earl Cornwallis was 'advanced to the dignity of Marquis Cornwallis', one step higher in the English peerage, marquis (or marquess) being the second-highest rank in the aristocratic hierarchy. He was made a general in 1793. His seven-year tenure having come to an end in 1793, he was scheduled to depart for England that year.

John Shore, who had been a member of Cornwallis's council, was to be his successor. The appointment was finalized towards the end of 1792. This was more of a stop-gap measure. The government had to resort to it because it was difficult to immediately nominate a high-profile successor to Cornwallis. The British government was preoccupied with the war in Europe and found it difficult to decide on a new governor-general. Shore was a safe bet: he was non-controversial, experienced, and competent enough to head the EIC's government in India for a few years.

The new appointee arrived in Calcutta in March 1793. Cornwallis did not relinquish office till October, so that for seven months Shore resided near Calcutta in a state of uncertainty, while in the meantime the outgoing governor-general was busy carrying out a series of revenue, judicial, and administrative changes, including the Permanent Settlement.[19] There was, all this while, a possibility that Cornwallis might be persuaded to stay on in India due to tensions between Britain and France in the wake of the French Revolution, which would mean that Shore would not be asked to take over.

In all, fifty-one regulations were passed by the governor-general's council in 1793 before Cornwallis handed over charge to Shore. Forty-eight of these regulations, all enacted in May, constituted what came to be known as the 'Cornwallis Code'. Regulations—the nomenclature then used for legislation enacted by presidency councils—were part of the delegated or

---

[19]'A Regulation for enacting into a Regulation certain Articles of a Proclamation, bearing date the 22nd March 1793: Passed by the Governor-General in Council on the 1st May 1793', *Regulations passed by the Governor General in Council of Bengal with an Index and Glossary*, Vol. 1, London, 1793, 1794, and 1795, 1828.

subordinate legislation enacted by the governor-general's council or by the Madras or Bombay councils. The principal legislation was enacted by the British Parliament, while authority was delegated to the councils to enact subordinate legislation.

Cornwallis finally departed in October, arriving in England at the beginning of the following year. By now, Britain was at war with France, and Europe was in ferment with the outbreak of the French Revolutionary Wars. Cornwallis with his conservative outlook was, of course, strongly anti-Jacobin and wholeheartedly supported his government in its war effort. A few weeks after he was back in England, Cornwallis was summoned to give evidence in the Hastings trial. He appeared before the House of Lords tribunal on 9 April and testified in favour of his predecessor. Cornwallis's opinion on matters relating to India carried considerable weight, and his statement, recorded towards the fag end of the long trial, contributed to the exoneration of Hastings.

Amidst the critical situation with which Britain and its allies were faced at the beginning of 1794, when dealing with an uprising in Warsaw against Russia that diverted their military focus, and at a time when the Prussians were threatening to withdraw from the fight against the French, Cornwallis was informed in May that he had been deputed to command a contingent of the king's troops in Europe, for which purpose he was to initially proceed to Flanders. This turned out to be a brief trip. His formal appointment to the command never came about. His duties, while he was on the Continent, were more of a diplomatic nature, and he was recalled in July.

In a surprise development, while he was in England, Cornwallis was suddenly requested to assume office once again as governor-general in India. He acceded to this request and was appointed for a second time in February 1797. The main task before him—and this was the primary reason for his reappointment—was to resolve the crisis in the Company's army brought about by a proposal to amalgamate it with the king's army.

On his return journey in 1793, Cornwallis had prepared a draft for a scheme for amalgamating the two. While he was in India, he had been pondering over such a scheme. His draft became the basis of consultations in London between the government and the directors, and between the directors and officials in Calcutta. When officers of the EIC army learnt of the plan to combine the two armies, they began to mobilize opinion in India and Britain against any such move.

In view of hostilities with France and the possibility that the French would join hands with Mysore against the British, a unified army in the subcontinent was a matter of priority for the Pitt administration. On the other hand, the EIC's military officials, especially in Bengal and northern India, were opposed to the amalgamation because this would reduce their autonomy, make them subservient to royal officers, and limit their avenues for promotion. The widespread discontent that ensued, virtually amounting to a mutiny, could not be easily ignored by London.

Orders for the reorganization of the armed forces reached Calcutta at the end of 1796. Governor-general Shore and his commander-in-chief, Robert Abercromby, found it very difficult to handle the repercussions of decisions taken by London. Abercromby failed to persuade the Company's officers to accept a revised version of the Cornwallis plan. The modified scheme worked out by the government did not imply the formal takeover of the EIC army by the Crown, placing it instead in the service of the king. Nevertheless—and this caused great resentment—it involved doing away with the prevailing system of promotions by seniority and a drastic reduction of allowances.

Abercromby was an appointee of the government. He belonged to the king's army and had been governor of the Bombay presidency from 1790 to 1792. He was made commander-in-chief in India when Cornwallis relinquished charge, and the military office was separated from that of the governor-general. At the same time, there was an ambiguity about the status of Abercromby, in his capacity as the commander of British forces, vis-à-vis the commanders-in-chief of the three components of the EIC's army (Bengal Army, Madras Army, and Bombay Army), each of which had its own chief. Abercromby was therefore unable to enforce discipline in this situation of crisis.

The fiercest opposition to the scheme came from officers of the Bengal Army. The officers constituted a committee of representatives to argue their case in London. During negotiations with these representatives, the British government indicated its willingness to make some further concessions. Cornwallis was opposed to these concessions. Moreover, the government, which had earlier received a petition from the committee of representatives remonstrating against the appointment of Cornwallis, refused to give him discretionary powers over the Company's army in his capacity as governor-general. Rebuffed, Cornwallis tendered his resignation in August 1797 without having assumed office.

Bengal army officers had strongly asserted that they were not 'slaves' and could not be made to change their employers without their consent. The revised scheme was finally abandoned, and amalgamation would not be attempted again for the remaining period of Company rule.

In an incisive analysis of the fate of the Cornwallis army reorganization plan, Raymond Callahan notes that 'Cornwallis' efforts to remodel the Indian army and their frustration at the hands of the Bengal army provide the basis for some modification in the view that Cornwallis was a great success in India'.[20] This aspect of his Indian career has been completely overshadowed in the historiography of the period by details of his administrative reorganization, revenue policy, and invasion of Mysore. Callahan draws attention to similarities in Cornwallis's attitude towards the Company's army and the loyalist militias of America during the War of Independence. These militias might have helped the British cause in the conflict.

---

[20]Raymond A. Callahan, 'Cornwallis and the Indian Army, 1786-1797', *Military Affairs*, Vol. 34, No. 3, 1970, p. 96.

Cornwallis was disdainful of the one and contemptuous of the other. In the case of the former, 'he allowed the lack of smartness in the Company's service and the low status of its officers to blind him to the fact that it was a perfectly adequate military force for its purposes'.[21]

As one of Pitt's (and Dundas's) troubleshooters, Cornwallis was sent to Ireland in 1798 as lord lieutenant and commander-in-chief to put down a serious rebellion that had engulfed the colony. The lord lieutenant was head of the government and personal representative of the British monarch in Ireland. An uprising led by the outlawed Society of United Irishmen had broken out in Ireland on 23 May 1798, which the incumbent lord lieutenant, Lord Camden, was unable to deal with. The society, formed in 1791, was inspired by the revolutionary and republican ideals of the French Revolution and had been assured of French assistance in its struggle against English rule.

Camden's repressive regime had been unable to crush the United Irishmen movement. Nor were the ruthless methods of one of the English commanders in Ireland, Gerard Lake (better known in Indian history for his role in the conquest of Delhi in 1803), entirely effective in foiling the plans of United Irishmen for an insurrection, even though the society was weakened organizationally by his persecution. If anything, Lake's brutality aggravated the situation.

Cornwallis took over in June and initiated a vigorous campaign to put an end to the rebellion. The operations against the rebels culminated in the Battle of Ballinamuck in September 1798. Ballinamuck is located about 130 km from Dublin. The Irish rebels were joined by a small French force in this confrontation, which ended with the victory of the English army led by Cornwallis. This was followed by large-scale executions of rebels. It is estimated that nearly thirty thousand people, mostly poor Irish peasants, perished in the rebellion. With the defeat at Ballinamuck, it was no longer

---

[21]Ibid., p. 96.

possible to sustain the struggle. Cornwallis had violently wiped out the resistance movement.

Three years later, Ireland was forcibly 'united' with Britain. The Act of Union (1800) which came into force in 1801 extinguished the limited autonomy allowed to Ireland and abolished the Irish Parliament.[22] Britain is still grappling with the consequences of that act. The acquiescence of a section of the Anglo–Irish landowning elite, who had generally opposed the union, was gained by creating several new peers for manufacturing a majority in favour of the government in the Irish House of Lords when the proposal was debated.

Cornwallis's experience in the revenue administration of Bengal, especially while working out the details of the Permanent Settlement, was useful to him while finalizing recommendations for the 'Act of Union peerages', as these were called. He ensured that these peers were men with substantial landed wealth and therefore had a stake in maintaining stability. Their chances of being elected 'representative peers' would be higher, and they would be seen to be representing Ireland in the (British) House of Lords. He 'meticulously itemised the rent rolls of the various aspirants', confirming that 'all were satisfactory (between £5,000 and £12,000 a year or more)'.[23]

Cornwallis died in 1805. In 1806, when the House of Commons was discussing a proposal for erecting a memorial for him in London, an Irish member strongly opposed the motion, reminding the house of the corrupt practices that were indulged in during Cornwallis's tenure as lord lieutenant for effecting the union (see chapter V, below). The deceased, in the opinion of the member, was not entitled to any public memorial, given

---

[22]Following the Act of Union, Irish peers were represented in the British House of Lords by twenty-eight peers elected from among themselves. These 'representative peers' as they were called, were elected for life. The remaining Irish peers were entitled to sit in the (British) House of Commons. The Irish peerage continued to be replenished after the Act of Union with the creation of new peers, in the Irish peerage. Further, existing and newly created peers continued to be promoted in the Irish peerage.

[23]Malcomson, 'The Irish Peerage and the Act of Union', pp. 291–92.

his large share in the immoral acts of the administration over which he presided. Among these acts was the nomination of peers who could be relied upon to support the government policies for effecting union.

ᴄᴏ

Meanwhile, in India, Shore had been replaced by Richard Wellesley as governor-general of the EIC's possessions. Wellesley arrived in Calcutta in May 1798. Shore was promptly recalled due to his supposed inept handling of the mess created by the scheme for reorganizing the army. The crisis, as we have seen, was not of his making. The plan had been envisaged by Cornwallis. Shore's appointment had all along been considered as tentative, notwithstanding that his tenure lasted for five years. It was felt that in view of this tentativeness, his recall would not be seen as a personal rebuke.

Colonial historiography has tended to avoid mention of the army reorganization fiasco. This has not been difficult, as Shore's tenure has been eclipsed by those of his more celebrated predecessor and successor, both depicted as towering imperial figures. Roberts in his textbook devotes a brief paragraph to the issue without clarifying Cornwallis's part in it. He quotes Cornwallis's statement about the inadvisability of appointing a Company servant as the head of its government in India, suggesting that this was the cause of Shore's failure and supersession.

According to Cornwallis: 'Such is the present temper of the British part of the community in India ... that nobody but a person who has never been in the service [of the Company] can be competent to govern our possessions with that energy and vigour which is essential to our political safety and internal prosperity'.[24]

The short biography of the governor-general authored by W.S. Seton-Karr in the *Rulers of India* series, published at the

---

[24]Roberts, *History of British India*, p. 242.

end of the nineteenth century, gives a brief account of the uproar in the army without even hinting at how Cornwallis might have been responsible for it.[25]

Mill, in his *History*, goes into the details of a controversy over the nomination of Lord Robert Hobart (governor of the Madras presidency, 1793–98) as Shore's successor prior to Wellesley's appointment, and the denial of the post to Hobart. The issue is quite unrelated to Cornwallis's resignation or the army question. Hobart, who had been eyeing the post since the end of Cornwallis's tenure in 1793, was given an assurance when Shore was appointed that he would succeed Shore. The British government backtracked on its commitment to him and had to sanction a generous pension to compensate Hobart for the 'breach of faith'. The pension was paid by the EIC's subjects in India. Mill makes no reference to the army problem in his account of the transition.[26]

Hobart occupies a place in the history of British colonialism in Asia for his role in the conquest of Sri Lanka (Ceylon). As governor of Madras, he was entrusted, during the conflict with France, with the responsibility of 'protecting' Dutch possessions on the island which, it was feared, might be taken over by the French. The Dutch ruled over portions of Sri Lanka. The Netherlands had come under French occupation in 1795, and the exiled stadtholder of the Dutch Republic, William V, had appealed to the British for help in defending Dutch colonies. Using this as a pretext, the government ordered that a naval fleet be sent to the island to seize Dutch-ruled territory in Sri Lanka. The Dutch possessions were eventually annexed by Britain, and Ceylon became a Crown colony. Wellesley had advocated making it a part of the EIC's empire in India but was overruled by London. Dutch control had been mainly confined to coastal areas. The British absorbed the entire island, thereby

---

[25]W. S. Seton-Karr, *The Marquess of Cornwallis*, Oxford: Clarendon Press, 1890, pp. 161–62.
[26]James Mill, *The History of British India*, Vol. 6, Fourth Edition, London: James Madden, 1858, pp. 71–72.

putting an end to the kingdom of Kandy, which had survived in the inner highlands under Portuguese, and then under Dutch ascendancy. The Hobart governorship of Madras is of more than passing interest, not least because one of the suggestions put forth when his pension was under consideration was that it be paid out of the revenues of Ceylon, initially regarded as an extension of the presidency.

With the appointment of Shore, an EIC employee of humble social origins had once again occupied the seat of the governor-general. As has been noted, for the aristocratic Cornwallis, such an appointment amounted to degrading the office. Shore came from an 'India family'; several of its male members had been in the service of the Company for three generations.

John's father had passed away when he was still a small child. Given the family's connections with the Company, it was not difficult to get an assurance that the son would be taken on as a writer when he came of age. At the age of seventeen, John was sent to an institution in a suburb of London to gain some familiarity with bookkeeping and accountancy to prepare him for the writership. This was an essential qualification for the appointment. Having acquired the necessary basic instruction, he embarked for India in 1768, arriving in Bengal via Madras at the beginning of 1769. Shore would later remark that he 'began life without connections and friends; and had scarcely a letter of introduction'.[27]

Within two years of his arrival, he was assigned to work in the revenue establishment at the Murshidabad headquarters as an assistant. Murshidabad was the seat of the nawab, and formally still the capital of the province. His promotion, within such a short time, to a position in which he exercised independent civil and fiscal judicial authority, reflected the acute shortage of personnel for carrying out administrative work in the vast region of eastern India acquired by the

---

[27]Lord Teignmouth, *Memoir of the Life and Correspondence of John Lord Teignmouth*, Vol. 1, London: Hatchard and Son, 1843, p. 24. Lord Teignmouth was the eldest son of Shore.

Company, and the ad hoc manner in which it attempted to govern these areas.

Shore's entire career after this, before he became governor-general, was in the revenue branch of the colonial administration. He spent nearly three decades of his life in India, with two intervals during which he was in Britain. His first and longest spell lasted till 1785; the second from 1786 to 1789 as a member of the supreme council; and the third, as governor-general, from 1793 till his final return in 1798.

As a member of the council under Cornwallis, Shore was Cornwallis's chief adviser on revenue matters, and his inputs were vital for formulating the Permanent Settlement scheme. Quite early in his career, he had commenced a serious study of the languages relevant to his administrative work, especially Persian and Hindustani, and while at Murshidabad was also given the job of Persian translator in the revenue department.

Shore and William Jones had a shared interest in 'oriental' languages, and they were sufficiently close to each other for Jones's wife to request Shore to write a biography of her late husband after his death. Jones had passed away in Calcutta in 1794 at the age of forty-seven. Shore's biography of his friend was published in 1804. He penned it while living in retirement in England. The account of the last twelve years of Jones's life, his most productive in terms of his 'oriental' studies, was 'chiefly supplied by my [Shore's] own recollection, assisted by information collected from his writings and correspondence'.[28] The two spent their spare time studying Persian literature and regularly sent to each other classical works in the language.

Company servants who acquired proficiency in languages, mainly Persian at this stage, formed a close-knit select circle, which included Hastings, Macpherson, and Shore. Unlike someone like Cornwallis, they were well-versed in Persianate culture. In his biography of Jones, Shore's reminiscences are mainly about the intellectual collaboration among members

---

[28]Ibid., p. viii.

of this circle. Shore took a keen interest in the activities of the Asiatic Society and succeeded Jones as its president following the latter's death. He remained president till the end of his tenure.

In the Indian phase of his life, which lasted till 1798, Shore maintained intimate relationships with several local women whom he took as his concubines.[29] Of these, the most well-known was Bibi Shore, or Chand Bibi. There were a few other women as well, many of whom bore him children. One of these offspring, his eldest son John (also known as Jack) born in 1772, figures in his records as the most visible of his 'Anglo–Bengali' children. John (Jack), whose mother was someone other than Chand Bibi, was sent to Britain when he was twelve years old, was brought up and educated by his uncle, and then became an indigo planter and trader in India.

Shore fathered four children whose mothers were part of his extended Indian family. It was not unusual in the early period of colonial rule for Company servants to have households with Indian concubines. High officials such as Shore could maintain families in India without being embarrassed back home about their native women companions or the offspring of these unions. Several wills are extant for the decades prior to circa 1830 of Englishmen posted in India, providing for their Indian families after their death. Nevertheless, the Anglo–Indian children did not have a share in ancestral property, nor could they inherit aristocratic titles. They were destined to remain inferior members of the larger family with their European counterparts. What is more, the women companions, even if they were provided for, were left to their own devices once their male English partners had returned home.

Thus, Chand Bibi found another companion, Charles Rothman, when Shore left for England. She bore Rothman a

[29]The following account of the Indian wives of Shore, and his children from them is based on Sarah Pearson, 'Making Britain in Empire: John Shore, Nation and Race in the Eighteenth-Century East India Company World', unpublished Ph.D. dissertation, University of Bristol, 2020, pp. 68–74.

daughter in 1802, who was named Eliza. Shore had by now settled down to the life of a respectable aristocrat advocating evangelical virtues. In the two-volume biography of his father published in 1843, Shore's British-born son erased the story of the family which had been left behind in India. This is not surprising, especially given the date of publication of the biography. By the 1840s, it was considered improper to acknowledge sexual relationships with non-white women.

Shore had been honoured with a baronetcy in 1792—a state honour in Britain that ranks higher than a knighthood, yet does not make the person upon whom it is bestowed a member of the aristocracy or peerage. Then, in 1797, he was made a peer, in the Irish peerage, with the title Baron Teignmouth. Barons, as we have noted, are at the lowest level of the peerage. Henceforth, he would be known as Lord Teignmouth—quite a rise in his social status when we recall that he came from a family of middle-level Company employees and started his life as a copying clerk. Teignmouth became a member of the Board of Control in 1807, thereby retaining a direct connection with the entity he had governed for almost five years. Except for being part of the larger group of colonial policymakers in London, he does not seem to have had much to do with politics in England, and devoted more of his time to the British and Foreign Bible Society. The society was formed in 1804, initially to print and distribute the Bible in the Welsh language, in Wales. Shore presided over the society for thirty years, from its founding until his death. He passed away in 1834 at the age of eighty-two.

V

TIPU AND AFTER

The prominence of Shore's successor, Lord Wellesley (Richard Colley Wellesley) is, to some extent, due to the fame of his younger brother Arthur, known as the Duke of Wellington from 1814 onwards, who commanded the victorious British army against Napoleon's forces at Waterloo (June 1815). Arthur became a cult figure, and his prominence as an icon of the empire steadily increased during the nineteenth century with the expansion of the British Empire. Richard partook of his glory. Post Waterloo, Arthur came to be regarded as Britain's greatest military commander, a reputation he enjoyed until the First World War produced its own heroes—without seriously diminishing his stature.

Arthur acquired his initial experience in warfare in India, where his brother unleashed major wars on the subcontinent, the two most important being the Fourth Anglo–Mysore War and the Second Anglo–Maratha War. Arthur played a crucial role in the latter and participated in a minor capacity in the former.

The two brothers were from a landed but not affluent (Anglican) Protestant Anglo–Irish family. Anglo–Irish families had been settled in Ireland for several generations and were a privileged minority dominating the Irish people, who mostly belonged to the Catholic Church and were excluded from political power. The family controlled one seat in the Irish Parliament.

Richard's father, Garrett Wesley, an Irish peer, passed away in 1781 when Richard was twenty-one years old. As Garrett's eldest son, he had to take on the responsibility of looking after his five siblings—a sister and four younger brothers. He succeeded to his father's aristocratic titles as Earl of Mornington and Viscount Wellesley, and later took the surname Wellesley, as did Arthur.

Richard was studying at Oxford when his father died and had to leave without taking a degree. In 1780, he was elected to the Irish House of Commons as a member for the family-controlled constituency of Trim, which he represented till 1781 when, upon succeeding to his father's titles, he became a member of the Irish House of Lords. Subsequently, he was a member of the English House of Commons, between 1784 and 1797, during which period he remained a minor political figure, often complaining that his career was not advancing as rapidly as he would have wished.

Richard served his apprenticeship in the colonial enterprise as a member of the Board of Control between 1793 and 1797. He was one of the junior commissioners on the board. This was 'not a particularly good training for governing India because Dundas refused to allow his colleagues to do anything'.[1] Wellesley was frequently absent from board meetings, which is understandable. There is nothing to suggest that he stood out as being more experienced than his colleagues, and the prime minister's decision, firstly to send him as governor of the Madras presidency and then as governor-general of India had more to do with the controversy over the denial of the governor-generalship to Hobart, factional disputes among the Company's directors, and the confusion caused by the appointment of Cornwallis, followed by the cancellation of that appointment.

Richard had been constantly lobbying for a political promotion, and when Hobart was recalled from Madras, he was nominated to succeed him as governor of the presidency. Cornwallis's resignation on the eve of his departure created

---

[1]Edward Ingram (ed.), 'Introduction', *Two Views of British India: The Private Correspondence of Mr Dundas and Lord Wellesley: 1798-1801*, Bath: Adams & Dart, 1970, p. 1.

the possibility of proceeding to Calcutta instead of Madras. Wellesley would have been quite satisfied with the lesser job, as governor of Madras. Another ambition of his was fulfilled when he was made a British peer—Baron Wellesley—in October 1797 before he embarked for India (Cornwallis, it may be recalled, had resigned in August). Arthur had been in India since 1796 as a lieutenant-colonel in the royal army. Another brother, Henry, accompanied Richard as his private secretary. Though an appointee of the government, Wellesley, like Cornwallis before him, was formally an employee of the Company.

At this stage, the new governor-general's information about India was mainly derived from the EIC's papers, which he would have come across as a member of the Board of Control, and Orme's *History of the Military Transactions of the British Nation in Indostan*.

Whereas Orme's *History* is exceptionally detailed, as a source of information on India it has its limitations. It only covers the period from the mid-1740s to the early 1760s, and focuses on the EIC's political and military entanglements in Bengal and the Coromandel. We learn that he had begun reading Orme's volumes when he intervened in the debate on Warren Hastings in the House of Commons.

Wellesley had also requested one of his patrons for a copy of Dow's English translation of the *Tarikh* of Firishta (*The History of Hindostan*), and François Bernier's *Travels in the Mogul Empire*. We do not know whether he managed to obtain them or read them. In other words, he possessed only a cursory knowledge of the subcontinent when he set out for Calcutta. Besides, we need to bear in mind that, for someone interested in India's past, there was very little material in English at this time.

Wellesley reached Calcutta in May 1798. Shore had left for home in March, and Hobart had departed from Madras about a month before that. The governor-general was quite annoyed that Arthur, who was then in Calcutta, had not been present to welcome him when he disembarked, and turned up much later to meet his brother. 'This episode really disgusted me,' Richard wrote to Hyacinthe Roland, his first wife, 'and has caused a coldness between us which I am afraid will last all our lives'.[2] He seems to have overreacted to his brother's lapse.

Wellesley had a long love affair with Hyacinthe before they married in 1794. The two had a live-in relationship for several years, during which they had five children. All the children were born before the marriage. As none of them were considered legitimate, they were barred from inheriting Wellesley's aristocratic titles. When Wellesley eventually travelled to India, Hyacinthe did not accompany him. He was unable to persuade her to join him. Wellesley is known to have had quite a few relationships after his marriage with other European women, some of whom bore him children. His inconsistency was one of the reasons for the growing distance between him and Hyacinthe after their marriage. The couple formally separated in 1810, and he married a second time in 1825. One of his sons from Hyacinthe, Gerald Wellesley, was employed in the EIC's establishment in India, where he was posted in Indore as a resident at the court of the Holkar ruler. While at Indore, he simultaneously presided over the EIC's opium enterprise in central India as the opium agent, a key position in the opium department.

In her biography of Richard, *The Eldest Brother* (1973), Iris Butler makes use of the ample correspondence between Hyacinthe and him, spread over more than two decades, to provide a more exhaustive account of the years that Wellesley spent in India. These letters are part of the private papers of the family, which were in the possession of Field-Marshal Michael Carver, the great-great-great-grandson of the governor-general, and were not available for purposes of historical research until Carver allowed access to them for the biography by Butler. The letters, now at the University of Southampton (Carver

---

[2]Iris Butler, *The Eldest Brother: The Marquess Wellesley, The Duke of Wellington's Eldest Brother*, London: Hodder and Stoughton, 1973, p. 142.

Manuscripts), shed much light on aspects of Wellesley's life and career that had hitherto either been concealed or were unknown to his biographers before the publication of *The Eldest Brother.* Several biographies of Wellesley were published in the nineteenth century, followed by a long gap toward the end of the century, when historical interest in him declined, only to revive later with new source material on his life.

One of the first tasks that Wellesley took up after assuming office was the construction in Calcutta of an official residence for the governor-general. Government House (now Raj Bhavan), as this building was called, was, till the imperial capital shifted to Delhi at the beginning of the twentieth century, the official residence of the governor-general of the British Indian empire.

The construction of Government House commenced in February 1799. There was no elaborate ceremony for laying the foundation stone since Wellesley had to rush to Madras on Christmas Day 1798 to settle scores with Tipu (usually spelt Tippoo by Wellesley and other colonial officials). When it was completed in 1803, Government House dominated the Calcutta skyline.

A splendid fête was organized by Wellesley in March 1803, marking the inauguration of the stately residence. This had been preceded by a magnificent breakfast party at the site, with over seven hundred guests, held in April 1802 to celebrate the victory at Seringapatam and the death of Tipu. The 1802 breakfast was perhaps the first official entertainment organized at Government House, which was then still under construction.

Government House itself stood where the original Fort William (no longer extant) was located during the days of the military conflict with Siraj-ud-Daula. This was the city's most impressive building; the imposing structure was visible in all its magnificence from every direction.

Various buildings in Calcutta had housed the governors-general prior to Wellesley's decision to construct a grand new residence. Lord Curzon, in his *Story of the Viceroys and Government Houses* identified at least six buildings in

Calcutta that had served as official abodes of the governors-general down to 1799, when the construction of Wellesley's Government House commenced.[3] Many of these structures were not particularly ostentatious.

Wellesley had initiated the project without seeking the approval of the Court of Directors and was strongly criticized by the court for this as well as the enormous expense incurred in constructing the palatial structure. Whereas he later claimed that he had communicated the estimates for the project to London, no such document has been traced.

The building was designed by Charles Wyatt of the famous 'Wyatt dynasty' of British architects. The design was inspired by a well-known English country house— Kedleston Hall in Derbyshire. In the late eighteenth century, Kedleston Hall was considered a neoclassical masterpiece. It may be mentioned that Kedleston Hall was the seat of the Curzon family, and Lord Curzon when he resided in Government House as governor-general exactly a century later, wrote an account, referred to earlier, in which he described in considerable detail the similarities and differences between the two buildings.

The design for Kedleston, generally attributed to Robert Adam, also bore the architectural imprint of James Paine. Both were leading architects of the period. Paine had been associated with the preparation of a design for Kedleston Hall during the initial stages; he was subsequently replaced by Adam (Paine himself had replaced the original architect, Mathew Brettingham). Adam ultimately completed the project. In the process, many of the elements of Paine's design were either modified or discarded. Nevertheless, after work on the building was completed in 1765 or thereabouts, Paine published the original design for Kedleston Hall in his *Plans, Elevations and Sections of Noblemen and Gentlemen's Houses* (1783).

Wyatt seems to have relied on the published Paine design

---

[3]Marquis Curzon of Kedleston, *British Government in India: The Story of the Viceroys and Government Houses*, Vol. 1, London: Cassell and Co., 1925.

while working out his own scheme for the Government House. For instance, Paine's unutilized design for a domed circular arrangement for the south front of Kedleston Hall might have been of use to Wyatt for conceptualizing the Calcutta building. Wyatt and his contemporaries, such as John Goldingham in Madras and Samuel Russell in Hyderabad, were seeking to define an architectural style that would be relevant to the Company's Indian empire against the backdrop of Wellesley's military successes, resulting in territorial expansion on a massive scale. The final war against Mysore was followed by campaigns against the Marathas, mainly with the objective of destroying the power of the Sindia and Holkar chiefs (Second Anglo–Maratha War, 1802–05). An appropriate architectural style was required to announce the political ascendancy of the Company.

In its basic design, the Government House comprises a central rectangular block with four detached wings, one at each corner. The wings are connected to the main block by curved corridors in the shape of quadrants. This design approximates Paine's design for Kedleston Hall, as published in 1783. The southern wings and corresponding corridors were not constructed at Kedleston. The floor plan of Government House, including the wings, resembles a square; the floor plan of Kedleston is rectangular. One major difference between the two is that the material used for the latter is Derbyshire sandstone. Locally available burnt-clay bricks were used for Government House; these were plastered with a sand-lime blend and then whitewashed. The overall effect of Government House is, therefore, quite different from that of Kedleston Hall.

In her study of the urban landscape of colonial Calcutta and the ways in which architectural spaces were reconfigured, Swati Chattopadhyay has pointed out that the interior of Government House was strongly influenced by contemporary colonial structures in Calcutta.[4] These had absorbed local traditions,

---

[4]Swati Chattopadhyay, *Representing Calcutta: Modernity, Nationalism, and The Colonial Uncanny*, London: Routledge, 2005, pp. 109–35.

so that space was configured in a manner appropriate to the social requirements of the colonial elite. In this, there was a divergence from the design of Kedleston and other aristocratic residences in the metropole.

The presence of extensive retinues of servants, attendants, 'native' underlings, housekeepers, etc. made it difficult to have spatial arrangements based on European notions of privacy. Servants were constantly present in very large numbers. Lord Minto, the first occupant after Wellesley, was quite unprepared to cope with the 'incessant entourage' which surrounded him in Government House, 'The first night I went to bed at Calcutta I was followed by fourteen persons in white muslin gowns into the dressing-room'.

It made sense, therefore, to make rooms and halls accessible from several points. The passages were designed to facilitate the movement of servants from one point to another. There are hardly any discrete closed-off spaces in Government House— something that the spouses of several governors-general found disconcerting. Surveying the layout of his residence, Minto noted that, 'The doors are open, the partitions are open or transparent also, and it is the business of a certain number to keep an eye upon me, and see if I want the particular service which each is allowed by his caste to render me'.[5] Incidentally, no space was allocated within the complex for accommodating servants; they lived outside it.

The boundaries of the nearly twenty acres of open space that surrounded the built structure were marked by iron fencing, with four monumental gateways. The gateways are large, arched structures—Roman triumphal arches in their conception—each with a decorative lion at the top. The lions face the main building from their respective locations, each holding a globe or sphere in one of its front paws.

The lion has traditionally been a symbol of power. Kedleston

---

[5]Countess of Minto, *Lord Minto in India: Life and Letters of Gilbert Eliot, First Earl of Minto, 1807 to 1814*, London: Longmans, Green, & Co., London, 1880, p. 30. Countess of Minto was the grandniece of Lord Minto.

as the inspiration is evident here as well. In the park of Kedleston Hall, there is the life-sized figure of a lion mounted on a pedestal, its front right paw resting on a globe. The Kedleston lion had as its model the lions that adorned the entrance of the Villa Medici in Rome, built in the sixteenth century.

∽

The topmost priority for the EIC when Wellesley took over was the destruction of the Mysore kingdom. Not only had the kingdom been the most steadfast among the leading political entities of southern India in its opposition to the Company, Tipu's friendship with revolutionary France also made his hostility particularly dangerous at a time when Britain was engaged in a deadly conflict with the French. Wellesley had already begun thinking in terms of launching a fresh offensive against Mysore by the time he reached India. It was immaterial that there had been no provocation on the part of Tipu, unless his admiration for the revolutionary regime in France could be regarded in such a light. Wellesley had been busy inventing a justification for invading Mysore since 1798. As Edward Ingram, editor of the published private correspondence between Dundas and Wellesley, has shown, there is absolutely no evidence that Tipu was planning to launch an attack against the British at the beginning of the 1790s. The Madras government assessed that having lost half his territories, Tipu was unlikely to risk another war with the British. On the other hand, the governor-general was unwilling to accept such an assessment, and 'Throughout 1798 and [early] 1799, Wellesley [wrote] as if Tipu Sultan was about to attack the British: in fact the British were about to attack him'.[6]

Wellesley, during his lifetime, ensured that many of the passages in his official correspondence which might reveal that he was responsible for unleashing the war that led to the final extinction of Tipu's kingdom, were removed from the

---

[6]Ingram, *Two Views of British India*, p. 5.

published version of these documents. Montgomery Martin, who has chronicled the history of the British Empire in a vast corpus of voluminous writings on the subject, undertook the publication of his private papers in collaboration with—and most probably at the suggestion of—Wellesley himself. The compilation, eventually published in five volumes (*The Despatches, Minutes and Correspondence of The Marquess Wellesley, K.G.* [Knight Companion of the Order of the Garter], *during the Administration in India*, 1836-7), was prepared 'under Wellesley's own supervision'. The letters in these volumes 'contain repeated minor alterations and frequent major omissions'.[7]

In contrast to the sanitized image of the governor-general presented in the Martin volumes, the letters in the Ingram collection 'reveal that Wellesley was a bad-tempered and overbearing man. Even allowing for the exaggeration of eighteenth-century writing, they also reveal that he was ungenerous'.[8] The Martin–Wellesley documentation was intended to demonstrate that Tipu was guilty of being friendly with the French. In colonial historiography, this has been seen as a grave provocation, sufficient to justify a renewed assault on Mysore. What needs to be underlined is that Mysore was an independent kingdom; its ruler had the prerogative of choosing his allies without any reference to the EIC.

The 1799 invasion of the Mysore kingdom ordered by Wellesley, known as the Fourth Anglo–Mysore War, ended in the conquest of the kingdom. This had been a long-cherished goal of the EIC.

The 'allied armies' as Wellesley preferred to call the invading force—consisting of Company contingents, Hyderabad troops commanded by British officers, and regiments of the king's army—launched an offensive without any provocation. The royal regiments included the 33rd Foot Regiment (later renamed

---

[7]Ibid., p. 1.
[8]Ibid., p. 11.

Duke of Wellington's Regiment), led by the governor-general's brother, who had commanded the regiment since its arrival in India in 1796. The 33rd was to join contingents from the Hyderabad state and this combined force was placed under Arthur.

The main body of troops, the 'grand army', led by Major-General George Harris, who had participated in the campaigns of the Third Anglo–Mysore War, commenced its march from Vellore in February. Orders had been sent to the Madras government in October 1798 to prepare for the invasion several months before the actual operation.

The British tried to deceive Tipu by pretending to be serious about diplomatic exchanges initiated by Wellesley in the intervening months. As late as the first half of April 1799, when Harris was about to storm the citadel of Seringapatam, a momentary lull in the fighting prompted Tipu to send a message to him enquiring: 'I have adhered firmly to treaties; what then is the meaning of the advance of the English armies, and the occurrence of hostilities? Inform me.'[9]

Yet another force, consisting of soldiers of the Bombay Army, was marching eastwards towards Seringapatam via Cannanore, while the Hyderabad contingents approached Mysore territories from the north. All these columns began to converge near Tipu's capital in the latter half of March.

Harris had been given instructions to negotiate with Tipu upon reaching the outskirts of Seringapatam and carried with him the draft of a treaty embodying terms for the cessation of hostilities. He modified the draft treaty on his own, making the terms even harsher than those stated by Wellesley. Tipu would have to relinquish half of what remained of his territories, would have to pay an indemnity of two crore rupees, and would have to hand over four of his sons and four of his generals as hostages.

---

[9]Denys M. Forrest, *Tiger of Mysore: Life and Death of Tipu Sultan*, Mumbai: Allied Publishers, 1970, p. 285.

The original draft demanded three of the eldest sons as hostages. Harris independently increased the number, adding that the actual hostages from among Tipu's sons and generals would be named by him. These conditions were unacceptable to Tipu, and he refused to sign the treaty.

There had been a pause in the fighting while negotiations relating to the treaty were in progress. The operations now resumed with bombardment of Seringapatam Fort. It is well established that the British managed to enter the fort with the help of a small section of Mysore officials who had gone over to the enemy. Nevertheless, when they entered the fort on 4 May, the resistance encountered by them was ferocious. Tipu himself had been constantly on the move within the fort, directing its defence and personally engaging in combat as an ordinary soldier. He was killed while fighting, and his body was discovered with much difficulty in a pile of corpses 'in the gateway on the north face of the fort':[10]

> The number of the dead, and the darkness of the place, made it difficult to distinguish one person from another, and the scene was altogether shocking; but, aware of the great political importance of ascertaining, beyond the possibility of doubt, the death of Tippoo, the bodies were ordered to be dragged out, and the killedar [qiladar, keeper of the fort], and the other two persons, were desired to examine them one after another. This, however, appeared endless; and, as it now was becoming dark, a light was procured, and I accompanied the killedar into the gateway. During the search, we discovered a wounded person lying under the Sultaun's palankeen [palanquin]: this man was afterwards ascertained to be Rajah Cawn, one of Tippoo's most confidential servants; he had attended his master during the whole of the day,

---

[10]'Major (Alexander) Allan's Account of … finding the Body of Tippoo Sultaun', Alexander Beatson, 'Appendix XLII', *A View of the Origin and Conduct of the War with Tippoo Sultaun*, London: G & W Nicol, 1800, pp. cxxx-cxxxi.

and, on being made acquainted with the object of our search, he pointed out the spot where the Sultaun had fallen. By a faint glimmering light, it was difficult for the killedar to recognize the features; but the body being brought out, and satisfactorily proved to be that of the Sultaun, was conveyed in a palankeen to the palace, where it was again recognized by the eunuchs and other servants of the family.

When Tippoo was brought from under the gateway, his eyes were open, and the body was so warm, that for a few moments Colonel [Arthur] Wellesley and myself were doubtful whether he was not alive: on feeling his pulse and heart, that doubt was removed. He had four wounds, three in the body, and one in the temple; the ball having entered a little above the right ear, and lodged in the cheek.

British officials, keen to ascertain the circumstances in which Tipu had died, questioned several eyewitnesses—mainly his attendants and soldiers—who confirmed that their master had been fighting courageously right till the tragic end. As soon as he realized that the British had managed to break into the fort, he rallied his soldiers to check the advancing column.[11]

> While any of his troops remained with him, the sultaun continued to dispute the ground, until he approached the passage across the ditch to the gate of the inner fort. Here he complained of pain and weakness in one of his legs, in which he had received a bad wound when very young; and, ordering his horse to be brought, he mounted: but seeing the Europeans still advancing on both the ramparts, he made for the gate, followed by his palankeen, and a number of officers, troops, and servants.

---

[11]Anon. (Theodore Hook), *The Life of …Sir David Baird*, Vol. 1, London: Richard Bentley, 1832, pp. 216–17.

Tipu was severely wounded in attempting to close the gate, receiving gunshot injuries in at least two places, which caused him to fall.

> The fallen sultaun was immediately raised by some of his adherents, and placed in his palankeen, under the arch, on one side of the gateway, where he lay, or sat, for some minutes, faint and exhausted, till some Europeans entered the gateway. A serjeant, who has survived, relates, that one of the soldiers seized the sultaun's sword-belt, which was very rich, and attempted to pull it off: that the sultaun, who still held his sword in his hand, made a cut at the soldier with all his remaining strength, and wounded him about the knee; on which he put his piece [gun] to his shoulder and shot the sultaun through the temple when he instantly expired.

The soldier who shot dead Tipu has been identified as Christenau, a private (ordinary soldier of the lowest rank), in the de Meuron regiment.

This was a Swiss regiment 'owned' by Charles Daniel de Meuron, which had been part of the English king's army since 1795, when de Meuron switched his allegiance from the VOC to the English following the British occupation of Ceylon, where the regiment had been stationed by the Dutch company. The de Meuron regiment fought at Seringapatam under Lieutenant Colonel Henri David de Meuron-Motiers. It was one of the eight European regiments of the 'grand army' which had set out from Vellore.

While the majority of the soldiers in the regiment were Swiss, it also had recruits from German states and other parts of Europe. Christenau is described as a 'Brunswicker', indicating that he might have hailed from Brunswick (Braunschweig) in Lower Saxony.[12]

---

[12]David C. J. Howell, 'An Account of His Majesty's De Meuron Regiment 1795-1816, During Campaigns in Ceylon, India, the Mediterranean and Canada', *The Napoleon Series* [online facsimile].

With the defeat and death of Tipu Sultan, Seringapatam was placed under Arthur Wellesley. Soon after the fort had been occupied, Seringapatam was formally declared a prize, which meant that the entire city could be 'legitimately' plundered by the victorious armed forces. All soldiers and officers received a share of the booty according to a fixed proportion determined by their place in the hierarchy. The commander-in-chief, Harris, was entitled to one-eighth of the prize. The troops were permitted to vandalize the city and forcibly rob its inhabitants of their belongings, officially till noon of the following day.

Brutal violence on a massive scale was perpetrated by the plundering troops throughout the night and the first half of 5 May. The treasure seized by the men, both within and outside the fort, created mini-fortunes for the soldiers, some of whom amassed wealth that was to become part of folklore in Britain about the pillage of Tipu's fabulously rich kingdom.

Arthur reported to the governor-general that:

> It was impossible to expect that after the labour which the troops had undergone in working up to the place, and the various successes they had had in six different affairs with Tippoo's troops, in all of which they had come to the bayonet with them, they should not have looked to the plunder of this place. Nothing, therefore, can have exceeded what was done on the night of the 4th. Scarcely a house in the town was left unplundered, and I understand that in camp jewels of the greatest value, bars of gold, have been offered for sale in the bazaars of the army by our soldiers, sepoys, and followers. ... [The people] are returning to their houses and beginning again to follow their occupations, but the property of every one is gone.[13]

The appointment by Lord Mornington (Wellesley) of his brother to administer the capital of Mysore caused much resentment

---

[13]Duke of Wellington, *Supplementary Despatches and Memoranda of Field Marshal Arthur Duke of Wellington ... : India, 1797-1805*, Vol. 1, London: John Murray, 1858, p. 212.

among some of the senior officers, who saw the appointment as another instance of the governor-general's nepotism (the first being the nomination of Arthur as commander of the Hyderabad contingent), especially as Arthur was not directly involved in the storming of the fort. Major-General David Baird, who was the senior officer and had led the successful charge, was indignant that he had been overlooked: 'Before the sweat was dry on my brow, I was superseded by an inferior officer.'[14]

Baird was a veteran of the campaigns against Mysore. He had been captured, along with other British soldiers, during the Second Anglo–Mysore War and held captive for several years before he was released. He also took part in Cornwallis's invasion of Mysore.

After handing over Seringapatam Fort to Arthur, Baird wrote an unusually strong letter to Harris on 6 May expressing his indignation. The letter concluded with the request that it may be forwarded to the commander-in-chief of the royal army, the Duke of York: 'I request that copies of this letter may be transmitted to his Royal Highness the Duke of York, Commander-in-chief, for the information of his Majesty, that, at the same time he is informed of my having been twice superseded by Colonel Wellesley …'.[15]

Baird was promptly pulled up for having written a 'very improper letter' and for having shown a 'total want of respect and discretion', holding 'sentiments so opposite to the principles of military subordination'.[16]

In his reply, Baird reiterated his grievance, adding that he had certainly not been disrespectful while making his representation. If, however, Harris felt that he was guilty of a transgression, he was willing to submit himself to a general court-martial, 'from which I can have nothing to fear'.[17] In

---

[14]Ibid., p. 226.
[15]Ibid., p. 237.
[16]Ibid., pp. 238–39.
[17]Ibid., p. 240.

writings of the post-Waterloo period, when Arthur Wellesley came to be regarded as a demi-god, the bitterness caused by the supersession of Baird was downplayed or simply ignored in accounts of the war against Tipu.

When Arthur learnt of this correspondence, he tried to assuage Baird's feelings by sending to him a valuable ceremonial sword of Tipu, seized from the interior of the palace. A fresh complication arose when the prize committee of the army—the committee constituted to assess the value of plundered objects and distribute them in accordance with the rank of respective soldiers—intervened to point out that the sword could not be gifted by the new commandant as it did not belong to him. It had to be returned to the committee since it was part of the collective booty.

Finally, a compromise was worked out. The sword was returned to the committee, which handed it over to the commander-in-chief, who then presented it to Baird 'in the name of the army, as a testimonial of their high admiration of his courage and conduct in the assault'.[18] The sword remained in the possession of the Baird family until recently. It was auctioned in 2003 when an Indian business tycoon bought it, and it was put up for auction again in 2023 when it fetched over £14 million—a record for such objects.

There is a footnote to this incident which suggests that the field officers serving under Baird were convinced that the politics of commemoration had resulted in denying the recognition that was due to their commander. Exactly a month after the capture of the fort, they informed Baird that they had placed an order with the English firm of 'Messrs. Jeffreys and Jones to make a dress sword, valued at two hundred guineas, bearing the following inscription:—"SERINGAPATAM, taken by storm the 4th May, 1799," on one side, and on the other, "Presented by the Field Officers who personally served under

---

[18]Ibid., p. 243.

Major-General Baird on that occasion"'.[19] They hoped that Baird would accept their token of appreciation, for which they had jointly contributed—which he did. The sword is now in the National Museum of Scotland, Edinburgh.

Following the conquest of Tipu's Mysore, the Company reconstituted the kingdom, reducing it to the status of a 'native' state. It was divested of a large portion of its territory and placed under a descendant of the Wodeyar dynasty, which had been supplanted by Haidar Ali. As a 'native' or princely state, it retained some internal autonomy, while being subject to the overall authority of the EIC. For half a century in the nineteenth century, the state was directly administered by the British until the so-called 'rendition' of Mysore in 1881, when the administration was handed back to the Wodeyar rulers. The Wodeyars had merely had a ceremonial presence for the preceding fifty years, between 1831 and 1881, when the state was administered by British officials.

The military operations against Tipu in the Fourth Anglo–Mysore War had been preceded by the signing of a treaty with Hyderabad, which formally reduced the state to the status of a subordinate ally of the Company. This treaty, concluded in 1798, imposed a subsidy, payable to the EIC, of nearly 25 lakh rupees per annum on Hyderabad, for troops 'with guns, artillerymen, and other necessary appurtenances' to be placed by the EIC in its territories. Besides, the nizam had to disband his army of 14,000 well-trained men, at that time commanded by an officer of French origin named Jean-Pierre Piron, who was a Jacobin sympathizer. Ironically, this efficient fighting force was used against Tipu, an ally of the French republicans, in the Fourth Anglo–Mysore War.

Under the provisions of the 'subsidiary' treaty, all military personnel of French origin serving in the state were to be dismissed. Wellesley's first Hyderabad treaty, the treaty of 1798, is supposed to have inaugurated what is usually referred to as

---

[19]Ibid., p. 244.

the 'subsidiary alliance' system. However, it was only one of a series of actions which, since the Carnatic Wars, had rendered Hyderabad subservient—first, to the French, and then to the English East India companies.

The genesis of the system may be traced back to French involvement in the politics of Hyderabad in the 1750s. The Compagnie's ascendancy at Hyderabad, lasting for nearly eight years, made it possible for the French to penetrate and undermine the independence of the state. This was done by using the resources of Hyderabad itself, thus minimizing the cost of colonial expansion. The French arrangements in Hyderabad were to provide the inspiration for the English company's system of 'subsidiary' alliances.

The model was further developed in Awadh when Hastings prevailed upon Shuja-ud-Daula to pay a subsidy for a contingent of EIC troops stationed in his territories. The Company could use these troops to control Awadh, and maintain them out of the revenues of the state. This would become the key element of the 'subsidiary alliance' system, which was extended to several states under Wellesley.

The system of 'subsidiary alliances' wherein the EIC coerced Indian states to accept its 'protection', was essentially a strategy of colonial expansion whereby the respective states were subjugated without actual annexation, although in some cases annexation might be the eventual outcome. James Mill candidly admitted in the testimony he presented to the select committee of the House of Commons in 1832, when the British Parliament was considering the renewal of the EIC's charter, that, 'It appears to me that the subsidiary alliance does not take away the spirit of sovereignty by degrees from those princes; this is taken from them along with the sovereignty at the first step. It does not remain to be done by degrees. We begin by taking the military power, and when we have taken that, we have taken all'.[20]

---

[20]*Select Committee on the Affairs of the East India Company, Minutes of Evidence,*

Hyderabad and Awadh were the two major states that were initially subordinated by the Company through a series of subsidiary treaties. Shortly after the end of the Third Carnatic War, the Company signed a treaty with Hyderabad in 1766 whereby it undertook to render military aid to the state whenever requested. An annual sum of nine lakh rupees had to be regularly given to the Company for this purpose. Subsequently, the Northern Circars (sarkars or districts) were ceded by Hyderabad in lieu of the payment. These districts were situated in the coastal regions of (present-day) Andhra Pradesh and Odisha, lying between the Krishna River in the south and the Mahanadi River in the north. Vishakhapatnam was part of the Northern Circars.

Another treaty was signed in 1768 by which Hyderabad could requisition two battalions of the EIC's army when needed, against the subsidy it was providing. On the eve of the campaigns against Tipu in the Third Anglo–Mysore War, the terms of the 1768 treaty were reiterated, while it was clearly understood that the two battalions would be available specifically for the EIC's war against Mysore—an ingenious formula that reduced the military expenses of the British.

As yet, the subsidiary force (i.e., the contingents for which a subsidy was extracted by the Company) was not permanently stationed in Hyderabad, and, indeed was dismissed by the nizam in 1795. The force was recalled by the Hyderabad court to assist in tackling a rebellion in the state led by the incumbent ruler's eldest son. The nizam's own army, which had been reorganized in the preceding years, was instrumental in suppressing the rebellion. In the campaign against the rebels, Hyderabad troops were led by the nizam's French commander, François de Raymond (also known as Michel Raymond).[21]

---

16 February 1832, House of Commons, 735-vi, 1832, evidence of James Mill, p. 7.
[21]Herbert Compton, who has provided brief biographies of several 'military adventurers' of the period in his authoritative work on the subject, mentions both names, but considers François de Raymond as the correct one. Herbert Compton, *A Particular Account of the European Military Adventurers of Hindustan,*

Raymond was later given charge of the Hyderabad gun-foundry, established in the state capital for producing cannons and ammunition for the nizam's army. Raymond died a few months before the 1798 treaty with Hyderabad was signed and was succeeded by a European officer from Alsace, Colonel Jean-Pierre Piron (not to be confused with General Perron, who served in the armies of Maratha chiefs). Piron (d. 1805) is described as 'an outrageous Jacobin, and in close touch with the French Republican faction in Mysore'. The sipahis of his corps had the motto 'Liberté et Constitution' embroidered on their uniforms. A prominent EIC official, John Malcolm, who knew Piron fairly well, disliked him for being a 'violent democrat'.[22]

The 'total annihilation of the French faction at Hyderabad' in 1798 became an occasion for great jubilation, as 'the very existence of so formidable a French faction in the heart of the Deccan would have rendered a contest with Tippoo Sultaun, which appeared inevitable, extremely precarious, and even hazardous'.[23]

It was under Wellesley that subsidiary alliances became a regular feature of the Company's expansionist policy, with subsidiary forces permanently stationed in states that were incorporated into the system. Under the provisions of the 1798 subsidiary treaty with Hyderabad, which was followed up by another treaty in 1800 formalizing the division of territory acquired from Tipu at the end of the Fourth Anglo–Mysore War, ten thousand troops of the Company's army were stationed in the Hyderabad territories 'in perpetuity'. The troops were recruited mostly from the Madras presidency. The subsidiary force consisted of eight battalions of native infantry, each comprising 1,000 sipahis; two regiments of native cavalry of 500 sawars each; and the 'requisite complement of guns,

1784-1803, London: T. Fisher Unwin, 1892, p. 382.
[22]Ibid., pp. 379–80.
[23]Beatson, *A View of the Origin and Conduct of the War with Tippoo Sultaun*, pp. 50–51.

European artillerymen, lascars and pioneers [the latter for light engineering and construction tasks], fully equipped with warlike stores and ammunition'.

Some of the other subsidiary alliances in southern India were linked to the campaigns against Tipu in the 1790s and served after 1799 to subjugate the respective political entities in the region. In 1791, a treaty had been signed with Cochin, placing it under British 'protection'. An annual tribute amounting to nearly half the total revenue of the state was levied by the Company for providing security to the state. In 1795 a subsidiary treaty was concluded with Travancore which, along with a supplementary agreement of 1805, gave to the Company the right of unlimited interference in its affairs in return for military 'protection'.

After the Battle of Seringapatam, a subsidiary treaty was signed with the Wodeyar ruler of a truncated Mysore in 1799. Bangalore was developed into a vast cantonment to station the Company's troops in the state. The tribute levied on the Mysore state steadily drained away its resources, leading to widespread agrarian discontent, which became the justification for taking over the administration of the state. As we have noted, the state remained under the direct control of the British for the next fifty years. Bangalore became the largest British cantonment in south India in the nineteenth century. While the city of Bangalore itself was under the Mysore ruler, the cantonment was under the British. Mysore, where the ruler usually resided, was marginalized as an urban centre.

In the case of Awadh, the long process of subjugating it through the device of subsidiary treaties was set in motion soon after the Battle of Buxar. Under one of the provisions of the Treaty of 1765, a brigade of the Company's army was placed at the disposal of Shuja-ud-Daula. Another treaty, the Treaty of Banaras signed in 1773, specified more concretely the terms on which the subsidiary force was to be made available to Awadh— at the rate of ₹210,000 per month for a brigade comprising two battalions of Europeans, six battalions of sipahis (with European officers), and one company of artillery. On the accession of Asaf-ud-Daula in 1775, yet another treaty was signed whereby the subsidy was enhanced to ₹260,000 per month for a brigade.

Awadh could never recover from the huge burden of payments for subsidiary forces, which paved the way for the annexation of its territories. In the first phase, more than half the territories of the state were 'ceded' to the EIC in 1801, which thereby became a leading north Indian power. This was another major territorial acquisition of the Wellesley era. The vast area acquired by the Company included the low-lying tracts of present-day Uttarakhand, Bareilly and surrounding areas, much of eastern Uttar Pradesh (present boundaries), including Gorakhpur, as well as lands situated on the right bank of the Ganga. Awadh was confined to a relatively small region extending eastwards from the Ganga to the foothills of Nepal. The territories taken from Awadh were later reorganized to form an administrative unit named North-Western Provinces. What remained of Awadh would be annexed in 1856, thereby obliterating the state.

∽

Wellesley was raised to the rank of a marquis in December 1799 for having conquered Mysore. He was upset that his elevation was in the Irish peerage, rather than the British. In the British peerage, he continued to be a baron. At the highest levels of political authority in Britain, the importance attached to Wellesley's achievement in India was not sufficient to elevate him to a marquisate in the British peerage. He had to be content with the lesser honour.

In the protocol relating to peerages, the superior title took precedence over the inferior and therefore Wellesley would be known as Marquess Wellesley. On the other hand, Arthur progressed steadily in the English peerage, from viscount (1809) to earl (1812) to marquis (1812) to duke (1814) for his military exploits in the years preceding Waterloo. Waterloo gave him a pre-eminent place in the imperial pantheon of the nineteenth century. Foreign governments too rushed to bestow honours on him. The Dutch made him prince of Waterloo, with 2,600 acres of land attached to the title. The land was located in Belgium, which emerged as an independent state in the early 1830s. The duke received a regular income from the land, which his descendants continue to enjoy.

A popular campaign in Belgium, currently ongoing, has been seeking to terminate this arrangement, which, it is argued, was thrust upon the country by Britain after it triumphed over the French.

By the time Richard Wellesley died in 1852, even the triumph at Seringapatam was being attributed to Arthur, a story that is repeated in several biographical accounts. It is pertinent that Baird never progressed beyond a baronetcy, or hereditary knighthood. Thus, he never became a peer. Baird was made a baronet in 1809. Wellesley might have been partly responsible for his marginalization. Baird had received a congratulatory letter from the governor-general following the Seringapatam battle, stating that he had been recommended for either a pension from the Company (of which he was not an employee; he was an officer in the king's army) or a state honour. The state honour being referred to was induction into the knightly Order of the Bath.

The Order of the Bath was an order of chivalry with roots in the knightly orders of medieval England. This particular order had been revived in the early eighteenth century. It was one of the four senior knightly orders in the United Kingdom. The topmost, or seniormost of these orders in the United Kingdom was (and is) the Order of the Garter. In the latter half of the eighteenth century, admission into the Order of the Bath was the most sought-after token of public recognition for military achievements and is still supposed to be the highest military order attainable. Membership of the Order of the Bath, before its membership was greatly enlarged after the Napoleonic Wars, was confined to a small number of members—initially thirty-five. Induction into the order was therefore a very special honour. Admission involved elaborate ceremonial conducted in public, most of the ritual having been invented at the time of the revival of the order. When an investiture ceremony was organized in 1788, more than 2,500 tickets were issued to spectators. The demand was so great that these were bought at prices far above the actual rates for the tickets.

From the point of view of public recognition of his services, being admitted to the order might have been preferable to a pension for Baird. However, he got neither. His biographer, Theodore Hook, remarks that it is difficult to ascertain whether Wellesley 'actually ever did make the application in his favour to the British government'.[24]

Arthur was given several other military and political assignments in India between 1799 and 1805, benefitting from his elder brother's official position as the top colonial administrator. He returned to England in 1805, where he arrived in September of that year. His elder brother was recalled the same year, while the younger brother, Henry (initially Richard's private secretary), had already returned in 1803.

In the Second Anglo–Maratha War (1802–05), another major war inflicted by his brother Richard on the subcontinent, Arthur achieved renown on the battlefield of Assaye (1803). This was the first time that he was given command of the army. The battle was among the toughest he fought in his long military career. Assaye is situated in the central part of the present-day state of Maharashtra, close to Aurangabad. The Battle of Assaye was one of the key confrontations of a war encompassing central, western, and northern India.

The EIC's main opponents in the war were the two most powerful Maratha warlords, Yashwant Rao Holkar and Daulat Rao Sindia. At Assaye, the British forces were pitted against Sindia's army, which was joined by the army of another Maratha warlord, Raghoji Bhonsle II. The Bhonsles ruled from Nagpur. British losses in the battle were severe. Arthur had seriously

---

[24]Hook, *Sir David Baird*, p. 246.

underestimated the military capabilities of the two chiefs. Randolf Cooper in his study of the Second Anglo–Maratha War comments that, 'Maratha artillery was more advanced than that of the British on several counts. Wellesley himself conceded there was no comparison in the quality of design and manufacture and ... it featured greater technical innovation and a more advanced method of application'.[25]

According to a British officer who was present at the battle, 'Nothing could surpass the skill or bravery displayed by their golumdauze [golandaz, cannoneer], as our loss fully testified. When taken, their guns were all found laid a few degrees below the point blank, just what they ought to be for the discharge of grape or canister at a short distance'.[26]

This was the war that placed Mughal Delhi under the Company's control. Delhi was occupied in 1803 following the defeat, at the Battle of Patparganj, of Sindia's troops, who had guarded the imperial capital since the 1780s. British troops were led by Lieutenant General Lake, who, as we have seen, had 'dealt furiously with the rebels' in Ireland a few years earlier. The EIC took over the civil and military administration of the city and its environs. Henceforth, the imperial capital was governed by the EIC on behalf of the emperor.

The British suffered several reverses in the Second Anglo–Maratha War, most notably at Mukandwara Pass near Kota and at Bharatpur. A British force led by Col. William Monson was defeated by Yashwant Rao Holkar at the Battle of Mukandwara Pass in July 1804. The British lost five infantry battalions and six companies of artillery in the battle.

The strategically located Lohagarh Fort at Bharatpur was besieged in January 1805 by British troops commanded by Lake. The ruler of Bharatpur had aligned himself with Yashwant Rao. The siege was a failure, and the unsuccessful attempts to

---

[25]Randolf G. S. Cooper, 'Wellington and the Marathas in 1803', *The International History Review*, Vol. 11, No. 1, 1989, p. 32.
[26]John Blakiston, *Twelve Years' Military Adventure in Three Quarters of the Globe*, Vol. 1, London: Henry Colburn, 1829, p. 176.

storm it resulted in massive casualties, running into thousands. Eventually, a compromise was negotiated between Lake and the ruler of Bharatpur.

The Second Anglo–Maratha War actually ended in a stalemate, the tangible gains for the British being their ascendancy at Pune and the acquisition of some territory mainly in northern India. Sindia and Holkar territories were confined south of the Chambal River, and their military strength was curtailed.

In England, there was growing opposition to Wellesley's policies mainly because of the enormous financial burden of the prolonged warfare. The directors were annoyed with the governor-general, whom they found increasingly unmanageable and unwilling to heed their instructions. In the House of Commons, Philip Francis was among the most vocal critics of Wellesley. But the most powerful denunciation of Wellesley's policies came from a younger member of the house, James Paull. Paull had spent several years in India as a private trader in Awadh. He was in the cloth export business (the EIC did not deal in the commodity any longer), which he conducted from his base in Lucknow.

Paull returned to England in 1805. He was elected to the House of Commons that year and, in his opening speech, launched an attack on the governor-general, in whose administration he stated, 'We have seen India deluged with blood, its princes dethroned, its ancient families ruined, and the spoils of our nearest allies added to the resources of the company, without exciting a sentiment of disapprobation on the part of the British legislature'.[27]

Paull had initially come to India as a writer in the Company's establishment. Subsequently, when he set himself up as a private trader, he occasionally sought the intervention of EIC officials in disputes with local authorities. As a private

---

[27]Hansard, 'Papers Relating to the Nabob of Oude', House of Commons Debates, 25 June 1805, Vol. 5, Col. 562, available at https://api.parliament.uk/historic-hansard/commons/1805/jun/25/papers-relating-to-the-nabob-of-oude.

merchant, he could not have carried out his enterprise without the tacit consent of the Company.

Most of the writings that mention Paull's crusade in Parliament against Wellesley, if at all they do, have derived much of their information about his occupation as a trader in Awadh from Peter Auber's *Rise and Progress of the British Power in India*. Auber's work was published in 1837 as a semi-official history of the Company's political activities in India up to the Charter Act of 1833, filling gaps in Mill's *History of British India* (1817), which stopped at 1805. Auber had retired as secretary to the Court of Directors. He had in his private possession several crucial documents, apart from the access he was provided to the official archive. We need to bear in mind that Mill was not an employee of the Company when he wrote his *History*—he joined the EIC's service in 1819, and worked at its head office in London.

Auber reproduces a lengthy letter of Paull addressed to John Malcolm, written in 1803, in which he thanks the governor-general for assistance in resolving a dispute with the Awadh court. Malcolm was then Wellesley's secretary. The personal references in the letter indicate that Paull knew Malcolm and several other members of the governor-general's retinue quite well. More importantly, he had intimate knowledge of the situation in Awadh, where he had resided for over a decade. Not surprisingly, Wellesley's friends viewed him as a serious threat when he turned against the colonial establishment, even though the erstwhile governor-general dismissed him upon his return to London as an 'obscure and low man'.[28]

In undertaking to expose the misdeeds of Wellesley, Paull had set himself a difficult task, the more so as his adversary was a nobleman 'of extensive influence, and possessing powerful connexions in both houses of parliament' whereas he 'was a new man and a very young member of this House'. He lamented 'that Lord Wellesley's spirit of aggrandizement, his

---

[28]Butler, *The Eldest Brother*, p. 371.

love of power, and insatiable ambition have led him into errors and mistakes, that have shook to its base our very existence in India, and to consequent acts of great injustice and oppression'.

The principal charge against the governor-general related to the annexation of a large portion of Awadh in 1801. Compared to this, the injustice done to Chait Singh by Hastings was, in his view, a minor offence, and yet, 'Mr. Hastings was impeached by the Commons of Great Britain'. Between these two issues, there was 'this marked and essential distinction, that Chyt Sing resisted demands that he thought oppressive, whereas the Nabob Vizier, the Prince of Oude, submitted to every demand, however illegal, however oppressive, however unjust'.

Secondly, Wellesley had 'violated the laws of his country, having in defiance of an Act of Parliament appointed his own brother [Henry] to a station of dignity, trust, and emolument that he was incompetent to hold'. [29]

Henry had been appointed lieutenant-governor of the territories that Awadh was compelled to cede to the Company in 1801. Wellesley's friends and relatives in Parliament immediately rushed to defend the governor-general on the latter charge. The president of the Board of Control, Lord Castlereagh, declared that, 'Mr Henry Wellesley was placed by the marquis, his brother, at the head of a commission in the province of Oude, for the purpose of placing the revenues and establishments of that country on a proper footing, in which service he actively and successfully employed himself, but for which he received no emolument, except what he derived from the office which he before held, and which he continued at that period to hold, that of private secretary to the governor-general. So far, indeed, from deriving any additional advantages from his employment in Oude, his health was seriously injured by his exertions whilst employed upon that service'.

Henry's elder brother, the second eldest of the Wellesley brothers, William Wellesley-Pole (the surname was changed

---

[29]Hansard, 'Papers Relating to the Nabob of Oude', Cols. 562–65.

following an inheritance), who was a member of the House of Commons for over twenty years, also intervened to defend his brothers. In one of his rare speeches in the House, he rejected the allegations, denying 'that Mr Henry Wellesley derived any emolument from his mission to Oude'. Paull's response was 'that the situation Mr Henry Wellesley was appointed to, was one of great trust, honour, and emolument, as would appear when the papers were laid upon the table; a situation in fact that made him second only to Marquis Wellesley, who was second to no other man in pomp and magnificence on this earth'.[30]

When the matter was again raised in the House a few months later, in January 1806, Paull gave notice for more papers to be tabled in addition to those that he had listed when he spoke in June 1805, and which had been ordered by the government to be printed for circulation among members, but were not yet forthcoming. He emphatically stated that 'He bore no animosity to Lord Wellesley personally; he would exert his honest endeavours to prosecute him to conviction, as the enemy to the happiness and prosperity of India, and to the best interests of the mother country; he could consider him in no light but that of a great state delinquent, in the situation that Mr Hastings stood on his return from abroad, with this essential difference, that what was undefined crime in the case of Mr Hastings, was positive criminality in the case of Lord Wellesley'.[31]

Straightaway, a Wellesley loyalist, Thomas Metcalfe, known for his obsequiousness, was on his feet to defend the governor-general. He was opposed to the tabling of papers demanded by Paull, as they could provide confidential information to the French. Furthermore that, at a time when Britain was at war with France, it was inappropriate that such an issue be raised in the House—in other words that it was not in the

---

[30]Ibid., Cols. 565–66.
[31]Hansard, 'Papers Relating to the Nabob of Oude', House of Commons Debates, 27 January 1806, Vol. 6, Col. 38, available at https://api.parliament.uk/historic-hansard/commons/1806/jan/27/affairs-of-india#S1V0006P0_18060127_HOC_2.

interest of the nation for Parliament to enquire into Wellesley's actions in India.

Metcalfe had served for twenty years in the Company's army. He had risen to the post of agent for military stores, a position that gave him ample opportunities for making money. Many of his contemporaries had a poor opinion of him, one of whom called him 'the time-serving, pompous, and sycophantic little Major Metcalfe'.[32]

Upon Metcalfe's return to England, Dundas helped him to get elected as a director of the EIC. In the Court of Directors, he refused to go along with the other members when they expressed their disapproval over the war launched by Wellesley against the Maratha chiefs and declined to sign a letter of censure, which was to be sent to the governor-general. And while none of the other directors attended a ceremonial dinner organized in honour of Wellesley when he returned home in 1806, Metcalfe was very much present.

Two of Metcalfe's sons, Charles and Thomas, are well-known figures in the history of nineteenth-century India. Both were employees of the EIC. Charles became a member of the governor-general's council, while Thomas was for nearly two decades the principal colonial official in Delhi, till his death in 1853. Remnants of the grand mansion in Delhi built by Thomas Metcalfe junior, Metcalfe House, are still extant.

In the debate on the Wellesley issue in 1806, the senior Metcalfe failed to convince members of his point of view. The House endorsed Paull's demand for the relevant documents to be made available. Nevertheless, Paull's attempt to mobilize support for the impeachment of the governor-general, along the lines of the Hastings impeachment, was unsuccessful. This is not to say that his endeavours did not damage Wellesley's reputation. On the contrary, this 'villain of no great intrinsic importance,' as he was characterized, 'was to do Richard Wellesley great injury'.[33]

---

[32]Benjamin Mee cited in Alfred Spencer (ed.), *Memoirs of William Hickey*, Vol. 4, Fifth Edition, London: Hurst & Blackett, 1950, p. 89.
[33]Butler, *The Eldest Brother*, p. 356.

The death of Pitt in January 1806, while in office, brought about political realignments which weakened the anti-Wellesley combination in Parliament, making it difficult for Paull to pursue the impeachment agenda on his own. Parliament was dissolved in October, and Paull did not win in the ensuing general election. The debate resumed shortly after the newly elected House assembled, with Lord Folkestone (William Pleydell Bouverie) now taking the lead in censuring Wellesley.

Folkestone, a member with 'radical tendencies', preferred to have Wellesley's actions denounced in the House through resolutions against him, rather than going ahead with the complicated—and as in the case of Hastings, possibly futile—attempt at impeachment. Parliament was again dissolved in April 1807, and after fresh elections, the House met in June.

Following a preliminary discussion on 29 June, Folkestone moved his first resolution against Wellesley several months later on 9 March 1808. The resolution was on the issue of the territories acquired from Awadh. He accused the former governor-general of having constantly harassed the subedar or nawab, Saadat Ali, with 'renewed and increasing applications' to pay for troops imposed on him. Awadh simply did not have the resources to pay the huge 'subsidy' demanded by the EIC, and its territories were taken over in lieu of monetary payment.

The annexation, he contended, was preceded by 'a very protracted negociation, in which, on the one side, is displayed all the arts of chicanery, accompanied with threats the most undisguised, and language of reproach and reviling the most contemptuous and unmerited, while on the other, patient forbearing, and earnest supplication were alone manifested'. Eventually, 'the unhappy nabob was compelled to yield to the Company a portion of territory of the alledged (sic.) annual income of one crore and 35 lakh rupees...in perpetual sovereignty, and to deprive himself even of all efficient government over the remainder'.[34]

---

[34]Hansard, 'Conduct Of Marquis Wellesley—Oude Charge', House of Commons

There was a lengthy and acrimonious debate on the motion, with Wellesley's supporters vociferously rejecting allegations of wrongdoing. In his speech, Folkestone drew attention to the propaganda conducted outside Parliament for mobilizing public opinion in favour of Wellesley. Pamphlets 'were distributed gratis, not only to members of that House, but in like manner through all the principal taverns and coffee houses in London'.[35]

Over a period of three years, Wellesley had to spend as much as £30,000 to counter the campaign against him. Part of the expense was incurred in maintaining a regular office with clerical staff to take care of the paperwork. Simultaneously, the relationship with Hyacinthe was on the verge of breaking down. He had acquired a reputation for philandering, which was also one of the reasons for his political marginalization. Butler reproduces a long letter written around this time by Hyacinthe to her husband, in which she complains about his relationships with prostitutes. She had restrained herself from writing to him about his 'whoring' but could no longer remain silent: 'Up till now I have refrained, with great care, from telling you of your reputation for debauchery and the jokes that are made about it.' She vents her anger against an associate of his who had become notorious as 'Lord Wellesley's provider, picking up two-guinea [a coin equal to a little more than one pound sterling] girls from the pavements, to whom you pay their weight in gold, as all old men do'.[36]

The Folkestone resolution was put to the vote on 15 March 1808 after a further debate on it. The motion in favour got thirty-one votes, while 182 members voted against it. Another resolution was then moved, applauding the services of Wellesley, and was adopted with 180 in favour and 29 against. This terminated the move to censure the former governor-general.

Debates, 9 March 1808, Vol. 10, Cols. 993–1004, available at https://hansard.parliament.uk/Commons/1808-03-09/debates/705348b9-44dc-43bf-b620-e9d3f45633b5/ConductOfMarquisWellesley%E2%80%94OudeCharge#main-content.
[35]Ibid.
[36]Butler, *The Eldest Brother*, p. 387.

In 1809, the Order of the Garter was conferred on him much against the wishes of George III. It was with difficulty that the prime minister was able to persuade the king to bestow the honour on Wellesley. The politically fluid situation in Britain, against the backdrop of the war, afforded an opening for him in the ministry. He became secretary of state (minister) for foreign affairs in the Tory administration of Spencer Perceval, whose ministry comprised 'somewhat second-rate material', as none of the more eminent figures in Parliament were willing to join the ministry.[37]

Perceval, an ultra-conservative Tory, was prime minister from 1809 to 1812. He was shot dead in the lobby of the House of Commons in May 1812—the only prime minister of the country to be assassinated. Wellesley had resigned a few months before the assassination due to differences over the conduct of the war against Napoleon, which he wanted to be carried out with greater vigour, and because he disagreed with the hardline stance of Perceval on the question of rights for Catholics in Ireland. On the latter question, Wellesley had urged a more moderate policy, not a radical change. Perceval was opposed to any change whatsoever, refusing even the slightest concession. Wellesley considered Perceval to be an incompetent prime minister, declaring in the end that he was not willing to serve 'under' him.

In the political crisis that ensued due to the slaying of the prime minister, Wellesley began to explore the possibility, upon authorization from the royal court, of forming a government with himself at the head. His bid for the premiership was unsuccessful. The two years and two months that he was foreign secretary was his only stint as a cabinet minister. Wellesley held no office for the next nine years, from 1812 to 1821. Between 1821 and 1828, and again for a few months in 1833–34, he served as lord lieutenant of Ireland. Politically, this was a demotion for him.

---

[37]Ibid., p. 422.

His brother, Arthur, had a long career as a leading Tory politician after 1815, overlapping with the key positions he held in the army. Arthur, Duke of Wellington, was prime minister from 1828 to 1830, and for a few weeks at the end of 1834. He was a cabinet minister without portfolio from 1841 to 1846. Wellington was simultaneously commander-in-chief of the royal army from 1842 until he died in 1852. He was the only British prime minister in the nineteenth century to have personal experience in India, where he spent nearly a decade. Richard passed away in 1842 at the age of eighty-two (he was thirty-eight when he came to India as governor-general), ten years before Arthur's death.

∽

When Wellesley had been recalled from Bengal in 1805, Cornwallis was once again sent out as governor-general after a gap of twelve years. He reached Calcutta in July, a month before his predecessor departed for England. In November 1804, the government had decided on replacing Wellesley, preferably with Cornwallis if he was willing to go to India for a second time. Cornwallis was nearly sixty-seven at this time. When approached, he had indicated his willingness to accept the appointment, especially as he had been offered no other position by the government in the past few years and was living in semi-retirement. It was difficult to resist the temptation of wielding absolute power. The appointment was officially announced in January 1805. Cornwallis's term lasted for just two months. Soon after his arrival, he proceeded by boat on the Ganga to undertake a tour of the recently annexed Awadh territories. During the journey, his health—already somewhat impaired when he had departed from England—began to deteriorate. On 29 September, he was shifted from the boat in which he was travelling to an official dwelling in Ghazipur. He died on 5 October and was buried in that city. The place of his burial is marked by a simple tomb built with donations from 'British inhabitants of Calcutta'. News of Cornwallis's death reached

England within about a week of the demise of Pitt, so that it did not receive even the token attention that might have been due to a well-known governor-general who had expired while in office. Parliament formally mourned his death on 3 February 1806, with several members paying tribute to his memory. Here, too, a speaker struck a discordant note, disagreeing with the adulatory reference made by Castlereagh (president of the Board of Control) to the role played by Cornwallis in helping to bring about the 'union' with Ireland. The dissent came from Charles O'Hara. Intervening in the debate on a motion, following Castlereagh's speech, for putting up a public statue of the deceased in London, O'Hara stated that, 'he could by no means give a vote for funeral honours to the memory of a man, who had had so principal a share in that transaction [the union], which he looked on as mischievous and fatal to the interests of Ireland'. Moreover, 'when he recollected also the shameful and barefaced corruption, which was openly carried on, for the purpose of carrying that fatal measure, and which reflected the greatest disgrace on the justice of this country, and called to mind the high part the Marquis Cornwallis filled in the scene of that transaction, he must oppose the motion'.[38] O'Hara was an Irish member of the House of Commons who had consistently opposed the union. The motion for erecting a monument commemorating Cornwallis was adopted. The statue, sculpted by Charles Rossi, was put up in St Paul's Cathedral in 1807—one among the several national monuments that celebrate military victories that led to the creation of the British Empire.

---

[38]Hansard, 'Papers Relating to the Nabob of Oude', Vol. 6, Col. 126.

VI

SETTLING DOWN

During the Peninsular War and in the final phase of the conflict with France, Britain had to concentrate all its resources on the fight against Napoleon. The Peninsular War, lasting from 1808 to 1814, was the confrontation between the two powers on the Iberian front, involving Portugal and Spain as well. Arthur Wellesley's reputation as a military leader of outstanding ability was acquired in peninsular campaigns. The EIC's territorial expansion temporarily ceased in these years, and resumed in 1814. Meanwhile, the Charter Act of 1813 ended the Company's monopoly over trade with India, something it had enjoyed for over two centuries. With the final defeat of Napoleon at Waterloo, France was no longer a threat to British colonial supremacy. Britain was to remain the dominant world power till the end of the century.

In India, a fresh round of expansion commenced in 1814 with an offensive against the kingdom of Nepal. The kingdom was invaded by British forces when the Kathmandu durbar refused to comply with an ultimatum to give up its possession of recently occupied lowlands bordering Gorakhpur. Gorakhpur was among the districts which the Company had taken from Awadh in 1801. There was also a row over Nepalese occupation of lowlands adjacent to the foothills of Kumaon and Garhwal, especially the Dun Valley.

Lord Moira—after 1816 also known as the Marquess of Hastings (governor-general, 1813–23)—used the border disputes in the two sectors as a pretext for attacking the kingdom. The Anglo–Nepal war lasted till 1816. It was a difficult war for the British, who lost an officer of the rank of major-general, Robert

Gillespie, at the outset of the campaign. The Treaty of Sagauli signed at the end of the war recognized the independence of the kingdom. The British annexed Kumaon, Garhwal, and the Dun Valley. Among the several Himalayan tracts which were acquired by the Company at the end of the war were the hills on which Simla (now Shimla) was to come up later in the century, as the summer capital of the British Empire. Moira was honoured with a British peerage in 1816–17, becoming the marquess of Hastings, for his additions to the EIC's territories at the expense of Nepal.[1]

The Nepal war was followed by the Third Anglo–Maratha War (1817–18). This was a confrontation between the Company and almost all the leading Maratha chiefs. The war carried forward the agendas of the Second Anglo–Maratha War, of which, in many ways, it was a continuation. The major outcome of the Third Anglo–Maratha War, for the British, was the extinction of the institution of the peshwa, and the annexation of territories in western Maharashtra that had been directly ruled from Pune, the seat of the peshwas.

The history of the Maratha empire in the latter half of the eighteenth century is the history of a 'confederacy' headed by the peshwa, comprising Sindia, Holkar, Bhonsle, and Gaikwad dynasties, all of whom acknowledged the peshwa as their nominal overlord. Defeat in the Battle of Panipat (1761) in which the Marathas were fighting against Ahmad Shah Durrani and his allies, was a major calamity for the formidable Maratha army and the peshwa. In the aftermath of the defeat, the principal warlords gradually became entirely autonomous. Pune became a distant reality for them as the century wore on. At the same time, they continued to be involved in factional tussles at the court, an indication of the symbolic importance of the peshwa's position for legitimizing the authority of the Maratha chiefs.

---

[1] The numerous aristocratic titles that Moira (Francis Rawdon-Hastings) had, and the variations in his surname, can at times be confusing. I have used Lord Hastings's pre-1816 title, Lord Moira, throughout rather than Lord Hastings, to avoid confusion.

For over two decades after the 1770s, the powerful Pune minister Nana Fadnavis held sway at the peshwa's court, whereas Mahadji Sindia (d. 1794) was the most powerful Maratha ruler. The waning of Nana Fadnavis's influence in the late 1790s and his death in 1800 led to factional realignments and the intensification of quarrels at the Pune court. The minister had earlier been outmanoeuvred in a contest over succession when Baji Rao II (r. 1796–1818) succeeded Sawai Madhav Rao (Madhav Rao II) as the peshwa, mainly with Daulat Rao Sindia's support. Daulat Rao had succeeded Mahadji as ruler of Sindia territories. Nana Fadnavis had opposed Baji Rao's claim. The succession and Nana Fadnavis's death were followed by a violent conflict between Daulat Rao and the incumbent Holkar chief, Yashwant Rao.

In 1801, Yashwant Rao invaded Ujjain, which was at that time the Sindia capital. Later in the same year, Sindia troops invaded the Holkar capital, Indore. Yashwant Rao then retaliated by inflicting a defeat on the combined forces of Baji Rao and Daulat Rao near Pune (1802). This sequence of events formed the backdrop of the Second Anglo–Maratha War. Baji Rao was restored to peshwaship with British support. As the price for its support, the Company compelled Baji Rao to sign a subsidiary treaty, which further increased its capacity to intervene in Maratha affairs.

Given that, together the Maratha-ruled states had a subcontinental presence, their subjugation had been at the top of the EIC's expansionist agenda after the destruction of Tipu's Mysore. The Second Anglo–Maratha War left the task unfinished. Another offensive would be required to fully subjugate the Marathas.

At the end of the Third Anglo–Maratha War, Sindia, Holkar, and Bhonsle accepted British supremacy, and Baji Rao II's territories were annexed. Baji Rao, accompanied by his family and retainers, was exiled to Bithur near Kanpur and allotted a small pension. He was utterly forgotten till his name resurfaced in the context of the uprising of 1857 at Kanpur, in which his adopted son and successor, Nana Saheb, played a prominent part.

Baji Rao passed away in 1851. The EIC refused to acknowledge Nana Saheb as his successor, discontinuing the pension. After the defeat of the rebels at Kanpur in 1857, the British alleged that the denial of Nana Saheb's claims by the Company's authorities in London had given him a strong personal motive to hatch a conspiracy against the EIC. The mutiny in the EIC's Bengal Army was a product of this conspiracy. The British held him responsible for the killing of Europeans in Kanpur in 1857. In the popular British imagination, Nana Saheb came to be perceived as the arch-villain in the revolt, the evil mastermind of the massacres of Kanpur. An elaborate memorial was built by the British at the site of the massacres within a few years of the suppression of the revolt. The centrepiece of the memorial was a well, where a sculpture of an 'angel of pity' or 'angel of resurrection' was erected in memory of the European victims, with the following inscription on the pedestal: 'Sacred to the perpetual memory of a great company of Christian people—chiefly women and children—who, near this spot, were cruelly massacred by the followers of the rebel, Nana Dhoondopunt of Bithoor, and cast, the dying with the dead, into the well below, on the XVth day of July 1857.' Thus was the lie about Baji Rao's successor endlessly perpetuated. The war of 1817–18 had a long afterlife.

The Third Anglo–Maratha War overlapped with an all-out campaign against the Pindaris, referred to as 'freebooters' in colonial writings and in textbooks that reproduce colonial stereotypes. 'Pindari' was a label used by administrators for diverse communities which were not part of settled agrarian society. They were a product of processes of social differentiation in the tribal belt of central India, especially the tracts lying south of the Narmada. These processes were, in turn, linked to the dislocation and disruption caused by Mughal and Maratha empire-building, subsequently hastened by colonial intervention in the region.

After the Second Anglo–Maratha War, the Pindaris had been regularly used as cheap auxiliaries by the Sindias and Holkars in military conflicts. The outcome of the war had not been favourable for these states: they lost territories and resources, which compelled them to reduce their military strength. Moreover, the sudden defection of several officers of European descent from the Sindia and Holkar armies to the British side during, and at the end of, the war had had an adverse impact on the military organization of these states. These circumstances had increased their reliance on the Pindaris.

At the outset of the renewed campaign against Maratha-ruled states, Moira announced his intention to annihilate the Pindari presence in Sindia and Holkar spheres of influence in central India and the Malwa plateau. This provided justification for military mobilization on a massive scale.

Malwa was the core region of Sindia and Holkar power. The plateau is located at the junction of northern, central, and western India, most of it lying in the western portion of present-day Madhya Pradesh, with a few patches spilling over into neighbouring south-eastern Rajasthan. Numerous rulers, ranging from the powerful Sindias to the petty Rajput chieftains of Amjhera and Sitamau, controlled different parts of the plateau at the turn of the century.

The Sindias possessed the largest chunk of territory, although some of their territories were situated adjacent to, but outside, Malwa proper. Gwalior, the Sindia capital from circa 1810 onwards, itself lies on the northern edge of Malwa. The territories of the Maratha chiefs in this region, among which were Dhar and Dewas ruled by separate branches of the Puwars, were scattered over the entire plateau.

The manner in which the Pune court initially assigned different zones to Maratha warlords for the collection of its share of agrarian surpluses in what had been the Mughal suba of Malwa, prevented these chiefs from controlling contiguous areas. The dispersed tracts for which each chief was responsible were intermixed with those of the others so that when these warlords began asserting their independence, their states lacked territorial cohesion.

For the campaign against the Pindaris, two colonial armies were to converge on Malwa, one from the north and the other from the south. The southern army was commanded by Lieutenant-General T. Hislop, and the northern army was led by Moira himself. The governor-general was concurrently the commander-in-chief of British forces in India. He had a long military career before being appointed governor-general, during which he had fought in the war against the American revolutionaries as a junior officer under Cornwallis, and had been the commander-in-chief of the royal army in Scotland for several years in the first decade of the nineteenth century. The total strength of the two armies assembled for the anti-Pindari offensive was 120,000. Most of the Pindari bands simply dissolved without offering any open resistance in the field. The greatly exaggerated Pindari menace had been obliterated by the beginning of 1818.

At the end of the Second Anglo–Maratha War, Sindia and Holkar territories had been confined mostly to Malwa and some other areas situated between the Chambal and Narmada Rivers, while the EIC was able to extend its control to the Ganga–Jamuna Doab and northern India. The Third Anglo–Maratha war allowed the EIC to consolidate its position further and to acquire a vast stretch of territory in western India. It is worth bearing in mind that, unlike in southern and eastern India, the Company was not a territorial power of any consequence in western India till 1818. Bombay, Surat, Bharuch, and Kheda were its only possessions. It now took over an estimated 130,000 square kilometres of territory by extinguishing the peshwa's rule. The peshwa's domain, broadly corresponding to present-day western Maharashtra, was attached to the Bombay presidency. Besides, all of Gujarat was brought under the Company's authority, its droves of princely rulers henceforth supervised by the Bombay government. As a consequence of the Third Anglo–Maratha War, the EIC also gained control over the Rajput-ruled states of Rajasthan—a bonus for the Company. Most of these states had been under either Sindia or Holkar dominance.

The Gaikwad chief, ruling over large parts of Gujarat from Baroda, had signed a subsidiary treaty in 1802, thereby losing his independence. The Baroda state was incorporated into the empire as a princely state and, along with Hyderabad and Mysore, was among the three foremost 'native' states in the hierarchy constructed later in the century by colonial officials. As for the Saurashtra/Kathiawad region of Gujarat, with nearly four hundred princely states, most of which were petty chieftaincies owing allegiance to the Gaikwads, it came to have the largest regional concentration of indirectly ruled political entities in the British empire in India. These had earlier been subject to Maratha control. Most of these states were too weak and insignificant to be able to withstand colonial meddling, making it easy for the British to discipline them. On the other hand, in Malwa and central India, the Sindias continued to be militarily potent in the post-1818 period. A major campaign had to be launched in 1843–44 to curtail the power that soldiers of the Sindia army continued to wield even after 1818.

ॐ

Moira had an unusually long tenure of nearly ten years as governor-general. He was an intimate friend of the king, George IV (r. 1820–30). George IV had been the de facto monarch since 1811, acting as regent on behalf of his father, George III. George III's insanity had necessitated such an arrangement. Moira and George had been friends for several years before the latter became the regent.

As heir apparent (Prince of Wales), George had borrowed heavily from his friend to support an opulent lifestyle. The loans were never repaid. Moira belonged to a wealthy Irish aristocratic family inheriting, as the eldest son, its vast estates. His own expensive tastes, his financial support to the exiled

French royal family after the Revolution, and loans to George had exhausted his considerable resources within a few years of his return from the American campaign at the end of 1782. These were years in which he began to aspire to a place in the ministry.

Having been made an English peer as Baron of Rawdon in 1783, he became a member of the (British) House of Lords and thereby commenced his parliamentary career in Britain. Differences with Prime Minister Pitt prevented Moira from realizing his political ambitions. His friendship with the Prince of Wales dates back to this period. In 1797 he attempted, with the backing of the prince, to replace Pitt as prime minister and form a new ministry. His efforts failed, and he was ridiculed by his opponents for having foolishly assumed that he could find sufficient support for the parliamentary manoeuvre.

Moira tried his hand at forming a ministry again in 1812. After Wellesley's unsuccessful bid to become prime minister following Perceval's death, the regent asked Moira to attempt to put together a cabinet. However, Moira was unable to accomplish the task due to inadequate support among the various parliamentary factions to which he appealed. Each faction consisted of a small number of individuals owing loyalty to an influential member. The faction could be either Whig or Tory in terms of its broad ideological position. Therefore, ministry formation was more a matter of persuading prominent individuals who cumulatively had sufficient support in Parliament, and together had a common outlook on at least key issues. Moira was unable to muster a majority. This was to be his 'last attempt ... to enter the mainstream of British politics'.[2]

Prior to the experiment in government formation, the regent had proposed sending Moira as governor-general to India. The offer had been declined at that time. Now, several months later, it suddenly seemed attractive to Moira. His appointment

---

[2]Paul David Nelson, *Francis Rawdon-Hastings, Marquess of Hastings: Soldier, Peer of the Realm, Governor-General of India*, Madison: Fairleigh Dickinson University Press, 2005, p. 145.

was announced in November 1812. In the meantime, a Tory ministry had assumed office under Lord Liverpool. Liverpool had temporarily headed the government upon Perceval's assassination. He remained prime minister for fifteen years, till 1827—that is, for almost the entire duration of the regency and the reign of George IV.

As we have noted, Moira was also appointed commander-in-chief of British forces in India. He expected a separate remuneration for his military appointment. The decision in this matter was left to the EIC, which would have had to make the additional payment had it been generous enough to sanction two salaries to Moira. The governor-general had to be content with just one salary. He received no extra pay in his capacity as the principal British military commander in India. The question of the salary was of vital importance for Moira in view of his financial difficulties.

The decision of the cabinet regarding the appointment of Moira as governor-general—the regent had left the prime minister with no choice in the matter—had still to be approved by the Court of Directors; the EIC was the paymaster. This was not a mere formality, as is indicated by the outcome of the voting. It is pertinent that the issue required a vote, which, as it turned out, was not unanimous. Seventeen directors voted in favour of the appointment, while six opposed it. The division on Moira's concurrent military command was fourteen in favour and seven against. No reference was made to the additional allowance of the governor-general in his capacity as commander-in-chief.

The Company thereby saved the £20,000 that it would have had to pay Moira annually for nine years for the military post, defeating his hope of using his dual employment to make himself financially solvent. The loans he had taken in the preceding years amounted to £270,000 in 1807. The sum increased further while he was in India.

Given his complete lack of knowledge of the political entity he was going to govern, Moira got in touch with a few senior retired Company officials with experience in India. These included Warren Hastings. Six years before this, shortly after the death of Pitt, Warren Hastings had approached Moira with the request that he use his influence with the Prince of Wales so that he might advise the government to confer some honour on him. Pitt was perceived to be hostile to Hastings. Hastings recorded his March 1806 meeting with Moira (Pitt passed away in the last week of January) in some detail. The latter was very courteous when his predecessor called on him at his residence, yet the meeting had no concrete outcome.

In May 1812, a few days after the assassination of Perceval, when he might have heard rumours about the possibility of Moira becoming prime minister, Warren Hastings promptly wrote to the regent, offering his services 'to be employed in any way which Your Royal Highness may think it proper to command them'.[3] While it is unlikely that the regent would have mentioned the veteran EIC official's letter to Moira amidst the hectic turmoil of the summer of 1812, some casual reference in a conversation in the context of the latest Indian appointment might have suggested Warren Hastings's name to Moira when he was looking for information about Indian affairs on the eve of his departure.

Hastings was only too eager to give detailed advice on how to govern the EIC's territories. Of course, the former governor-general's views were easily available in the Company's archives, and Moira might have consulted the relevant memoranda and correspondence whenever necessary, directly or in the form of summaries prepared by his secretarial staff. For the time being, a conversation with the knowledgeable Hastings would have been useful as a preliminary introduction to the colony he had been called upon to administer.

On the other hand, the impeachment and trial of Hastings had discredited EIC personnel occupying positions at the highest level of its establishment in India and had created conditions

---

[3]Warren Hastings cited in Lawson, *Private Life of Warren Hastings*, p. 192.

for the British state to have a decisive say in the selection of the governor-general. The appointment of the governor-general became the exclusive preserve of the cabinet and the monarch by the end of the century, subject to formal approval by the Court of Directors. In the closing years of George III's reign and under George IV (including the regency), the monarch, rather than the cabinet, personally exercised greater control over the appointment. The appointment of the commander-in-chief of the British forces in India, including the Company's army, especially came to be regarded as a royal prerogative.

We need to bear in mind that, whenever the distinction between EIC officers and king's officers was blurred, it caused tensions that could have serious ramifications, as happened when Cornwallis attempted to formally amalgamate the two distinct military formations. On taking over as commander-in-chief, Moira superseded George Nugent, also an officer drawn from the king's army (commander-in-chief of British forces in India, 1811–13). Nugent was unhappy that he had been unceremoniously replaced by the governor-general. The Court of Directors then appointed him as commander-in-chief of the EIC's Bengal Army, which, from his point of view, amounted to a demotion. Nugent resigned his EIC command in 1814, much to the satisfaction of Moira. He went back to England, deeply embittered at having been dislodged.

Nevertheless, the large salary of £20,000 per annum, which Nugent had enjoyed as commander-in-chief, was not transferred to Moira. The return to England terminated Nugent's military career. He seems to have expressed his displeasure openly— something that was not appreciated by the military establishment.

The later years of Moira's tenure were rocked by scandal, hastening his return. Besides, his hold over the supreme council had weakened by 1819. He had already been in office for six years (he had initially planned to spend five years in India) and was not used to opposition from members of the council. Moira was annoyed that some of the members were beginning to assert themselves. He was also losing the confidence of the cabinet, particularly of the president of the Board of Control, George Canning.[4] As president of the board, Canning was the minister for Indian affairs in the cabinet.

Ultimately, it was Moira's disgrace over official support extended by him to the Palmer agency house in its shady dealings with Hyderabad that forced him to resign. The allegations of personal corruption against Moira were never properly investigated. William Palmer & Co. was one of the biggest European financial-cum-commercial concerns operating in India. Such firms conducted their businesses with the approval of the EIC. The firm had given massive loans to Hyderabad, having obtained the personal authorization of the governor-general for loaning these amounts to the state. Repayment of the loans involved a huge fraud, thereby swindling Hyderabad of at least sixty lakh rupees. Both Canning and the prime minister felt that Moira had been wrong in authorizing Palmer to carry out its financial operations in the state. Liverpool's intervention on the issue made it impossible for Moira to continue. He had lost the favour of the king as well.

Moira was furious when he was abruptly informed by the Court of Directors in 1822 that it was in the process of finalizing his successor. He departed from India in January 1823, 'a tired, angry old man'.[5] He died three years later, leaving a most bizarre instruction in a will he wrote when he was on his deathbed. According to the note, his right hand was to be 'cut off and preserved, so as that it may be put with ... [his wife's] body into the coffin when it shall please the almighty to decree the union of our spirits'.[6] When Moira's wife died sixteen years later, his preserved hand was placed in her coffin.

Whereas Wellesley altered the landscape of Calcutta by implanting a grand building inspired by European architecture

---

[4]Canning's son, Charles Canning, became governor-general and headed the colonial government during the revolt of 1857. All references in this chapter are to the elder Canning.

[5]Nelson, *Francis Rawdon-Hastings*, p. 19.

[6]Ibid., p. 190.

for housing the governor-general, Moira, during his tenure, introduced British–Irish court etiquette in a city that was emerging as the imperial capital. Wellesley and Moira, between them, transformed the character of the EIC's headquarters in India.

Calcutta had grown over the years as a Company town entirely dominated by European writers, factors and merchants, and Indians connected to the EIC. Its culture reflected the non-elite (European) social origins of those who exercised power, namely senior officials of the Company whose extensive political and military authority had been acquired relatively recently, just half a century ago. Aristocratic presence from Cornwallis onwards had only had a limited influence so far. Aristocratic European women were unknown to Calcutta. Cornwallis's wife had passed away before he came to India, and Wellesley was not accompanied by Hyacinthe. Shore was a veteran India hand and, as we have seen, maintained social ties with his Indian family while living in Calcutta. He would have reinforced rather than undermined the Company's social protocol that had evolved since the days of Clive, incorporating several features of Mughal ceremonial.

Cornwallis's successor, after he died in 1805, was Lord Minto (d. 1814). He assumed office in 1807. George Barlow, a senior member of the council, was the acting governor-general in the intervening two years. Minto had been a long-standing parliamentary figure; he had assisted Burke in the trial of Warren Hastings. He was president of the Board of Control in the short-lived ministry formed after Pitt's death but was not a member of the cabinet. He was requested to become governor-general due to differences between the cabinet and the Court of Directors on the choice of a full-fledged governor-general to replace Barlow. Neither was willing to confirm Barlow in his position.

Minto's appointment was a compromise, since the directors declined to accept the cabinet's nominee, Lord Lauderdale. Lauderdale was one of the most controversial political figures of Britain in the 1780s and 1790s. He had opposed war with France and was a fierce critic of the Company. Lauderdale himself withdrew his name as a candidate for the governor-generalship when his main sponsor in the cabinet, Charles Fox, fell seriously ill. Fox died in September 1806. Minto's name was put forward by the cabinet to break the deadlock.

Minto's first halt upon reaching India in June 1807 was Madras, where he spent two weeks en route to Calcutta. He was received by William Bentinck, who was then on his way out as governor of the Madras presidency, having been recalled for his inept handling of a mutiny in the Company's army. Minto had not yet taken charge as governor-general and therefore interacted with Bentinck only informally. The EIC's instructions required him to open the sealed commission he was carrying with him upon arrival in Calcutta, and not earlier. That would confirm his assumption of office. The practice of giving a sealed commission to the governor-general-designate before his departure from London was a survival from the days when the captain of a Company fleet or ship would be provided with a sealed commission by the Court of Directors, before setting out on a voyage to the East Indies.

Minto's wife, too, did not travel to India. Moira was the first of the aristocratic governors-general who was accompanied by his wife, Lady Loudoun, during his stay in India. Moira's wife had an independent title as a peer—Countess of Loudoun —a title she had inherited in her own right from her father, the Earl of Loudoun (she was the only child of the earl). Together, Moira and Loudoun refashioned the public image of the governor-general, projecting his imperial status and insisting on strict adherence to British royal ceremonial.

The ceremonial associated with the governor-general was relatively relaxed till the end of the century when Wellesley began making changes that would end 'ill-bred familiarity'.[7] According to Lord Curzon, who became governor-general

---

[7]Curzon, *British Government in India*, Vol. I, p. 210.

a century after Wellesley, Wellesley 'elevated the spectacular to the level of an exact science'.[8] What Curzon overlooked was that Wellesley did not have sufficient time to replace the practices of Company administrators with those derived from British aristocratic traditions. Moreover, Cornwallis, his only aristocratic predecessor, had left behind no significant cultural legacy that Wellesley could have carried forward to make sweeping changes in ceremonial. Cornwallis had even been critical of the as yet restrained fanfare with which he was received upon his arrival in Calcutta in 1786. Minto, coming a few years after the Wellesley innovations, expressed his annoyance over the large retinue which escorted him when he went out for his morning and evening 'airing', in a letter to his wife, 'I am always followed by an officer and six troopers of the body-guard. These cannot be dispensed with. Four syces or horse-keepers with fly-flappers ran alongside of the horses till I positively rebelled against this annoyance. Everybody, European and native, salaams as I pass, and the natives, who swarm, draw up in lines and touch the ground almost with their heads.' The arrangements for travelling in a palki or palanquin were particularly elaborate: 'Thirty people go before in two lines which extend a great way forward. They carry gold and silver maces and halberds, and embroidered fans, and cows' tails to keep the flies off, besides two orderly sepoys and two troopers. All these run on foot at a round trot, some of them proclaiming my titles.'[9]

Warren Hastings had considered it important to broadcast his status as an omnipotent ruler by surrounding himself with a splendidly mounted contingent of bodyguards when he was on the move. In 1773, he reorganized the small cavalry, which had acted as the bodyguard of the Bengal governor since the early 1760s, into a formal contingent mainly for ceremonial purposes. The reorganized contingent was called 'The Governor's Troop

---

[8]Ibid., p. 208.
[9]Countess of Minto, *Lord Minto in India*, p. 29.

of Moguls', referring to the community among Muslims from which the troops were initially recruited (the soldiers of the pre-1773 bodyguard were European).

In the early nineteenth century, the bodyguard did occasionally take part in fighting but was eventually confined to ceremonial duties and parades. This mounted escort was to remain a permanent feature of the governor-general's establishment until the end of colonial rule. While seeking the sanction of the Court of Directors for the expense incurred in raising the contingent, consisting of 100 sawars, or horsemen, Hastings denied that he was being ostentatious. The number was reduced to fifty by Macpherson during his brief tenure, then progressively increased until its strength had reached 500 by mid-century. The number was fixed at 120 after the revolt.

The Moira dispensation ushered in a grand style that would reflect British imperial, as distinct from Company, power. With Loudoun installed in the recently-built palatial residence of the foremost British official in Calcutta, it was possible to secure the willing collaboration of European women in the settlement, particularly wives of senior Company officials. The conventions of the Government House were substantially modified so that they resembled those of the British royal court. One of the prominent officials of the Company, who was a favourite of Moira, Charles D'Oyly was, however, not too impressed by the attempts of the couple to develop a style 'which forms its model on the Rules of a Court in Europe'. He found their conduct quite jarring in the setting of Company-dominated Calcutta: 'I am sorry both Lord Moira and Lady Loudoun are so enveloped in formality and grandeur, for there is no approach to anything like intimacy.'[10] Major, later General, William Palmer (d. 1816), who had been secretary of Warren Hastings and whose son, William Palmer, was founder of the firm that defrauded Hyderabad of its revenues, in a letter addressed to his former

---

[10]Sydney C. Grier (ed.), *The Letters of Warren Hastings to His Wife*, Edinburgh: William Blackwood, 1905, p. 427.

chief, with whom he continued to correspond, described some of the changes of the Moira dispensation and concluded with the remark, 'A Household Establishment is formed resembling that of Royalty—probably modelled on that of the Castle of Dublin'.[11] Palmer was referring to the practices of Dublin Castle as a source of inspiration for Moira. The governor-general was replicating the etiquette of Dublin Castle, which, in turn, replicated the etiquette of the royal court in London. Moira had ample opportunity to be acquainted with Dublin Castle as a small boy.

Dublin Castle was the headquarters of the Irish administration, the seat of the lord lieutenant. The lord lieutenant governed Ireland on behalf of the British Crown, and was the personal representative of the monarch. As the personal representative of the monarch, he had the title of viceroy. The ceremonial of the viceroy's court was based on that of the monarch's court. These are the conventions that Moira imported into Calcutta, giving the governor-general a quasi-regal status. He saw himself as 'surrogate monarch' similar to—but on a grander scale—the viceroy of Ireland.

In an essay on how the British aristocracy 'transformed the culture of imperial governance' in India and Moira's contribution to the process, Ashley Cohen notes that 'By introducing Dublin Castle etiquette, Moira effectively renovated the trappings of his new office so that it more closely resembled the post he would have preferred [lord lieutenant of Ireland], recasting the governor-general as viceroy. This was a highly significant step, and one that has been overlooked as a precursor to the wholesale monarchicalization of the colonial government after the Mutiny of 1857'.[12]

The title of viceroy mentioned by Cohen is that which was used in the context of Ireland by the lord lieutenant in his capacity as the personal representative of the monarch. From

---

[11]Grier, *Letters of Warren Hastings*, p. 426.
[12]Ashley L. Cohen, 'The "Aristocratic Imperialists" of Late Georgian and Regency Britain', *Eighteenth-Century Studies*, Vol. 50, No. 1, 2016, pp. 13–14.

1858 onwards, the governor-general of India had the additional title of viceroy. As viceroy, he was deputizing for the monarch. The protocol followed in Calcutta and other presidency towns conformed to the EIC's managerial hierarchy, in which senior merchants and high-ranking military officers (in the EIC army) were placed at the top of the order of precedence, just below the governor-general, the commander-in-chief, and members of the supreme council. This was an inversion of the rules of precedency that prevailed at home, in which the aristocracy stood at the apex, having its own complicated hierarchy.

'In Britain,' Cohen observes, 'the ultimate determinant of rank was the peerage, but in India generations of EIC servants recruited from the middling orders had created an alternative measure of social status, where EIC and military seniority prevailed. The result was [that] ... commerce was elevated above noble birth and "Senior Merchant's wives" outranked the likes of Lady Elizabeth Murray, wife of Sir Evan John Murray MacGregor, second Baronet, and daughter of the Duke of Atholl'.[13]

With encouragement from either Moira or Loudoun, some of the aristocratic wives in the settlement appealed to the regent to intervene in disagreements over the order of precedence. In May 1814, he ruled in favour of aristocratic privilege, aligning 'colonial precedency with metropolitan conventions'.[14]

Once the war in Europe was over, and Napoleon had been trounced, the much-exaggerated fear of French intrusion into the Indian subcontinent subsided. Moira and his wife had ample time, particularly after the Nepal and Maratha wars, to impose their aristocratic ideas of ceremonial on the English community in Calcutta. Loudoun took charge of initiating the women into the knowledge of the intricacies of British high culture, the source of Government House etiquette. For example, the women

---

[13]Ibid., p. 15.
[14]Ibid., p. 16.

were taught to wear formal court dress, which included a head-dress with ostrich plumes. Lady Loudoun decreed that the dress code for formal entertainment at Government House would be, for the women, regency-style costume with appropriate head ornamentation.

The British travel writer Emma Roberts, who visited Calcutta in the second quarter of the nineteenth century, mentions in her travelogue that many women 'were prevented from attending in consequence of the dearth of ostrich feathers, the whole of the supply being speedily bought up; and, as it was not considered allowable to substitute native products, there was no alternative but to remain at home'.[15]

The following account of current fashions in London would indicate the fascination with ostrich feathers under the regency:

> Feathers were worn very large and high in the earlier years of the century. There was little taste shown in the disposition of the plumes. The Princess of Wales [Caroline of Brunswick, spouse of George IV, Princess of Wales, 1795–1820; Queen 1820–21] [d. 1821], who, though she did not enjoy the reputation of her husband for perfect dressing, was, of course, regarded as a leader of fashion, wore large ostrich feathers rising straight up from the top of her head. ... Ostrich feathers were generally used, but there were also worn the gorgeous plumes of the Bird of Paradise and feathers culled from the pheasant and the macaw.[16]

Loudoun's endeavours to enforce the code rigorously were not entirely successful, and under Moira's successors there might have been a relaxation of these rigid norms. Roberts commented that expatriates were not inclined to adopt the manners of the mother country in a hurry: 'Few had been accustomed

[15]Emma Roberts, *Scenes and Characteristics of Hindostan ...etc.*, Vol. 3, London: W. H. Allen, 1835, p. 75.

[16]Georgiana Hill, *A History of English Dress from the Saxon Period to the Present Day*, Vol. 2, London: Richard Bentley, 1893, pp. 293–94.

to European courts; and, having once established rules and regulations of their own, they stoutly resisted all attempts at alteration and innovation, every arrival being obliged to submit to the customs of the colony.'[17] This does not mean that Moira's measures were transient: 'It was, nevertheless, under him that the final stages of the transformation from the old India, which [Warren] Hastings knew, to pre-Mutiny India took place.'[18]

Already under Warren Hastings, the ritual at some of the official events had an imperial flavour, signifying the authority of the British monarch, notwithstanding that the EIC acknowledged the sovereignty of the Mughal emperor. The governor-general was required by the directors to entertain on a lavish scale, at the Company's expense, on the birth anniversaries of the king and the queen, and on New Year's Day. The firing of gun salutes on the occasion of the king's birthday would have proclaimed the majesty of the English monarch to the 'native' inhabitants of Calcutta. According to a contemporary account:

> At that period the King's birthday was celebrated with much pomp, the Governor-General always giving a dinner to the gentlemen of the Settlement and a ball and supper to the ladies at night, at which entertainments everybody ... appeared in full dress.... The Governor-General presided at the dinner-table. Upon the cloth being removed, he gave as first toast, The King; then, The Queen and Royal Family; The East India Company; The Army and Navy; The Commander-in-Chief; Success to the British arms in India—each toast being followed by a salute of twenty-one guns.[19]

The austere Cornwallis hosted splendid receptions on these occasions, which highlighted the governor-general's connection

---

[17]Roberts, *Scenes and Characteristics*, Vol. 3, p. 75.
[18]Grier, *Letters of Warren Hastings*, p. 426.
[19]Alfred Spencer ed., *Memoirs of William Hickey*, London: Hurst and Blackett, Vol.II (1775-1782), Seventh Edition, n.d., p. 173.

with the king, and would conclude, as we know from the description of a dinner held in 1789, with the singing of the 'coronation' anthem. The anthem was composed for the coronation of George III in 1761. There was no notion of a 'national' anthem as yet. The singing of *God save the King*, which dates back to 1745, with earlier versions going back to the end of the seventeenth century, gained popularity in the latter half of the eighteenth century. Only gradually did it become Britain's national anthem. Colley points out that, 'Not until the early 1800s would this song come to be called the national *anthem*, a term that the British invented' (emphasis in the original).[20]

In the twenty years following the coronation, the song (*God save the King*) was performed only four times in London theatres, but ninety times in the next two decades, so that at the turn of the century 'Britons were regularly calling this rather dismal piece of music—as they had not done before—the *national* anthem' (emphasis in the original).[21] Following the victory in the Napoleonic Wars, it was sung as the 'national air' in the presence of the king, George IV, at his coronation in 1821.[22]

The coronation anthem sung at Cornwallis's gathering was an expression of loyalty to the monarch. Of the several anthems that were performed at George III's coronation, all composed by William Boyce, the anthem *O Lord grant the king a long life* is most likely to have been the one sung at the Calcutta reception referred to, since the occasion for the dinner in 1789 was thanksgiving for the recovery of the king from his first episode of insanity. At the coronation ceremony, this was the anthem for the procession from Westminster Hall to Westminster Abbey—viz., the entrance-anthem—and its

---

[20]Colley, *Britons*, p. 44.
[21]Ibid., p. 209.
[22]Matthias Range, *Music and Ceremonial at British Coronations, From James I to Elizabeth II*, Cambridge: Cambridge University Press, 2012, pp. 193–94.

wording was the most relevant for the thanksgiving.[23] Some of these gestures prefigured the conventions which were to become part of the official ceremonial which, from Moira onwards, placed the governor-general on an imperial pedestal and made the link between the Company state and the British monarch visible to its subjects.

A public avowal of loyalty to the king, implying an assertion of the sovereignty of the British crown, however, had its problems. In seeking legitimacy for its state, the EIC had, by the beginning of the nineteenth century, co-opted the Mughal court. Yet the court was not, strictly speaking, part of the colonial state or its exploitative machinery. The otherwise powerless Mughal rulers used the cultural capital at their disposal, with the residual appeal of imperial ceremonial, to retain a function that enabled them to be distinct from the colonial state. The last two emperors Akbar Shah (r. 1806–37) and Bahadur Shah (r. 1837–62),[24] following in the footsteps of Shah Alam (r. 1759–1806), projected themselves as custodians and interpreters of courtly etiquette.

The Company's adherence to this etiquette made it the model for the British empire in India, including its princely rulers. By adopting a model derived from Mughal traditions, the princely states could simultaneously empower themselves vis-à-vis the Company, while reinforcing the model itself.

It is not widely known that, over a period of more than ninety years since the 1765 durbar at Allahabad, there was only one occasion when the emperor—Akbar Shah in this case— granted an audience to the Company's chief functionary in India. This was when Lord Amherst, governor-general from 1823 to 1828, visited Delhi in 1827.

Amherst's visit to Delhi in 1827 took place soon after

---

[23]Ibid., p. 164.

[24]I have taken 1862, the year in which Bahadur Shah died, as the terminal year for his reign, rather than the conventional 1857 or 1858, since the last Mughal emperor did not formally surrender or transfer sovereignty upon being made captive in 1857. He remained in captivity till his death.

the conclusion of the First Anglo–Burmese War (1824–26). The fiercely fought war engulfed a large part of the north-eastern region of the subcontinent, and Burma, resulting in the defeat of the Burmese kingdom. The kingdom was ruled by the Kongbaung dynasty, which had unified most of what is present-day Burma by the middle of the eighteenth century and was gradually extending its rule to Manipur, the Jaintia Hills, Cachar, and Assam. The westward expansion of the Burmese kingdom brought it into conflict with the EIC. The Company had been pushing eastwards along the Brahmaputra River in the late eighteenth century, and had begun intervening in the internal affairs of the Ahom kingdom of Assam. This was the prelude to the colonial conquest of the entire region.

The First Anglo–Burmese War led to the signing of the Treaty of Yandabo in 1826. Under the provisions of the treaty, the Burmese had to pay a huge indemnity to the British, and had to give up their claims over Manipur, Assam, Cachar, and the Jaintia Hills. Burma was forced to cede valuable and strategically located territory in the southern part of the kingdom—Arakan and Tenasserim—lying on either side of the delta of the Irrawaddy River. The delta region and northern Burma continued to be part of the independent Kongbaung kingdom, with its capital at Ava (later shifted to Amarapura and then to Mandalay, both in the neighbourhood of Ava). The process of conquering Burma, which commenced under Amherst, was completed in the 1880s. Tragically, the last Mughal emperor, Akbar Shah's son and successor, would be transported to Burma after the revolt and die in captivity.

Other than the 1827 exception, there were at least three other occasions when the governor-general might have been admitted to the royal presence, but the refusal on the part of the emperor, in each of these instances, to allow any major alteration in established etiquette precluded the possibility of a meeting. Moira's request in 1814 for an audience with Akbar Shah had been declined since the emperor was unwilling to allow the governor-general to be seated in his presence. The governor-general, after all, merely represented the diwan of the eastern subas, and therefore did not rank very high in the Mughal imperial hierarchy.

The semi-official *Asiatic Journal*, in a report on Akbar Shah's refusal to grant an audience on the governor-general's terms, published several years later, recorded responses that have been generally overlooked or deliberately ignored in later or even contemporary writings:[25]

> The Marquess of Hastings, in notifying his intention of visiting the emperor, coupled it with the stipulation that he should have a chair, and be received on an equality; but this his majesty would not hear of; and his lordship, in consequence, would not enter Delhi at all, but came within a march, when Lady H[astings] visited the palace *incog* [incognita]. On the occasion of Lord Hastings' extraordinary demand, the old emperor remarked, that Lord H. was only the servant of a king and, therefore could not be received on terms of equality; a privilege only granted to crowned heads, and his granting such a request would be breaking in upon the very few remaining prerogatives left to him. The transaction altogether was much more creditable to the emperor than to the Marquess of Hastings, who, on this occasion as well as many others, allowed his extravagant vanity to get the better of his good sense; he took an ungenerous advantage of the power and influence of his office to demand the concession of an empty honour, which, without adding an iota to his dignity, would have degraded the source from whence he wished to extort it.

In 1831, Akbar Shah again refused to grant an audience to the governor-general, this time to Amherst's successor William Bentinck—as did Bahadur Shah in 1838 when Lord Auckland

---

[25]*The Asiatic Journal and Monthly Register*, Vol. 26, May–August, London, 1838, p. 202.

was in Delhi. Auckland was governor-general from 1836 to 1842. Thus, it was only once that a meeting did materialize— something that became possible due to the emperor agreeing to dispense with the requirement of having the governor-general remain standing, as did everyone else, in his presence. The concession was immediately regretted, the honour never to be accorded again, either by Akbar Shah or his successor:

> On the visit of Lord Amherst, his majesty received the Governor-general standing, and with an embrace; after which he mounted his throne and beckoned to his lordship to be seated in a chair placed for him near the throne. This was conceived to be so novel and extraordinary an innovation of established etiquette, that the natives declared, in their expressive language, that the sun of the house of Timoor had then set, never to rise again. His majesty was in great agitation during the first part of the interview and seemed to be playing a game which his own judgment condemned.[26]

As custodian and interpreter of Mughal courtly etiquette, the emperor was averse to any sort of deviation in the ceremonial. Barring the exception that had been made at the time of Amherst's visit, no public gesture that could be suggestive of the governor-general being the emperor's equal was admitted— for which reason the emperors never granted an audience to any governor-general except for one brief moment in 1827.

∽

The seven years from 1828 to 1835, when William Bentinck was governor-general, marked an interlude between the aggressive territorial expansion that followed the end of the Napoleonic Wars and the even more violent phase of large-scale warfare from the late 1830s to the early 1850s which completed the Company's conquest of the subcontinent. The consolidation of

---

[26]Ibid., p. 203.

colonial rule in these seven years prepared the ground for the expansionist thrust of the next fifteen years.

At the beginning of the 1830s, the attention of government and political circles in Britain was focused on demands for parliamentary reform which culminated in the Reform Act of 1832. The hectic political activity on the issue of reform in England coincided with consultations over the renewal of the EIC's charter by Parliament. The charter came up for renewal in 1833. The directors were busy mobilizing support for retaining some of their privileges in the new charter.

The Company's influence had steadily declined as the Lancashire cotton lobby, which had powered England's Industrial Revolution, began to have a bigger say in policymaking. It was difficult to resist the pressure to end the EIC's monopoly of the China trade, all the more so as ideas of free trade had begun to gain wide acceptance. Nevertheless, the patronage that directors could dispense due to the hold they had over appointments in India was an important privilege and worth fighting for. Appointments in the civil and military establishment in India were made exclusively on the basis of recommendations by the directors, each director being allotted an annual quota for nominating writers and cadets. Moreover, the actual governance of the empire was still in the hands of the Court of Directors. Since the charters provided the framework for governing the British empire in India, the provisions of the upcoming charter were a matter of vital concern for the Company's authorities in London.

The Charter Act of 1833 abolished the Company's monopoly of trade with China—its only remaining monopoly after 1813–14 when it had lost the monopoly over trade with India. The act also made changes in the composition and functioning of the governor-general's council. Law-making powers of the council were enhanced, and it was to have a member drawn from the legal profession in Britain to assist it in the making of laws. Thomas Macaulay was the first 'law member' of the new council. His initial meeting with Bentinck took place at the hill station of Ootacamund (Ooty) in June 1834, towards the close of Bentinck's tenure.

Bentinck had been camping at Ootacamund to direct military operations against the kingdom of Coorg situated to the west of Mysore. Coorg was annexed in April. A few years before the annexation of Coorg, the administration of Mysore had been taken over by the EIC in 1831. This amounted to annexation all but in name. The Wodeyar ruler of Mysore merely had a ceremonial presence for the next fifty years, while the actual administration was in the hands of colonial officials headed by a commissioner with wide-ranging powers. The annexation of Coorg took place shortly after Bentinck had taken over as commander-in-chief in 1833, a position he was to hold until the end of his tenure as governor-general. This was a continuation of a long military career, the highlight of which had been his command of British forces in the Mediterranean in the closing years of the Napoleonic Wars. Standard textbook accounts usually avoid mention of Bentinck's 'peaceful' annexations or his military career.

Bentinck belonged to one of the most powerful aristocratic families of England. His father, the Duke of Portland, had become prime minister in 1783. We have seen that Portland formally headed the Fox–North coalition of 1783. The coalition ministry had introduced an India Bill, which was rejected by the House of Lords through the intervention of George III, providing the king with an excuse to dismiss the ministry (see Chapter III). Portland was again prime minister from 1807–1809. William, the second son of the duke, opted for a military career when he came of age. He joined the army in 1791 and was a colonel by 1798. His father's influence, along with the extensive Portland family network, helped to accelerate his subsequent elevation to positions of authority.

In 1803, he managed to obtain the governorship of the Madras presidency at the unusually young age of twenty-nine. The duke saw this as a stepping stone to Bentinck's governor-generalship: 'In April 1802 his father... applied to Addington [prime minister, 1801–1804] to make Bentinck governor of Madras, "with a view to his succeeding at a proper time to the government general [sic.] of India".[27] There was nothing unusual in a prominent aristocratic father seeking favours for his son. The political realignments of the 1790s and early 1800s in Britain, in the wake of the French Revolution, created conditions in which such a request would have been acceded to with more alacrity than otherwise.

Ideological differences over the French Revolution had brought about a split among the Whigs in the early 1790s. Portland was the key organizational figure of the Whig parliamentarians in the last quarter of the eighteenth century and controlled the electoral machinery of the Whigs. The Whig 'party' was a 'party in that it had a common historical myth, common memories of struggles waged together [against the unrestrained power of the Crown], some kind of understood common attitudes, and an organization advanced for its time. It was also, much more than any late nineteenth- or twentieth-century party, an association of magnates and connections bound by ties of friendship and kin'.[28]

The Whig faction led by Portland joined hands with Pitt, who had emerged as a vehement opponent of the French Revolution and its principles. The alliance with Pitt implied support for a policy of offensive war against France in collaboration with reactionary regimes of Europe, and measures to quell radical tendencies at home. Pitt, for his part, needed the cooperation of the Portland Whigs, and it is not surprising that he helped the duke in getting the appointment for his son, even though he was not the prime minister at that moment.

Bentinck assumed office at a time when, with the partitioning of Tipu's kingdom, the process of integrating substantial recent additions to the presidency had just gotten underway. There

---

[27]R. G. Thorne (ed.), 'William Cavendish Bentinck', *The History of Parliament: The House of Commons 1790-1820*, London: Secker & Warburg, 1986.
[28]John Rosselli, *Lord William Bentinck: The Making of a Liberal Imperialist, 1774-1839*, Delhi: Thompson Press, 1974, p. 41.

was widespread discontent against the Company in Tamil Nadu and other parts of southern India. A number of local military chiefs—the Palaiyakkarars or Poligars—in central and southern Tamil Nadu, seriously challenged the EIC's authority from the late 1790s onwards. The military campaigns against these chiefs, known as the Poligar Wars, began in 1799 and continued till 1805 when the resistance of the anti-British Poligars was finally crushed.

The final stages of the Poligar Wars overlapped with the outbreak of a major mutiny in the Madras Army, which at this time was the largest of the three military formations of the Company, the other two being the Bengal Army and the Bombay Army. The displacement caused by the wars against Mysore, together with the disbanding of Tipu's large army, were the major underlying factors for the rebellion of Indian soldiers of the Madras Army in 1806. Sympathy for Tipu's family, both within and outside the army, intensified the anti-British sentiment prevailing in Tamil Nadu and the Malabar Coast. The latter was among the catchment areas for the recruitment of soldiers in the Company's army. The most efficient soldiers of the Mysore army had been absorbed by the EIC, and some of the rebels belonged to these recently inducted units.

Tipu's family was incarcerated in Vellore Fort after 1799. In the aftermath of the mutiny, which began on the night of 9/10 July 1806, members of the family were accused of having incited the Mysore sipahis of the Vellore garrison to rebel. One of Tipu's sons, Muiz-ud-din—who, it may be recalled, was one of the hostages who had been handed over to the British fourteen years earlier—was singled out as the main culprit. Subsequent research has established that neither Muiz-ud-din nor other members of the family had anything to do with the mutiny directly.

British officers stationed in the fort were attacked by the mutineers, and, in the fierce fighting that went on for several hours, heavy casualties were sustained by both sides. The British were able to overpower the Vellore rebels with enormous difficulty, with the arrival of European and Indian troops from neighbouring Arcot.

The reinforcements despatched from Arcot were commanded by Rollo Gillespie, who was later killed in the Nepal war. The soldiers under Gillespie suppressed the uprising ruthlessly. Several hundred rebels were massacred, and a larger number of non-combatant civilians were killed. Many of the rebels were pursued into the countryside, captured, and summarily executed by being blown from guns.

The operations extended to the other side of the peninsula, including the Malabar Coast. As late as November 1806, British officers of the subsidiary force stationed in Travancore were disarming and restraining Muslim soldiers under their command.

Tipu's family was banished to Bengal. Muiz-ud-Din was incarcerated in Calcutta, while other members of the family were dumped in an inhospitable location on the outskirts of the city and abandoned to a miserable fate.

An enquiry commission was set up soon after the mutiny had been suppressed, to investigate its causes and how the Madras government had responded to the crisis. The commission submitted its report in August. The report is our main source for reconstructing the events of 9–10 July 1806. The commission identified two causes of the mutiny, one of which was resentment over modifications in the sipahis' uniform, the second being the encouragement offered by the presence of Tipu's family in the fort.

Upon reviewing the report, the Court of Directors criticised Bentinck for failing to ascertain the views of the sipahis before going ahead with changes in their dress and appearance. The review concluded by censuring the Madras governor in severe terms: 'After weighing all the considerations connected with the business of Vellore, we felt ourselves unable any longer to continue that confidence to him which is so necessary for a person holding his situation to possess.'[29]

---

[29]W. J. Wilson (comp.), *History of the Madras Army*, Vol. 3, Chennai: Government Press, 1883, p. 200.

Bentinck was recalled. The commander-in-chief of the Madras Army, J. F. Cradock, too, was removed from his post. After his return to England, Bentinck made a representation to the Court of Directors in which he defended his conduct, conveying to it the humiliation he had experienced upon learning of their remarks: 'The mutiny at Vellore cannot be attributed to me directly or indirectly ... My dismissal was effected in a manner harsh and mortifying, and the forms which custom has prescribed to soften the severity of a misfortune at all events sufficiently severe were on this single occasion violated, as if for the express purpose of deepening my disgrace.'[30]

The court responded in 1809 by reiterating its position. There is a possibility that by promptly recalling Bentinck in 1807, the directors wished to pre-empt any move to promote him to the position of governor-general. Portland had taken over as prime minister for a second time at the end of March 1807; the directors' order for his son's dismissal is dated 15 April. It was known that the father 'hoped to foist him on the company directors as governor-general'. In any case, William 'had hoped to stay in that country until 1812 and make £100,000'.[31]

Bentinck resumed his military service upon returning home. He participated in campaigns of the Peninsular War, especially the Battle of Corunna in Spain (January 1809), in which the British were defeated and had to retreat before the French army. Thereafter, he was in England for two years. In 1811, he was sent to command British troops in Sicily (Richard Wellesley was foreign secretary at this time).

The large island of Sicily, in the Mediterranean, ruled by the Bourbon dynasty of Naples—which was a branch of the Bourbons of Spain—came under British 'protection' during the conflict with France. This was to pre-empt the French occupation of Sicily. In 1806 the king of Naples, Ferdinand IV, was forced to withdraw to Sicily when Napoleon's army

---

[30]Demetrius G. Boulger, *Lord William Bentinck*, Oxford: Clarendon Press, 1892, pp. 37–38.
[31]Thorne, 'William Cavendish Bentinck', *The History of Parliament*.

invaded the kingdom's territories on the mainland, declaring the end of Bourbon rule. British naval strength in the Mediterranean prevented the French from taking over the strategically located island. The Bourbon court-in-exile was subsidized by the British.

London, at one point, contemplated formal annexation of Sicily. A minister was posted by Britain in the capital, Palermo, and was the de facto governor of the island. Lord Amherst, later Bentinck's predecessor as governor-general in India, was also his predecessor as British minister in Sicily. When Amherst resigned in 1810, he was replaced by Bentinck, who was appointed commander-in-chief as well. The latter post made him commander of the British forces in the Mediterranean.

During his stay in Sicily, Bentinck attempted, on his own initiative, to make Sicily a constitutional monarchy. The experiment failed, leading to his removal in 1815. Before his recall, he had intervened in the affairs of several Italian states on the mainland, and in Sardinia, which caused much unease in London. These actions hastened his recall; he returned to England ten days before Waterloo.

For the next twelve years, Bentinck was in the political wilderness. He continued to lobby for the governor-generalship of India, which seems to have become the main ambition of his life. An opportunity to go to India did come his way in 1819 when the Court of Directors offered to nominate him governor of the Madras presidency a second time. This was the most coveted post in the EIC's empire in India after that of the governor-general. It was, therefore, difficult for Bentinck to dismiss the offer outright. He informed the court that he would be willing to accept the appointment on the condition that he was also made the commander-in-chief of the Madras Army. Canning, as the president of the Board of Control, was firmly against giving him both posts, notwithstanding that the directors were prepared to make the concession. The process of negotiation that preceded appointments of leading colonial administrators and military commanders is often overlooked in much of the historiography on British rule in India.

When the imminent departure of Moira necessitated a fresh nomination in 1822, Bentinck lobbied hard for the post of governor-general. As he had recently aligned himself with opponents of the government in Parliament, Liverpool was averse to making him governor-general. Canning, in a surprise move, given his standing in Parliament and British politics, was himself on the verge of proceeding to Calcutta as governor-general. He had been appointed to the post in March 1822. He gave up the idea of going to India when he was requested to become secretary of state for foreign affairs in Liverpool's ministry following the suicide, in August 1822, of the incumbent foreign minister, Lord Castlereagh. Canning relinquished his governor-generalship in September. Amherst was given the post. Bentinck was accommodated in the establishment attached to Canning.

In his biography of Bentinck, John Rosselli notes that the situation for him was quite bleak at this time since 'he had no job, no fortune, no fixed residence'; 'he was childless and deep in debt'.[32] His desperation accounts for the persistence with which he pursued the goal of obtaining the governor-generalship. For younger members of the aristocracy, the top job in India was one way of overcoming financial distress.

Liverpool's resignation in February 1827, due to a stroke, created a vacuum, and a new government was formed in April with Canning as prime minister. The formation of the Canning ministry coincided with the end of Amherst's tenure. In his search for Amherst's successor, Canning approached, one after the other, five potential nominees, none of whom was willing to go to India. As a last resort, he offered the post to Bentinck. Had the vacancy occurred before Liverpool suffered a stroke, or under Wellington, who became prime minister the following year, the appointment would most certainly have been denied to him.

---

[32]Rosselli, *Lord William Bentinck*, pp. 101 and 103.

Canning's death in August, after being in office for about four months, and the resignation of his successor Lord Goderich—whose son, Lord Ripon, became governor-general in the early 1880s—brought Wellington to the office. Wellington disliked Bentinck due to differences which dated back to the Peninsular War. It was fortunate for Bentinck that the decision was made before Canning's death. The directors accorded their approval, with only one member of the court voting against Bentinck. The new governor-general was on his way to India by February 1828.

After a preliminary residence in Calcutta for the first two years of his tenure, Bentinck spent the next two and a half years travelling in northern India, retreating to Simla each summer. Bentinck's annual sojourn in the hills marks the beginning of the colonial tradition in British India of moving to mountain locales in the hot weather, for which purpose 'hill-stations' were specifically developed in the latter half of the nineteenth century. Simla emerged as the imperial summer capital in the 1880s. Ootacamund, in the Nilgiri Mountains, was Bentinck's favoured retreat in the south; this would become the summer capital of the Madras government.

During the governor-general's long absence from Calcutta, the administrative work was handled by Charles Metcalfe, who was now a senior member of the council, making him a powerful figure. Metcalfe was the acting governor-general for a year before Lord Auckland assumed office. The Court of Directors was displeased that Bentinck should be away from Calcutta continuously for so long and function alone, without his council. The council was supposed to act as a check on the governor-general's authority. Bentinck, on the other hand, justified his absence by emphasizing the unsuitability of Calcutta as the seat of government given the vast territorial extent that the EIC's empire had acquired by the 1820s. He advocated shifting the seat of government, along with the council, to a suitable place in northern India, or a central location in the Company's domain, such as Aurangabad 'which

Aurangzeb once contemplated as his seat of empire'.[33]

Between 1829 and 1833, he carried on a lengthy correspondence with the Court of Directors on the subject of permanently transferring the seat of government out of Calcutta. All his proposals were turned down.

There is a legend that Bentinck, while he was undertaking his north Indian tour, visited the Taj Mahal while passing through Agra in 1831. He is supposed to have sanctioned the sale of the monument during his stopover. The main source for this story is a report in the newspaper *John Bull* published from Calcutta. *John Bull* had a large readership among British soldiers stationed in India, carrying stories that were of particular interest to them. The story in question is dated 26 July 1831. An extract from it was reproduced by the travel writer Fanny Parkes in her well-known travelogue *Wanderings of a Pilgrim, In Search of the Picturesque* (1850). According to the report:

> The Governor-General has sold the beautiful piece of architecture, called the Mootee Musjid, at Agra, for 125,000 rupees, ... and it is now being pulled down! The taj has also been offered for sale! But the price required has not been obtained. Two lacs, however, have been offered for it. Should the taj be pulled down, it is rumoured that disturbances may take place amongst the natives. If this be true, is it not shameful? ... By what authority does the Governor-General offer the taj for sale? Has he any right to molest the dead? To sell the tomb raised over an empress, which, from its extraordinary beauty is the wonder of the world? It is impossible the Court of Directors can sanction the sale of the tomb for the sake of its marble and gems.[34]

[33]'Letter of John Malcolm, 28 September 1830', C. H. Philips (ed.), *The Correspondence of William Cavendish Bentinck*, Vol. 1, Oxford: Oxford University Press, 1977, p. 517.
[34]Fanny Parkes (Parks), *Wanderings of a Pilgrim, In Search of the Picturesque*,

Oddly, the extract is inserted by Parkes in a description of the sacred sites of Allahabad, where she was residing in 1831, and follows a passage about her exploration of rare plants and flowers in and around that town. She gives no context; neither does she offer any comment.

In an article published in 1949, Percival Spear scrutinized the available evidence relating to Bentinck's scheme for disposing of the Taj.[35] Other than the report in *John Bull,* as reproduced in Parkes's journal, there is no reference to such a scheme in any contemporary source. The rumour had its origin in the sale of some marble from one of the royal baths in the Agra Fort, the details of which need not detain us.

Spear is of the view that the rumour was spread by disgruntled soldiers whose allowances had recently been withdrawn by the Company's government, which made the governor-general very unpopular. The version in *John Bull* might have been an attempt to give a sensational twist to gossip among troops in Agra, which substituted the marble in the Fort with the Taj Mahal. It must be seen as an expression of their resentment.[36] If at all there was such a plan, nothing was heard of it any further.

Bentinck's willingness to intervene energetically in some social and religious matters selectively, to bring to the subjects of the Company some of the accomplishments of modern Western civilization, made him, in the eyes of ideologues of empire and activists in Britain as well as a vocal section of the elite in India, a different sort of administrator—an ideal governor-general whose actions ought to have served as a model for his successors.

Vol. 1, London: Pelham Richardson, 1850, p. 220.

[35]Percival Spear, 'Bentinck and the Taj', *Journal of the Royal Asiatic Society of Great Britain and Ireland*, No. 2, 1949, pp. 180–87.

[36]I am not aware of any recently published research questioning Spear's conclusions. On the other hand, the story remains in circulation, reinforced by numerous posts on the internet which continue to repeat the tale of Bentinck's proposal to dismantle the monument and auction its marble.

One of his initiatives, the abolition of sati, has since been regarded by a wide range of opinion as marking a crucial step in the direction of reforming Indian society during the colonial period.[37] The agenda for such reform was set by the colonial state, and colonial officials and ideologues defined what constituted modernity. In turn, their understanding of what had to be reformed, and how to go about it, was shaped by ideas and movements in the metropole, as well as arguments of the intelligentsia in India on these issues. The diversity of indigenous positions on various social and religious questions might have necessitated compromises or, as happened very frequently, led to the privileging of one point of view over another.

We need to bear in mind that the process of codifying and institutionalizing sacred texts—identified by pandits and qazis selected by the EIC's establishment for the purpose of handling litigation in the Company's courts—was an ongoing one since the 1770s. The question of sati had come to the forefront at the turn of the century.

In 1805, during Cornwallis's second tenure as governor-general, the Nizamat Adalat in Calcutta, the provincial court for criminal cases, formally sought opinion on the 'practice' from a pandit attached to the Adalat. The pandit, Ghanshyam Surmono (Sharma), stated in his response that the rite was sanctioned by scripture, subject to it being voluntary. Strictly speaking, it was not mandated, but it was allowed by the scriptures because the woman who performs the action earns great spiritual merit.

It took the government nearly seven years to issue directives based on this opinion. According to the instructions, sati was not to be interfered with, unless it was being performed under coercion or if the widow was pregnant or had a child under three years of age. Every immolation required the presence of a

---

[37]Sati refers to the immolation ('self-immolation') of a widow, and to the woman who immolates herself on the funeral pyre of the dead husband.

magistrate, who was to record all the details and communicate them to the Nizamat Adalat.

Subsequently, instructions were issued in 1815 for compiling data pertaining to sati. Over the next thirteen years, 8,134 instances of sati were recorded. The interpretation of scripture in favour of sati did not go unchallenged from a section of the intelligentsia, which opposed the practice, and cited texts to substantiate their interpretation. Rammohun Roy (1772–1833) was the main spokesperson of the section in Bengal that vehemently opposed sati.

The enactment of Regulation XVII of 1829 (Bengal Code), which outlawed sati, has been hailed as the single most important achievement of the Bentinck regime. At an individual level, Bentinck's espousal of the abolition cause was critical for the legislation. Rammohun Roy had been mobilizing public opinion through his writings on the issue, which began to appear in 1818. Whereas Bentinck's predecessors had been unwilling to interfere with the custom so as not to appear to be meddling in the sphere of religion—something that the EIC was quite wary of—Bentinck decided to go ahead with criminalizing the practice. Roy's support was invaluable for countering the anti-abolition lobby.

Nationalist narratives of social reform in the nineteenth century, and the contribution of Indians to it, usually commence with the campaign against sati, the abolition of which is represented as the outcome of the efforts of social reformers in Bengal, led by Rammohun. The image of Rammohun teaming up with Bentinck to put an end to the inhuman practice has endured. This is the way textbooks tell the story of this defining moment. The initiative would endear Bentinck to nationalists, and would make Rammohun an icon of the crusade for women's emancipation in the twentieth century.

The complete eradication of the practice has been one of the issues on the agenda of the struggle for women's rights in independent India, as incidents of sati have taken place from time to time in some parts of the country after 1947.

The persistence of the practice was highlighted by a case of sati in 1987 in Rajasthan—the infamous burning of Roop Kanwar in the village of Deorala. This was among the last few known occurrences of the practice after Independence and led to massive mobilization by progressive women's organizations throughout India against sati as well as its glorification. These protests forced the government to enact comprehensive legislation criminalizing the practice, with stringent punishment for those responsible for abetting sati or coercing the victim.

Thus, Bentinck can be seen as a colonial administrator aligned with a progressive cause. The Deorala case also aroused considerable scholarly interest in debates on widow immolation during the colonial period. Several insightful writings on the subject began to appear in the 1980s, a small number of which were published before the Deorala tragedy—for instance, Lata Mani's well-known article on the production of an 'official discourse' on sati in the early nineteenth century (1985). Lata Mani argues that the encounters through which knowledge about colonial society was produced, based on certain shared assumptions of British policymakers and a section of the native intelligentsia, created a specific understanding of sati that focused on interpreting sacred texts. Opponents of sati and those who defended it, both argued by appealing to tradition, and colonial officials who were in favour of abolition insisted that they were upholding tradition.

The article was the first of several path-breaking essays by Lata Mani, which were followed by her influential work *Contentious Traditions* (1998).[38] As Rammohun and his allies saw it, sati had to be done away with because it was not sanctioned by scripture. Religious texts, according to them, emphasized ascetic widowhood; they did not prescribe sati.

---

[38]Lata Mani, 'Production of an Official Discourse on *Sati* in Early Nineteenth Century Bengal', Francis Barker et al. (eds.), *Europe and its Others*, Vol. 1, Colchester: University of Essex, 1985, pp. 107–27; Lata Mani, *Contentious Traditions: The Debate on Sati in Colonial India*, New Delhi: Oxford University Press, 1998.

Opponents of the practice did not put forth their case by arguing that sati was immoral or that immolation was horrific and extremely painful. In other words, 'the debate centers not on women, but on questions of scriptural interpretation'.[39]

Further, the abolition of sati was intended to assess the extent to which it might be possible for the colonial state to interfere in what were perceived to be religious matters, hitherto kept outside its purview. In her critique of some aspects of Lata Mani's study, Andrea Major contends that the abolition issue cannot be viewed in isolation, ignoring the intellectual milieu of contemporary Britain.[40]

Another problem with the study is that it is narrowly focused on Bengal, where, too, it concentrates on official perceptions and how they were formed, overlooking popular opinions as well as variations in customs within and outside Bengal. Popular perceptions and variations in the practice influenced, and were influenced by, official narratives.

Changes in attitudes towards suicide, insanity, and bodily pain at the beginning of the nineteenth century against the backdrop of social transformations brought about by the Industrial Revolution, determined British reactions in the metropole to reports of burning of widows. In order to comprehend how the debate unfolded, we need to pay attention to ideas prevalent both in Britain and in India, and their linkages at the specific historical juncture when the issue began to intrude upon the consciousness of colonial ideologues and policymakers.

For instance, attitudes towards suicide had undergone a significant change during the eighteenth century, paving the way for legislation in the early 1820s, which did away with the severity with which the state had dealt with such cases earlier. Traditionally, suicide was a grave sin from a religious point of view, and a monstrous crime in the eyes of the law, amounting

---

[39]Lata Mani, *Contentious Traditions*, p. 72.
[40]Andrea Major, *Pious Flames: European Encounters with Sati, 1500-1800*, New Delhi: Oxford University Press, 2006.

to self-killing of a king's subject. The dead body could not be interred in consecrated ground, and the property of the deceased was confiscated by the monarch. During the eighteenth century, there was increasingly a tendency to ascribe the act to the loss of sanity. As the person who had committed suicide was regarded as not having been in his senses momentarily, the harsh provisions for punishing the act were diluted somewhat by the Burial of Suicide Act of 1823 in Britain. Under the act, the deceased could, with some restrictions, be buried in a churchyard.

The intense debate over suicide, and the 1823 legislation, had implications for the question of sati. Sati, or rather 'voluntary' immolation, was equated with suicide. The enormous British interest in, and fascination with, sati towards the end of the eighteenth century and in the first two decades of the nineteenth century, was the outcome of an intense preoccupation with 'self-destruction' at a time when new laws about suicide were being enacted. Major remarks that, 'it may be possible ... to understand the early nineteenth-century obsession with sati as reflecting a desire to both debate and displace the delicate issue of suicide, as fascination with sati mirrored preoccupation with the self-destruction of British men and (more particularly) women at home'.[41] And the debate on sati had a bearing on British attitudes towards suicide as an ethical and legal question.

Rammohun Roy recognized that consistent propaganda was indispensable for countering the campaign of the anti-abolition lobby, which continued with full vigour even after the 1829 law. He published a brief tract in 1830 entitled *Abstract of the Arguments Regarding the Burning of Widows, Considered as a Religious Rite,* outlining the key arguments for the abolition of sati, and also drafted a petition addressed to the House of Commons, urging it to disregard the move by spokespersons of conservative and reactionary elements to have the law annulled.

---

[41]Major, *Pious Flames*, p. 160.

Rammohun's 1830 tract was written in response to a representation made to Bentinck by opponents of abolition. When the plea was rejected by Bentinck, anti-abolition activists formally filed an appeal before the privy council in London challenging the 1829 law. The privy council was the highest appellate court of the United Kingdom, and hence for the Company's territories. A recently formed organization in Bengal, the Dharma Sabha, had filed an appeal against the ban. Radhakanta Deb was the moving spirit of the Sabha.[42] He belonged to a wealthy landed family in Calcutta, which was closely aligned with the EIC since the days of Clive. He was one of the prominent figures of Bengali society who worked to thwart the efforts of those engaged in agitating for the abolition of sati.

The Dharma Sabha hired a Calcutta-based lawyer named Francis Bathie to file the appeal. Bathie enlisted the services of the well-known barrister and legal luminary, Stephen Lushington—otherwise a supporter of progressive causes such as the abolition of slavery—to argue the case before the council. Rammohun Roy was then in England and was invited by the Lord President of the Council to attend the proceedings in the case. Even though Rammohun had no role to play in the judicial process related to the appeal, he was present at all the three hearings in the case. The appeal was contested by the Company's legal team. The proceedings commenced in the last week of June 1832, ending with the appeal being dismissed in the second week of July.

Among the nine privy councillors who decided on the appeal was Bentinck's immediate predecessor Lord Amherst, who during his tenure had refrained from intervening in the matter. He, along with three other councillors, voted against the abolition, so that

---

[42]The brief outline of the history of the appeal which follows, is based mainly on Suzanne A. Blunn, 'Sati and its Abolition in British Social and Political Discourses c. 1832–1895', unpublished Ph.D. thesis, Birkbeck, University of London, 2024, pp. 34–75. Blunn's study devotes considerable space to the appeal and its outcome, and is the only detailed discussion of it in the extensive literature on the 1829 law.

the appeal was rejected by a narrow majority of one (four against and five for dismissal of the appeal). On the other hand, the consensus within political circles in Britain by the early 1830s was in favour of abolition. Amherst and two other members who had voted for rejecting the law, did not, however, agree to a proposal for suspending its implementation. Nor did Bathie's memorial on behalf of the appellants to the King-in Council in 1833, 'imploring your Majesty to condescend to grant some gracious assurance of your Majesty's determination to preserve from aggression or interference the religion of your Majesty's Hindoo subjects', bring any relief.[43]

Rammohun Roy's presence in London when the privy council took up the Dharma Sabha's appeal was a coincidence. He had travelled to England primarily to carry out a task assigned to him by the Mughal emperor. He had been sent by Akbar Shah as his official envoy to George IV to apprize the British monarch of the EIC's breach of faith in not adhering to the commitment it had made in 1765 to render to the imperial treasury the annual peshkash of twenty-six lakh rupees as the emperor's share of the revenues of Bengal, Bihar, and Orissa. As we have seen, Hastings had discontinued the remittance in the 1770s. When the Company took over the civil and military management of Delhi in 1803, it resumed partial payment of the peshkash, amounting to ₹11 lakh per annum. Shah Alam was assured that this was a provisional arrangement and that once the financial situation improved with the cessation of hostilities of the Second Anglo–Maratha War, the sum would be enhanced.

The war with the Marathas was more specifically against Yashwant Rao Holkar after 1803. For several years after the war, the EIC prevaricated, and by the late 1820s, had reneged on its commitment. Akbar Shah had pursued the matter vigorously since his accession.

---

[43]Jatindra Kumar Majumdar (ed.), *Raja Rammohun Roy and Progressive Movements in India: A Selection from Records (1775-1845)*, Calcutta: Art Press, 1941, p. 281.

The willingness to deviate from Mughal court protocol in 1827, when the emperor allowed Amherst to be seated in his presence, was actuated by his wish to resolve the issue. Amherst, however, was not inclined to recommend an increase in the peshkash. The governor-general's position was that the sum paid to the emperor was merely an allowance for his maintenance and had nothing to do with the Bengal peshkash. Sixty years after the grant of diwani, it was easy to pretend that there was no commitment on the part of the Company to remit the sum of twenty-six lakh rupees annually to the emperor as the imperial share of the revenues of the eastern provinces.

Once it became known that Amherst was not inclined to recommend an increase in the peshkash, Akbar Shah's advisors persuaded him to send an emissary to London to acquaint the British monarch with the Company's refusal to meet its obligations, enshrined in documents, towards the emperor. As the primary overlord of the Company, the British monarch was expected to discipline its officials. The name of Rammohun Roy, who at this time did not have the title of 'Raja', was put forth for the mission.

The proposal was given concrete shape by a prominent official at the court, Khwaja Farid (Khwaja Fariduddin Ahmad Khan), who persuaded Rammohun Roy to undertake the responsibility. Khwaja Farid was a maternal uncle of (Sir) Syed Ahmad Khan. Rammohun's family had been connected with the Mughal court for at least two generations. While summoning Rammohun to Delhi in 1828, the emperor made it a point to refer to services rendered to Shah Alam by Rammohun's grandfather, Brajabinod.

Rammohun was formally designated *elchi*—envoy, a Turco-Mongol word frequently used for a representative engaged in peace negotiations. As befitting his new status, the title of 'Raja' was conferred on him. Henceforth, he was known as Raja Rammohun Roy, though the Bentinck administration disputed the emperor's right to bestow the title. Rammohun astutely turned around the meaning of the conferment of the title, arguing that an envoy to the British monarch's court could not be a mere commoner.

Rammohun Roy arrived in England in April 1831. The Company's officials were, as might have been expected, hostile to him, but he had a circle of admirers among whom he was highly regarded as a celebrated scholar and social reformer. He was received with respect by an influential section of opinion-makers in England. Rammohun was able to meet the king, George IV's successor William IV (1830–37), and present Akbar Shah's epistle addressed to George IV. The letter had been drafted while George IV, who passed away in June 1830, was still on the throne. Rammohun departed for England in November, before news about the accession of the new king could have reached India. He was an invitee at the coronation ceremony of William IV held in September 1831.

The Company's hostility and the refusal of its London headquarters to officially inform Rammohun of the outcome of the directors' deliberations about the peshkash, left him in a state of despair. For over a year, he was unsure about where he stood with regard to the claim. Michael Fisher observes that 'despite his social prominence, publications, and successful public lectures, sermons, and private dialogues, he became despondent and ill over his slighted treatment by the directors, and by his financial difficulties'.[44]

Not that Rammohun Roy was unaware of the machinations of the EIC establishment when it came to an issue such as this. The Company fully comprehended the import of the argument set out in Akbar Shah's letter. With his knowledge of English legal terminology, Rammohun had given final shape to the letter which incorporated the Mughal emperor's understanding of his position—namely, that he was sovereign within his domain, although the Company had de facto authority. This basic premise was questioned neither by the British government nor by the directors. The acceptance of the letter, from one

---

[44]Michael H. Fisher, *Counterflows to Colonialism: Indian Travellers and Settlers in Britain, 1600-1857*, New Delhi: Permanent Black, 2004, pp. 257–59.

sovereign to another, itself amounted to a recognition of the Mughal emperor's status.

In his letter, Akbar Shah addressed the British monarch as 'My Brother,' declaring at the outset that he was writing to him 'with the language of fraternal equality'.[45] Mindful of his sovereign status, he stated in the concluding paragraph: 'I will not condescend to accept, and Your Majesty will disdain to confer as a favour that which is due as a right.'[46]

The mission did not yield much in monetary terms. In February 1833, the directors agreed to increase the peshkash from ₹12 lakh to ₹15 lakh per annum. An additional one lakh rupees had earlier been added to the provisional 'allowance' of ₹11 lakh per annum. Rammohun Roy was disappointed with the decision and did not recommend its acceptance. Due to procrastination by the Company, and because the political focus in England at that juncture was on the Reform Bill (leading to the Reform Act of 1832) and on the EIC's charter, there was considerable delay in arriving at a decision about Akbar Shah's claim. Rammohun Roy was contemplating his future course of action (he intended to reopen negotiations on the issue) when he died in September 1833 at Bristol, leaving the question of the peshkash unsettled.

Sabyasachi Bhattacharya has pointed out that Rammohun Roy's familiarity with the English legal and political framework made it possible for him 'to put a new spin on the question in dispute', situating it in the context of international law.[47] The juridical notion that he brought to the question was that an agreement between two parties—in this case, between the emperor and the Company—did not cease to be valid merely due to the inability of one of the parties to enforce it.

---

[45]Akbar Shah to King of England, Jatindra Kumar Majumdar (ed.), *Raja Ram Mohun Roy and the Last Moghuls: A Selection from Official Records (1803-1859)*, New Delhi, 1981, p. 196.
[46]Ibid., p. 202.
[47]Sabyasachi Bhattacharya, 'The Colonial State: Theory and Practice', General President's Address, Indian History Congress, 65th Session, Bareilly, 2004, p. 16.

In his letter, Akbar Shah demanded to know whether 'I become less entitled to the performance of the contract that has been entered into with my family because my ancestors were great and powerful, and I am feeble and helpless held down by those who make my weakness and degradation the excuse for their injustice? I cherish the confident persuasion that Your Majesty will not sanction the principle that in my case a National contract ought not to be fulfilled, because I am powerless to enforce its obligations'.[48]

With Rammohun Roy removed from the scene, there were no further negotiations with the directors about royal prerogatives and the figure of ₹3 lakh was taken as final. In January 1834, Calcutta received instructions that the emperor be informed of the offer to enhance the peshkash to ₹15 lakh annually on the condition that he would renounce all further claims. Left with no other option, the emperor reluctantly agreed to the settlement.

However, there was one more hurdle to be overcome. The Company, much to the emperor's surprise, put conditions on how the additional sum could be utilized—something that Akbar Shah was unwilling to concede. The actual arrangements for the payment of the additional sum were finalized by the Calcutta authorities, who imposed these conditions. Although the modalities had been left to the governor-general and his council, the imposition of conditions must have had the tacit support of the directors, who had been hostile to the emperor all along.

The main issue now was the emperor's determination to provide a regular allowance for the heirs of Raja Rammohun Roy out of the additional sum of ₹3 lakh. A memorandum drawn up in 1837 by Roy's close friend, Dwarkanath Tagore, succinctly described some of the developments pertaining to the peshkash question since the death of Rammohun Roy. The memorandum is unsigned and undated. It seems to have been

---

[48]Akbar Shah to King of England, Majumdar (ed.), *Raja Ram Mohun Roy and the Last Moghuls*, p. 201.

written to serve as a background note for some official of the Company. The document is superscribed, in pencil, 'Memo given by Dwarkanath Thakoor, on the distribution of the allowance to the King of Delhi'.[49]

From Tagore's memo, we learn that Bentinck's office received orders about the peshkash in January 1834. It took another two years for the decision of the Court of Directors to be formally conveyed to Akbar Shah. He was requested to provide a list of beneficiaries among whom the enhanced amount would be distributed, which he transmitted in April 1836. Rammohun's sons, Radhaprasad and Ramaprasad, together were to receive ₹22,500, i.e. 7.5% of the additional sum annually: and the rest would be distributed in varying proportions among members of the royal family. The allowance set aside for Radhaprasad and Ramaprasad was in keeping with the terms on which their father's services had been engaged.

Rammohun was entitled to a fee equivalent to one half of the entire additional amount, for the first year in which an enhanced amount would be received; and thereafter to 7.5% of the additional sum (₹60,000 for every 8 lakh of increase: ₹8 lakh must have been the minimum augmentation that would have been hoped for) annually 'for ever'.[50] Akbar Shah had made a solemn commitment to his envoy; he was firm that he could not forsake Rammohun Roy's heirs.

Having agreed to enhance the peshkash (a term that the British avoided using) so reluctantly, the EIC now declined to release the additional sum if a part of it was to go 'to individuals not being members of the Royal Family and who have no claim on the bounty of the British government'.[51] By dictating to the emperor the mode of disbursal of ₹3 lakh, it was seeking to nullify the claim itself. This the emperor could

---

[49]'Memorandum', (n.d.), National Archives of India (hereafter, NAI), Foreign Department, Political (henceforth FDP), 8 May 1837, No. 25 and KW.
[50]Ibid.
[51]Government of India to Akbar Shah, Majumdar (ed.), *Raja Ram Mohun Roy and the Last Moghuls*, p. 251.

not accept unless he was prepared to surrender his sovereign rights. The peshkash issue was not just a trivial monetary matter but revolved around the question of sovereignty, since it was ultimately tied to the Bengal tribute.

Despite his financial difficulties, Akbar Shah firmly stuck to his decision. In his reply to the Delhi resident's communication of January 1837 on the subject, he declared, 'It appears ... that Roy Radhaprusad and Roy Rumaprusad, the sons of Rajah Rammohun Roy (who went to England as an Ambassader [sic.] and who departed this life while engaged in my service) shall not have a single pice .... Consequently, I refuse to take the additional allowance [peshkash]'.[52]

The EIC, too, did not relent, and this was the status of the peshkash when Akbar Shah passed away in September 1837. When Bahadur Shah became emperor, he too, like his father, rejected the conditions sought to be imposed by the Company. The issue was destined to remain unresolved till the end of the Mughal monarchy. As Percival Spear puts it, 'the increase was never actually paid, the claims were never actually abandoned'.[53] Rammohun Roy's efforts to prevail upon the government in London to intervene in this matter were to no avail.

∽

Listing the 'important reforms' initiated by Bentinck, his biographer places, next to the abolition of 'widows' self-immolation', measures to 'suppress the religiously dedicated murderers called Thags'.[54] By setting in motion operations for the suppression of thuggee from 1830 onwards, Bentinck is

---

[52]'Memorandum', (n.d.), NAI, FDP, 8 May 1837, No. 25 and KW. The resident was the representative of the EIC at the Mughal court. As head of the administration he was also the principal colonial official in Delhi. Thomas Metcalfe, brother of Charles Metcalfe, was the resident at this time.
[53]Percival Spear, *Twilight of the Mughuls*, reprinted in *The Delhi Omnibus*, New Delhi: Oxford University, 2002, p. 49.
[54]Rosselli, *Lord William Bentinck*, p. 20.

supposed to have contributed significantly by making travel on the highways safe.

The curious history of the 'discovery' of thuggee (*thagi*) by colonial officials, and of its suppression, continues to baffle historians, as it is unclear whether we possess convincing evidence of the existence of such a phenomenon. Even if we were to ignore the more sensational accounts, much of the literature on the subject, including that which approaches the problem with sobriety, is overwhelmingly in favour of conceding that thuggee did exist. The present consensus is summed up by Kim Wagner in his study on this controversial subject. According to Wagner, 'thuggee cannot simply be reduced to a colonial construction'.[55]

Colonial officials initially came across offenders called thugs in the first decade of the nineteenth century, when the EIC was in the process of establishing its authority in frontier tracts of territories acquired recently from Awadh. These tracts included the inhospitable Chambal ravines, stretching along the loosely defined border between the Sindia state and the Ceded and Conquered Provinces of the Company. It was here that an incident occurred in 1812, which set afloat rumours of the presence of a body of outlaws who came to be referred to as thugs in colonial records. Thuggee was seen as a peculiar form of banditry perpetrated by thugs. 'Thug' (*thag*) was originally one of the several terms used locally for armed retainers of landholders, and occasionally for cheats and tricksters (this is the specific sense in which it continues to be used in common parlance). In the latter sense, it did not have the sinister connotations that it was to acquire in colonial records. It is pertinent that the term was originally used interchangeably with 'sipahi', and that the Sindia state formally collected a tax from zamindars in the area, called 'sipahi jama' based upon the number of armed retainers, or thugs, inhabiting a village.

---

[55]Kim A. Wagner, *Thuggee: Banditry and the British in Nineteenth-Century India*, South Asia edition, New Delhi: Primus Books, 2014, p. 231.

In other words, they were a traditional component of rural society, where they would have been used by landed elites to discipline the peasantry. It is likely that these armed retainers occasionally engaged in highway robbery—something that is not surprising, given the protection they received from locally influential clans to which they owed their allegiance.

The 1812 episode was a straightforward case of collective resistance to the high-handedness of Company officials. It took place in the village of Sindouse (Sindaus, in the Etawah district of Uttar Pradesh). Ravines are a typical feature of the landscape within which the village is located.

Finding it difficult to extract revenue from the area, the officials attempted to subdue refractory zamindars by a show of force and deputed N. J. Halhed (not to be confused with the well-known Orientalist) for this purpose. Halhed reported that 'the *zamindars* would not agree on a revenue settlement, nor did they allow the land to be measured'.[56]

As news spread of Halhed's plan to disarm the villagers, a small party of troops accompanying him was ambushed. The party was trapped in the ravines by villagers, and a young officer was killed in the confrontation. This episode was blown out of proportion in subsequent colonial reports.

Wagner draws attention to a report of 1809 containing a reference to thugs, suggesting that, before the Sindaus episode, British officials had already begun to define the term in the way that it was to figure in later accounts: 'This ... first allusion to thuggee contains many of the elements that were later to signify the British perception of the phenomenon: the thugs were a specific "set" or group, their ancient existence, the abomination and secrecy of their practice.'[57]

These elements were put together—almost entirely on the basis of hearsay—by officials hard-pressed to find the culprit or culprits who, in 1809, had murdered four sipahis of the

---

[56]Ibid., p. 72.
[57]Ibid., p. 41.

Company's army in Etawah. There seems to have been no proper enquiry: neither were the bodies examined systematically nor was the manner of killing established with any certainty. Yet an elaborate story about thugs was put into circulation without any evidence.

The murderers were elusive and could not be apprehended. Then in 1810, some culprits alleged to be thugs were taken into custody for the crime. One of the suspects, a sixteen-year-old boy, was made to turn approver. His testimony provided a few details that confirmed the existence of thuggee in the form outlined in the 1809 report. The testimony was considered to be of no value by the sessions court, and later by the Nizamat Adalat, due to its lack of consistency. Nevertheless, the testimony added to the growing thuggee archive, so that by the time a major operation for the elimination of thuggee was launched in the early 1830s, the colonial stereotype of the thug was well established and easily recognizable.

The campaign was directed by W.H. Sleeman, a military officer posted in the Sagar–Jabalpur area (in present-day Madhya Pradesh). As 'general superintendent for suppression of thug associations', Sleeman greatly magnified many of the features of this stereotype, making out the thug to be a bloodthirsty, vicious, cruel, and ruthless creature who murdered habitually. The mystery and elaborate ritual attributed to the thugs as members of a well-knit secret society of highway robbers-cum-assassins, whose tentacles extended to large parts of the subcontinent, were Sleeman's special contributions to the image of the thug.

A few of his embellishments, such as the humbug about the secret language or unique argot of the thugs, 'Ramasee', on which he proclaimed himself to be an expert, rendered the phenomenon of thuggee so bizarre as to be understood only in terms of an Orientalist fantasy.[58] Wagner notes that 'Sleeman

---

[58]W. H. Sleeman, *Ramaseeana, Or a Vocabulary of the Peculiar Language Used by the Thugs*, Calcutta: Military Orphan Press, 1836.

consistently emphasized the more exotic and sensational aspects of thuggee'. His frantic despatches, emphasizing the enormity of the conspiracy, proved useful to him for advancing his career.

Ultimately, Sleeman advanced his career by unleashing a reign of terror, especially in central India (he had his headquarters at Sagar and later at Jabalpur). He was made superintendent of a newly created 'Thuggee and Dacoity Department', enjoying almost unlimited powers. Sleeman's propagandist endeavours played an important role in convincing the Calcutta authorities of the need to set up such a department, with a large staff consisting of informers, special police, and mounted troops. The draconian provisions of Act XXX of 1836 ('For the Trial and Punishment of Thugs'), which allowed colonial officials to incarcerate anyone on suspicion of being a thug, led to thousands of innocent persons being put behind bars without any hope of ever being released. Strangely, the act did not define thuggee. Sleeman and his minions became adept at assembling testimonies of approvers—the only evidence they could ever produce—to punish suspects. Within a few years, it was announced that thuggee had been eradicated. The department itself remained in existence till the beginning of the twentieth century.

In view of the want of any independent authentication of the testimonies of approvers, or any evidence that cannot eventually be traced back to a tiny group of bureaucrats— posted mainly in the relatively more inaccessible tracts lying between the Chambal and Narmada Rivers, including officials of the department—one is compelled to regard thuggee as an invention of a group of functionaries of the colonial state.

This does not mean that crime, banditry, and highway robbery did not exist in those areas in which alleged thugs are supposed to have operated, or that the stereotype had no basis whatsoever. Stewart Gordon, in an essay that is one of the most insightful contributions to our understanding of the phenomenon, considers thug gangs to be 'locally-organized, small-scale marauding groups (given the name "Thugs" by the

British)', which in the writings of Sleeman became 'a hideous, widespread religious conspiracy'.[59]

In the period following the Second Anglo–Maratha War, and more so after the Third Anglo–Maratha war, the EIC was engaged in consolidating its vastly expanded empire, which now included large parts of central India. Radhika Singha has forcefully argued that consolidation necessitated dealing appropriately with 'men of the road'. The sheer diversity of wanderers that Singha catalogues in her study of thuggee, namely— 'mendicants, peripatetic professions, bands who frequented forest zones or the fringes of cultivation'—is an indication of the possibility of using the label of thug for disciplining a wide range of itinerant communities. These communities 'seemed to elude the reach of taxation and policing; their way of life was considered motley and suspect'.[60] Historically, the significance of the Bentinck era lies in the strengthening of the authority of the colonial state, greatly extending its reach, reinforced by changes in the legal framework, which enhanced the ability to enforce the state's authority ruthlessly.

By 1833–34 Bentinck's failing health had made it difficult for him to carry on his work as governor-general. He tendered his resignation and departed for home in March 1835. For a year after his departure, Charles Metcalfe officiated as governor-general. At the beginning of 1836, Lord Auckland took over. His tenure inaugurated a period of territorial expansion on a massive scale, lasting till the early 1850s. The widespread dislocation caused by the expansion became one of the main factors in the mass upheaval of 1857.

---

[59]Stewart Gordon, 'Scarf and Sword: Thugs, Marauders, and State-formation in 18th Century Malwa', *The Indian Economic and Social History Review*, Vol. 6, No. 4, 1969, p. 149.

[60]Radhika Singha, *A Despotism of Law: Crime and Justice in Early Colonial India*, New Delhi: Oxford University Press, 1998, p. 186.

VII

DALHOUSIE AND THE QUEST
FOR GLORY

The brief biography of Lord Dalhousie by Hunter, in the *Rulers of India* series, published in 1894, has the title, *The Marquess of Dalhousie and the Final Development of the Company's Rule*. This was one of two short volumes that Hunter contributed to the series, the other being a biography of Lord Mayo, governor-general from 1869 to 1872.[1] Mayo's tenure was cut short by his assassination during a tour to the Andamans.

In 1875, Hunter had published a two-volume biography of Mayo, to whose patronage he attributed the rapid advancement of his career as a bureaucrat.[2] A second edition was issued within a year of its publication, in 1876. Hunter was encouraged to write the volume on Mayo in the *Rulers of India* series partly due to the success of this more detailed biography of over 700 pages, and partly as an expression of his gratitude to his patron. The former work was a summary of the larger biography in about 200 pages—the standard length of volumes in the series.

On the other hand, the biography of Dalhousie was based on fresh research which, according to Hunter, was somewhat hampered by the former governor-general's instructions that his correspondence should not be made public for a period of

---

[1]William Wilson Hunter, *The Earl of Mayo and the Consolidation of the Queen's Rule in India*, Oxford: Clarendon Press, 1891.
[2]W. W. Hunter, *A Life of the Earl of Mayo: Fourth Viceroy of India*, London: Smith, Elder and Co., 1875.

fifty years after his death (Dalhousie died in 1860). The title was intended to indicate Dalhousie's place in the history of British India, reflecting the evaluation of the Dalhousie era by colonial ideologues in the high noon of empire. The Dalhousie era posed a difficult problem given the controversial nature of his governor-generalship. There were many who held that Dalhousie's actions were responsible for creating circumstances that eventually led to the outbreak of the revolt.

Hunter, in his introduction to the biography, states that 'the time has not yet come to pronounce a final judgment on Lord Dalhousie's work'. He hoped that, 'this little volume will, at any rate, correct the misunderstandings and half-knowledge which obscured Lord Dalhousie's administration at the time of his death'.

Hunter goes on to say that he had collated the published writings on Dalhousie and his administration, and official documents, for a fresh historical assessment of the period. He concludes the introduction with an awareness of the tentativeness of his assessment: 'The result, while not justifying a final verdict as to the far-reaching consequences of Lord Dalhousie's rule, will enable us to obtain a clear and impartial view not only of his measures but of the considerations which regulated his policy and of the motives which guided the man'.[3] For Hunter as well, as Dalhousie's biographer, it was not easy to reconcile the contradictory opinions of contemporaries.

Dalhousie was nominated as governor-general at the age of thirty-five, 'the youngest Governor-General who has ever sat in the seat of Warren Hastings and Lord Wellesley'.[4] It may be mentioned that Clive was barely thirty-two years old when he became 'master of Bengal'. The difference, of course, was that unlike Clive, Dalhousie was appointed directly to the highest post, with no experience or knowledge of India, and at

---

[3]William Wilson Hunter, *The Marquess of Dalhousie and the Final Development of the Company's Rule*, Oxford: Clarendon Press, 1894, pp. 17–18.
[4]L. J. Trotter, *Life of the Marquis of Dalhousie*, London: W. H. Allen & Co., 1889, p. 31.

a time when he had embarked on a successful political career in Britain, with the possibility of a place in the cabinet.

He was selected for the post partly because of the efficiency with which he had earlier handled paperwork as a member of the cabinet when he was president of the Board of Trade for a few months. More importantly, his appointment, which he does not appear to have lobbied for, was the result of political calculations of Prime Minister Lord John Russell, who, in a situation of fast-changing parliamentary alignments in Britain, was looking for allies among Dalhousie's friends.

Dalhousie, James Ramsay, first (and last) marquess and tenth earl of Dalhousie, belonged to a well-established family of Scottish chiefs, heads of the prominent Scottish clan Ramsay.[5] Dalhousie Castle, the hereditary seat of the chiefs for several generations, is located at a short distance from Edinburgh and is now a luxury hotel. The Ramsays fought against Charles I in the cause of Parliament in the early seventeenth century. The earldom dates back to the 1630s. We are told that after the English Civil War, the Ramsays (i.e. the Dalhousies) 'served in all the great campaigns of the eighteenth and nineteenth centuries on the Continent, in Canada, and in India'.[6]

Dalhousie senior, the ninth earl, George Ramsay, had joined the army in the 1780s as a commissioned officer. Financial worries prompted him to take up a military career. He became a major-general in 1808, fought in the Peninsular Wars under Wellington, and in 1815, was created a baron in the peerage of Britain. He had also represented the Scottish peers in the (British) House of Lords as one of the sixteen Scottish representative peers, since 1796.

At the end of the Napoleonic Wars, he sought, as did

---

[5]Dalhousie was elevated to the marquisate in 1849 to 'honour' him for the conquest of Punjab.

[6]George Way of Plean and Romilly Squire, *Scottish Clan and Family Encyclopedia*, New York: Barnes & Noble, 1998, p. 299.

several veterans of the war, an administrative position in the colonies—again primarily due to pecuniary difficulties.[7] George was appointed lieutenant-governor of the province of Nova Scotia in Canada in 1816. Halifax was the capital of the province. Within four years, he was elevated to the position of Governor-in-Chief of British North America. British North America was a colonial administrative entity broadly corresponding to Canada—the Dominion of Canada did not come into existence till 1867.

George's four-year-old son, James (James was the third son of George Ramsay), who had accompanied his father to Halifax, also went with his father to the seat of government, Quebec. James stayed in Quebec for two years before being sent to Britain for his schooling.

The governor was granted leave of absence in 1824 to visit Scotland for attending to the maintenance of his property. Besides, he had problems with his eyesight, due to which there was some uncertainty about his return to Quebec. Nevertheless, he returned in 1825. The remaining duration of his governorship was a troubled one. The constant tension between the governor and the legislature created a volatile situation. Differences with colleagues in Canada and lack of adequate support from the home authorities—especially the colonial secretary (minister for colonies), Lord Bathurst—made it difficult for him to govern effectively. Dalhousie senior's attempts to uphold the prerogatives of the Crown brought him into direct conflict with the legislature, culminating in an open clash with the speaker, Louis-Joseph Papineau.

Papineau, a towering political figure, championed the cause of protecting French–Canadian traditions, and in the 1820s emerged as a radical opponent to the interests of the

---

[7]The following account of George Ramsay's Canadian sojourn is based mainly on Peter Burroughs, 'George Ramsay, 9th Earl of Dalhousie', *Dictionary of Canadian Biography*, Vol. 7, University of Toronto/Université Laval, 2003, available at https://www.biographi.ca/en/bio/ramsay_george_7E.html; and William Lee-Warner, *The Life of the Marquis of Dalhousie*, Vol. 1, London: Macmillan, 1904, pp. 6–13.

British commercial groups in Canada. Bathurst's successor in London, William Huskisson, felt that Dalhousie would have to be removed if colonial rule in British North America was to be stabilized. The British could not risk turbulence in the region so soon after America had broken away from the empire. Dalhousie was shunted to another part of the empire in 1828 as commander-in-chief of British forces in India. His Scottish networks would have been useful to him in securing the support of Robert Dundas (son of Henry Dundas) for the nomination.[8]

Robert Dundas, like his father, was president of the Board of Control, between 1807 and 1812, and held the same office between July and September 1828. With his enormous influence he could easily have manoeuvred such a coveted posting in India for Dalhousie senior.

George Ramsay travelled from Quebec to India via Britain. He had been discouraged from halting too long in transit— which he was keen to do, in order to explain to cabinet ministers his actions in Canada. He considered this necessary in view of the growing criticism of his policies. Parliament constituted a select committee to examine some of the contentious issues which had dogged his administration. The report was critical of his conduct. Dalhousie senior refrained from appealing directly to his former military commander, Wellington, whom he found utterly cold and unresponsive.

He departed for India in July 1829, assuming charge in January 1830. He took over from Lord Combermere, commander-in-chief since 1825. Dalhousie was in office for two uneventful years and relinquished his post at the beginning of 1832. He suffered a stroke within a few months of his return and passed away in 1838.

A few years before his father returned from India, James (Dalhousie junior) contested, unsuccessfully, for Parliament as

---

[8]Henry Dundas became Viscount Melville in 1802. He died in 1811, and Robert Dundas succeeded to the title.

a Tory candidate from Edinburgh. He contested again, from a different constituency, in the next general election held in 1837 and won. This was the first election during Queen Victoria's reign. The Whigs had been in power before the election and once again secured a majority. It was just two years since the previous election had taken place. Another election—within two years—had been necessitated by the succession—namely the death of William IV and the accession of Victoria. This was a constitutional requirement (the provision requiring the election of a new Parliament upon every succession was dispensed with in 1867).

James's election more or less coincided with his father's final illness and death. He now succeeded to the peerage as the only surviving son of the ninth earl of Dalhousie, the other two sons having predeceased George Ramsay. In 1838, the tenth earl—the Dalhousie on whom this chapter focuses—became a member of the House of Lords (all subsequent references are to the tenth earl).

Yet another general election, held in 1841, resulted in the defeat of the Whigs placing the Tories in office after a considerable duration. Robert Peel became the prime minister. The formation of the Peel ministry marked the beginning of Dalhousie's political journey. In 1843, Peel made him vice-president of the Board of Trade, an important branch of the government. As vice-president of the Board he was a junior minister, working under W.E. Gladstone. Gladstone, who would dominate British politics from the 1860s till the end of the century, heading the government four times, was also at the beginning of a long innings. He was three years senior to Dalhousie. In 1841, Gladstone became vice-president of the Board, and its president in 1843 with Dalhousie as vice-president. When Gladstone resigned in 1845 over differences on a matter quite unrelated to the affairs of the Board, Dalhousie was promoted to president. In his capacity as president, he played a role in formulating policies for railways in their formative phase in Britain.

To follow the vicissitudes of Dalhousie's public life over the next few months, we need to refer to the acrimony in British politics generated by the demand for abolishing or lowering duties on the import of foodgrains. The question of the repeal of Corn Laws—the legislation relating to the imposition of high import duties on foodgrains—had gained urgency in the early forties due to rising prices of bread and shortages of wheat in Britain, especially in Ireland. A devastating famine in Ireland in 1845–46, aggravated by large-scale damage to the potato crop, on which the poor were dependent, caused nearly one million deaths.

The rationale of the existing tariff structure was that the import of cheap foodgrains would be detrimental to the interests of agriculturists in Britain. These laws had been enacted in 1815 and had been controversial ever since. Their effect over a period of time was that the price of food grains and bread remained high, raising the cost of living for the working class in a rapidly industrializing England. A sustained campaign for the repeal of the laws was undertaken from the mid-1830s onwards by anti-Corn Law associations. These associations were successful in mobilizing public opinion in favour of repeal.

The Tories were strongly committed to protection, as was an influential section of the Whigs, many of whom were wealthy landlords. Both had their base among big landowners and affluent farmers and therefore represented the interests of the landed elite. With mounting pressure from below, differences began to surface among the leaderships of the two parties—quite unexpectedly among the Tories as well. The dominant Whig faction, led by Russell, declared its support in November 1845 for doing away with the laws entirely. Peel was initially opposed to repeal but gradually altered his position. He began to think in terms of a substantial reduction in the tariff, stopping short of outright repeal.

Most of the prime minister's colleagues, many of them diehard Tories, were unwilling to dilute their stand on the laws and resisted proposals for introducing changes. Peel tendered his resignation following Russell's statement in favour of complete repeal. His continuation in office had become untenable, as Russell's views were a reflection of popular sentiment. However, though he was provided an opportunity by the queen to form a ministry that would act decisively in the matter, Russell was unable to form a government, as he could not muster a majority. The queen then asked Peel to continue as prime minister. Peel had resigned in the first week of December 1845; he was back in office towards the end of the month, with an assurance of Whig support on the issue of repeal.

Dalhousie was again made president of the Board of Trade, this time with a place in the cabinet. The exit of one of Peel's key ministerial colleagues, Lord Stanley (later, Lord Derby), who headed the Tory no-repeal faction, facilitated Dalhousie's induction into the cabinet. Incidentally, Gladstone too was back in the cabinet, now as secretary of state for war and colonies.

Peel moved rapidly to introduce the Corn Importation Bill in May 1846. The bill was passed in the last week of June. Immediately afterwards, the government was defeated in Parliament on an entirely different issue, leading to Peel's resignation. This brought to an end Dalhousie's short-lived stint as a cabinet minister, lasting six months. He firmly sided with Peel on the issue of repeal, and had effectively intervened in the debate on the bill in the House of Lords with a lengthy speech.

Dalhousie became part of the pro-repeal Tory faction in Parliament informally attached to Peel. The Peelites, as they came to be called, included Gladstone. The Peelites continued to be referred to by this label even after the death of Peel in 1850. They soon joined hands with the more progressive sections of the Whigs and other democratic elements in British politics to form the Liberal Party in the 1860s. From its foundation to its decline at the end of the century, Gladstone was the tallest leader of the party especially after the death of Lord Palmerston in 1865.

Russell became the prime minister following the resignation of the Peel ministry. He was in office for the next six years.

The numerical weakness of the Whig party in the House of Commons induced him to look for supporters among the Peelites. An offer was made to Dalhousie to join the ministry, which he declined, stating that his ideological position prevented him from accepting a ministerial berth in a government with a different political persuasion. Russell's subsequent invitation to head the newly formed railway board, too, was refused for the same reason. Given that the political situation was so fluid, and perhaps because of political differences, Dalhousie was not too enthusiastic about aligning openly with Russell. Soon, another opportunity came Dalhousie's way. The governor-general of Indian territories, Lord Hardinge (1844–48), was scheduled to retire at the end of 1847. Hardinge was an appointee of the Peel administration. Before being sent to India, he had been a member of the cabinet, as secretary at war (minister in charge of administrative aspects of the war office), from 1841 to 1844.

It is not clear what prompted Russell to choose Dalhousie as Hardinge's successor. Hardinge was a cabinet minister when he was appointed. He had earlier held the same portfolio in Wellington's government (1828–30). He was a veteran of the Peninsular War, and was still on active service. In 1852, he was made commander-in-chief of the British army when the post became vacant upon Wellington's death in that year. As commander-in-chief, Hardinge directed the military operations of the Crimean War (1853–56), and was promoted to the rank of field marshal in 1855, a year before he died at the age of seventy-one.

Significantly, he was the only exception in the first half of the nineteenth century to the unwritten rule that a governor-general had to be a peer. He was the younger son of a clergyman. His father was the rector, or parish priest, of a small town in northern England, and his family had some aristocratic connections. This made his social background very different from that of all the appointees of the nineteenth century, other than John Lawrence. Yet he was a high-ranking minister, and high-ranking military officer. No other member of the cabinet, at this level, had been sent out as governor-general prior to Hardinge. The nomination of Dalhousie as Hardinge's successor, notwithstanding his aristocratic lineage, could be interpreted as a downgrading of the governor-generalship by the Whig regime of Russell.

We know that Dalhousie, since the advent of the Peel ministry, had been hinting that he might be interested in an Indian office, even if he did not lobby for the post. To begin with, his name was floated by his adherents for the governorship of Bombay in 1846. Nothing came of this proposal. Several years earlier, in 1841, before he entered the ministry, there had been some speculation that he might be sent to Madras as governor. He had indicated that he would be willing to go. No offer, however, had materialized.

The nomination in 1847 as governor-general seems to have had its origin in consultations between the Court of Directors and the president of the Board of Control, John Hobhouse, regarding Hardinge's successor. Dalhousie's name figured in these consultations. It is likely that Wellington, who saw Dalhousie as his protégé and with whom the acolyte was in regular touch, nudged Russell to give him the job. Be that as it may, his name was formally suggested by Hobhouse. The EIC's directors promptly conveyed their concurrence. A formal offer was then made to Dalhousie, who replied that he would accept if he did not have to give up his political affiliation. This did not matter, as he would be abroad for at least five years and therefore absent from the political scene in Britain. The warrant, or official letter, of his appointment, was signed by the queen in August 1847.

Dalhousie was fully aware that a prolonged absence from Britain would slow down his political career. His strong preference for the governor-generalship, which would assure him an annual income of £25,000, was dictated by the financial troubles of his family. He could not have foreseen that he would return home in broken health after eight years, and be dead by 1860.

In keeping with the Company's tradition, the Court of Directors hosted a grand banquet in honour of the governor-general-designate on the eve of his departure. The function was held at the London Tavern, the customary venue for these dinners. The London Tavern was located in Bishopsgate Street, not far from the Company's headquarters at Leadenhall Street. It was 'a celebrated public house that was built on a scale previously unknown in London, and which set the pattern for a new kind of tavern that dominated the social, political, and cultural life of the metropolis until the middle of the nineteenth century'.[9]

We have at least two contemporary illustrations of farewell functions organized in the banqueting hall of the Tavern in the 1840s, depicting EIC ceremonial dinners organized on a lavish scale. One was a banquet for Dalhousie's predecessor, Hardinge (1844), and the other for Charles Napier (1849), who would play a key role in the military campaigns of Dalhousie's tenure. Napier was returning to India in 1849 upon his appointment as commander-in-chief. He had earlier been instrumental in the conquest of Sind. Wellington and Hardinge were present on the latter occasion. Dalhousie's farewell function was attended by the prime minister. It had become the custom for the directors to host a dinner for governors-general and other high officials at the London Tavern before they embarked on their voyage to India to take up an assignment.

Ian Newman, in his study of the place of taverns in the social history of late eighteenth-century England, has noted that the Company's association with the London establishment began in the 1790s. The London Tavern itself opened in 1768. A vast banqueting hall on the top floor of the tavern's three-storey structure, with high ceilings, Corinthian columns, numerous cut-glass chandeliers, and a gallery for women spectators, made it the first public space of its kind in London. The hall could

---

[9]Ian Newman, 'Edmund Burke in the Tavern', *European Romantic Review*, Vol. 24, No. 2, 2013, p. 127.

accommodate 300–500 guests. In the mid-nineteenth century, when London residents dined relatively early as compared to the later decades of the century, guests would be seated in the hall by six in the evening.

The establishment, it should be noted, was not a coffee shop or pub, bar, or 'alehouse'. Rather, it was a space patronized by the well-to-do for holding public gatherings and banquets. Many of the city's leading companies held annual meetings of their shareholders at the place. The directors of the EIC used it to organize receptions for dignitaries.

With the enormous resources at its disposal, derived from the exploitation of India (and China) for over two centuries, the Company could afford to entertain extravagantly. Newman notes that Burke had been critical of the dangerous and unhealthy influence exerted by such establishments on public opinion. For him, the problem with their presence was 'that privileged gentlemen gather in taverns, make toasts, and draw up resolutions which are quoted in newspapers and published in pamphlets to be quoted back at future meetings, then published again, in an endlessly repeating circuit, which circumvents any broader consensus-building and convinces the club members that their own opinions are held by all'.[10]

The sins of the Company could be easily ignored amidst the glorification of the empire at feasts such as those organized for Hardinge or Dalhousie. The governor-general-designate need not bother about the ugly realities of empire-building in the rarefied atmosphere of the London Tavern.

The feasting that had commenced in London before Dalhousie's departure continued upon his arrival in Calcutta. He disembarked in Calcutta in the second week of January 1848. The feasts were part of the ritual for the inauguration of every newly arrived governor-general. 'Since my arrival here on Wednesday,' Dalhousie noted in a letter, 'till to-day, when Lord Hardinge sailed, the festivities have been fearful. Two

[10]Newman, 'Edmund Burke in the Tavern', p. 137.

dinners of 150 each, two of 50, and a ball of 800, closed with a breakfast to 90.'[11] He was received ceremonially by Hardinge, who sailed for home shortly afterwards.

Christmas that year was celebrated by Dalhousie in Ludhiana. He had travelled for several weeks, partly upriver and partly overland, from Calcutta to the Company's outpost in eastern Punjab. Ludhiana had been in the Company's possession since 1809 when a treaty was signed with the powerful ruler of the Lahore kingdom, Ranjit Singh (r. 1801–1839). The treaty confined the British sphere of influence in Punjab to the region located south and east of the Sutlej River. Most of this region was under the rulers of relatively small states, of which Patiala was the largest. Besides Patiala, there were the states of Faridkot, Kapurthala, Jind, Nabha, Maler Kotla, and a few petty-chieftaincies. With the signing of the 1809 treaty, all these states, referred to collectively by the British as the 'cis-Sutlej states' ('on this side of the Sutlej'), were declared to be under the EIC's protection. Ludhiana was taken by the Company from the Jind ruler.

Ranjit Singh did not wish to get bogged down in a struggle with the British for control over these eastern Punjab states. He considered it wiser to concentrate on expanding his kingdom towards the west and the north. By the time of Ranjit Singh's death in June 1839, his kingdom, with its capital at Lahore, extended from the Sutlej in the east to the Khyber Pass in the west, from the frontier of Sind in the south to Kashmir and Jammu in the north (the latter two were part of his kingdom). Although there was no open confrontation between the EIC and Ranjit Singh for three decades, their relations were not always cordial. There were tensions over issues such as the attempt of the Company to penetrate the Indus River and flex its muscles in neighbouring Sind. Punjab was conquered within ten years of Ranjit Singh's death.

---

[11]Dalhousie's letter dated 18 January/7 February 1848, J. G. A. Baird (ed.), *Private Letters of the Marquess of Dalhousie*, Edinburgh: William Blackwood & Sons, 1910, p. 20.

British military mobilization for an invasion of Afghanistan had formed the prelude to two major colonial wars fought in Punjab in the 1840s, which ended in the conquest of the Lahore kingdom. Once the mobilization for the invasion of Afghanistan was underway, a large British force, designated as the Army of the Indus, commenced marching towards Kabul in early 1839, proceeding via Sind and the Bolan Pass. This had marked the beginning of the First Afghan War (1839–42).

The British had sought the support of Ranjit Singh for this campaign. Negotiations between the two culminated in an agreement signed in 1838, whereby the Punjab ruler was to provide some military assistance for the Afghanistan offensive. The campaign was ostensibly in support of one of the claimants to the Kabul throne, Shah Shuja (Shuja-ul-Mulk), a grandson of Ahmad Shah Durrani. Shah Shuja had been ousted by Shah Mahmud, his half-brother. Shuja was given asylum by Ranjit Singh. From 1815 onwards, the deposed ruler had been living in Ludhiana.

Further upheavals had followed in Afghanistan. Dost Mohammad, who belonged to a different clan (Barakzai), came to power in 1826. Subsequently, Shuja, who had been trying to mobilize support to regain power, launched an invasion of eastern Afghanistan in 1833, aided by Ranjit Singh. He had obtained the 'best wishes' of the British for the expedition. The offensive was a failure.

In the mid-1830s, the British committed themselves to the cause of restoring Shah Shuja as ruler, making him the instrument of their policy of expansion into Afghanistan. This policy was vigorously pursued by Auckland.

The Army of the Indus managed to restore Shah Shuja to power in August 1839 but could not keep him on the throne. Auckland had declared that the British would withdraw once the objective of restoring Shuja to power was achieved. However, it soon became apparent that the new ruler could not maintain his position if the British were to withdraw. Thus, it was decided that the Army of the Indus would stay on for some more time in Kabul.

Growing hostility to Shuja and to the British soon created a volatile situation. It was also clear that a large armed force, stationed at a considerable distance from the borders of the Indian empire, was an expensive proposition. A lengthy occupation of Kabul was financially unviable. Another cause of worry for the EIC was that the Lahore court was not enthusiastic about allowing the army to march through its territory so the return march from Afghanistan would have to take place along the more circuitous Sind route.

It is in this context that pressure began to be exerted on Punjab for active assistance, and suggestions for annexing the kingdom began to be floated by colonial policymakers. As conditions worsened in Afghanistan, the army was ordered to evacuate Kabul. The retreat from Kabul in the first week of January 1842 took place under very adverse weather conditions, and the troops were repeatedly attacked by local tribal warriors. Almost the entire force of 16,000 men—a large proportion of whom were Indian sipahis—was wiped out before the Khyber Pass had been crossed. This was the biggest defeat suffered by the British in their wars of the nineteenth century.

The to-and-fro movement of troops across Punjab during the Afghan war had made the colonial military establishment much better acquainted with the region. Improved knowledge of routes, resources, and internal conditions could now be used to further weaken the kingdom and prepare for an offensive. A large amount of information about Punjab had been collected and processed while working out the logistics for the Kabul expedition. This could be reoriented to attack an erstwhile ally. No wonder the Lahore officials had been unwilling to provide the British access to routes passing through Punjab on their way back from Kabul.

As soon as the British had recovered from the disaster of the Afghan war, colonial officials began planning for an attack on the kingdom of Punjab. The preparations coincided with, and were hastened by, the state of uncertainty prevailing in Lahore because of problems of succession. Three of Ranjit Singh's successors had died or were assassinated in quick succession within four years of his death: his eldest son, Kharak Singh; Kharak Singh's son, Nau Nihal Singh; and Kharak Singh's half-brother, Sher Singh. Some of the prominent courtiers, too, were killed in this short period. The kingdom's army stepped in to fill the political vacuum that had been created at the top by these deaths.

The formidable army of the Lahore kingdom, which owed its strength to Ranjit Singh's abilities as a military organizer, became the main player in the struggle for power at the Lahore court. The soldiers and their commanders mostly tended to act independently of the court. The durbar no longer had any effective control over the troops. These troops had constituted regimental councils (panchayats) through which they asserted themselves collectively.

After the assassination of Sher Singh in 1843, the army supported the claim of Dalip Singh, the youngest son of Ranjit Singh, to succeed as the maharaja. Dalip Singh was a minor, barely five years old at this time. His mother, Rani Jindán (Jind Kaur), was one of the wives of Ranjit Singh. In September 1843, Dalip Singh was proclaimed the ruler of Punjab, with Rani Jindan as the regent.

It was against the backdrop of these developments that the British launched an assault in December 1845 under Hardinge's command. The First Punjab War (1845–46) was won by the British at a very heavy cost. Their casualties in the war were unusually high. The British lost nearly 2,500 men in the crucial Battle of Sobraon. Sobraon is situated on the Sutlej, at a short distance from Ferozepur (Ferozepur had been in the EIC's possession since 1835). The Punjab army, whose soldiers fought on their own as their commanders had gone over to the British side, put up a very fierce resistance.

Given the enormous difficulties they encountered, the British decided not to annex the kingdom immediately. This would have involved prolonged fighting, for which the British lacked the strength at the time. Nevertheless, under the terms of the Treaty of Lahore (March 1846) negotiated at the end of the war, the fertile Jalandhar Doab lying between the Sutlej and the Beas was ceded to them, and Kashmir (along with Jammu) was detached from the kingdom and subsequently handed over to Gulab Singh. Gulab Singh was an influential warlord of the Lahore court, who had rendered useful help to the Company during the conflict.

Towards the end of 1846, a few months after the war had ended, a council of regency was constituted by the Lahore durbar under British pressure for administering the kingdom. The council consisted of nine Punjab chiefs—key state functionaries of the kingdom. The working of the council was supervised by the Company's representative at the Lahore court. Rani Jindan was completely marginalized in the process. This was the state of affairs when Dalhousie arrived in Ludhiana.

Towards the end of 1848, war was resumed against Punjab to complete the project for subjugating the kingdom. This was the purpose for which Dalhousie had journeyed to Ludhiana. From Ludhiana, he moved to Sobraon and thence to Ferozepur.

The first major battle of the Second Punjab War (1848–49) took place at Chillianwala, north of Lahore, on the banks of the Jhelum River, on 13 January 1849. The British were defeated. In colonial historiography, the battle is often described as having been indecisive, whereas in fact, the British were completely routed in the battle. A biography of Commander-in-chief Hugh Gough, who led the British forces at Chillianwala, while offering a defence of Gough's handling of the encounter, notes the 'vehement popular outcry' when news of the disaster reached Britain. Gough was 'accused of having made no preparations, of having wasted too much time in preparations, of being hasty, of being tardy, of ignorance of the elementary principles of military science, of excitement amounting to mania, of folly, and of inhumanity'.[12]

---

[12]Robert S. Rait, *The Life and Campaigns of Hugh First Viscount Gough Field-*

Gough was superseded by Charles Napier due to the debacle. We have already noted the elaborate banquet in his honour in the London Tavern on the eve of his departure. Unfortunately, the Punjab army was unable to take the victory at Chillianwala to its conclusion, as it lacked sufficient officers. Most of the experienced officers had already betrayed the soldiers. It was mainly the soldiers who fought this war.

After Chillianwala, another engagement on 22 February at Gujrat, near the Chenab River resulted in the defeat of the Punjab army. Ranjit Singh's kingdom was annexed. This became the province of (British) Punjab. Dalip Singh (d. 1893) was moved out of Punjab. He spent his entire adult life in forced exile.

Dalhousie followed up his success in Punjab with a war with Burma—the Second Anglo–Burmese War. Burma was invaded in April 1852. Rangoon was attacked and occupied. The important town of Pegu, lying northeast of Rangoon, was taken in June.

It may be recalled that parts of southern Burma had been annexed by the Company following the First Anglo–Burmese War. These formed two non-contiguous administrative units situated on either side of the Irrawaddy Delta, namely, Arakan and Tenasserim. Dalhousie's successful invasion of southern Burma allowed the EIC to annex the rich Irrawaddy Delta, along with the city of Rangoon, situated in the delta region. All the territories so far seized from the Kongbaung kingdom were constituted as the (British) province of Lower Burma.

The kingdom itself was extinguished in 1885–86 following the Third Anglo–Burmese War (1885–86) when northern Burma came under British rule. The last king of the Kongbaung dynasty, Thibaw (r. 1878–85), was made captive and transported to Ratnagiri in Maharashtra, where he passed away in 1916.

Thibaw's tragic story, his exile and death, forms part of the narrative in Amitav Ghosh's acclaimed novel, *The Glass Palace*. In the novel, the exiled Thibaw, while living in captivity in

<hr>

Marshal, Vol. 2, Westminster: A. Constable & Co., 1903, p. 240.

Ratnagiri, comes across a news item describing the London tour of the ruler of Siam, which mentions his stay at Buckingham Palace. This prompts him to comment on the twist of fate which had made a vassal of the rulers of Burma an honoured guest at the palace of the British monarch while Thibaw himself languished in exile, a prisoner of the British: '"When our ancestor, the great Alaungpaya, invaded Siam," Thebaw said to his daughters one day, "he sent a letter to the King of Ayutthya [the main city of the kingdom of Siam]. There was a copy in the Palace archives. This is what it said: *There is no rival for our glory and our karma; to place you beside us is to compare the … sun with a firefly; the divine amadryade of the heavens with an earthworm; Dhatarattha, the Hamsa king with a dung beetle.*' That is what our ancestors said to the King of Siam. But now they sleep in the Buckingham Palace while we lie buried in this dungheap".'[13]

To the new annexations under Dalhousie was added, in 1856, at the fag end of his tenure, the much-abridged, semi-independent state of Awadh. For about eighty years, since the death of Shuja-ud-Daula, the state had been subjugated by the Company. It had lost most of its autonomy in governing the portions that were left to it after the cession of 1801.

By the end of the eighteenth century, the EIC's resident in Awadh, the principal colonial official stationed in the state, had emerged as a parallel centre of authority. The capital of the state had been shifted by the nawab from Faizabad to Lucknow in the late 1770s. Here, the residency became increasingly powerful, eventually eclipsing the nawab's durbar. The presence of a Company resident at the Awadh court dates back to the time when Warren Hastings began intervening aggressively in the affairs of the state. Although a representative of the EIC had been posted regularly in Awadh since the 1770s, it was in the years 1785–94, when Edward Ives was resident, that the arrangement was stabilized.

---

[13]Amitav Ghosh, *The Glass Palace*, New Delhi: HarperCollins, 2006, p. 87.

To a large extent, the resident derived his authority from his control over the Awadh army. As we have already noted, the state paid for the maintenance of the troops—Indian soldiers and the EIC's British officers. Michael Fisher, in his study on the evolution of the residency system in British India, points out that the residents of Awadh deployed the army 'against selected defaulting landholders' to enhance their authority and that 'these troops provided [the resident] with base for his forays into the administration'. Further, 'the soldiers themselves—mostly born in Awadh—used the Resident to provide them and their families with protection from the Awadh administration. Thus, the Resident redirected much of Awadh's military potential into the Company's hands'.[14] The residency, rather than the palace, was the actual centre of power by the 1830s.

At the same time, colonial officials constantly spoke of 'misrule' in Awadh. Residents regularly dispatched reports to Calcutta, alleging that the rulers were incapable of governing the state, which in turn justified greater intervention by the EIC. In the 1830s, the directors had authorized Bentinck to take over the administration of the state. This would have implied reducing the 'King of Oudh' to the status of a titular ruler. The nawab (subedar) had assumed the title of 'badshah' in 1819 at the instigation of the British, thereby repudiating his allegiance to the Mughal emperor. Political developments in Lucknow, during Bentinck's tenure, prevented the resident from initiating any measures for taking over the administration. Under Dalhousie, decisive steps were taken to do away with whatever residual autonomy was left to Awadh. The directors endorsed his intervention. Sleeman, of thuggee notoriety, was rewarded for his anti-thug crusade by being appointed resident at Lucknow and set about preparing the ground for taking over the state. He assumed charge in January 1849 and, within

---

[14]Michael H. Fisher, *Indirect Rule in India: Residents and the Residency System, 1764-1858*, New Delhi: Oxford University Press, 1991, pp. 381–82.

a few months, had compiled a report on conditions in the state. The report upheld the Company's assertion that the administration of Awadh had collapsed. Sleeman was in favour of taking over the government immediately but did not go to the extent of recommending annexation. The British were to act as 'trustees' for the nawab's (king's) family, and the state was to be administered by Awadh personnel, supervised by Company officials. The resident undertook an extensive tour of the Awadh countryside, facilitated by the durbar, between December 1849 and February 1850 to gather more evidence for substantiating allegations of misrule. Sleeman's term ended in 1854. He was succeeded by James Outram, who prepared another report on conditions in Awadh, reiterating Sleeman's assessment. This was in keeping with the Company's policy of moving in the direction of annexation. By 1855, the British cabinet, the Board of Control, and the directors had resolved to formally make the state a part of the empire. Orders for annexation were received by the governor-general in the first week of 1856 (the despatch is dated 19 November 1855). Awadh was annexed in February 1856. Having accomplished the task, Dalhousie handed over charge to his successor, Lord Canning, at the end of the month.

The outgoing governor-general had been afflicted with a painful disease of the bone in one of his legs for some time. He received Canning at the top of the grand stairway leading up to the entrance of the governor-general's official residence, supporting himself on crutches, 'On the last day of the month— it was leap year—the new Governor-General, Lord Canning, passed up the broad flight of steps that led into Government House. Above him, dressed in full uniform and propped up on crutches, stood the retiring viceroy, backed by the members of his Council'.[15]

Dalhousie departed from Calcutta on 6 March. From the moment he left the imperial capital, he was of little consequence

---

[15]Trotter, *Dalhousie*, p. 189.

insofar as the EIC was concerned. He lived the last four years of his life in political obscurity. He complained bitterly to his friends about the shabby treatment he received from the London authorities as he approached the end of his tenure. A week after he departed from Calcutta, he wrote to a close friend: 'I have left India without receiving one word of thanks or civility from the Court of Directors or from H.M. [Her Majesty's] Government. For two mails [,] before I ceased to be G.-G.[,] the Chairman [of the EIC] did not write to me at all. For one mail I received no letter from the President of the Board of Control. After I ceased to be G.-G., I had letters from each, but not a civil word from either.'[16]

The letter is addressed to George Couper, with whom he kept up a regular correspondence, a selection from which was published in 1910 when Dalhousie's private papers became accessible to the public. Couper had been aide-de-camp to Dalhousie senior and was nearly twenty-five years older than Dalhousie junior.

No information had been received by Dalhousie before his departure from Calcutta about arrangements for the final lap of his homeward journey from Alexandria to England. The vessel he had boarded in the Bay of Bengal, the *Ferooz* (sic.), brought him as far as Egypt via the Red Sea. The journey thence overland to Alexandria was difficult for Dalhousie due to the excruciating pain in his leg caused by his ailment. He was upset that he was to complete his homeward journey aboard an uncomfortable 600-ton vessel, the *Caradoc*.

The *Caradoc* was a paddle-wheel steam vessel equipped with one gun. Built in the late 1840s, it was initially used for ferrying passengers across the Irish Sea from Holyhead in Wales to Dublin. This was a major sea route linking Britain and Ireland in the early nineteenth century. During the Crimean War, the vessel was deployed in the Mediterranean.

---

[16]Dalhousie's letter dated 12 March 1856, Baird (ed.), *Private Letters of the Marquess of Dalhousie*, pp. 371–72.

Writing to Couper from Cairo, where he halted briefly, Dalhousie expressed his disgust at the pettiness shown by the government in sending the *Caradoc* to fetch him, 'I am deeply and justly dissatisfied that the Government should have sent me a Holyhead ferryboat to bring me back from an eight years' government of the Indian Empire.'[17]

At Malta, en route to England, he transferred to a somewhat more comfortable vessel, the *Tribune*, for the passage to Southampton. Nevertheless, before embarking on the final stage of his journey, he communicated his resentment to Wood, who was then the first lord of the admiralty (and had earlier been the president of the Board of Control). 'I have written to Sir C. Wood,' he informed Couper, 'making no personal complaint, but representing on behalf of the great office I have held so long, that the selection of a Holyhead packet-boat [small vessel for carrying mail] to convey a Governor-General to England neither shows the consideration which is due to his high official rank nor maintains him and the Government he serves in the position they ought to hold ...'.[18]

His mood improved when, during a short pause at Gibraltar, he learnt that the Company had proposed an annual pension of £5,000 for him, 'I have just learnt from the newspaper that the court have settled £5,000 a year on me. The court is very bountiful, and I am grateful. Will their vote be confirmed [by the Court of Proprietors and the government]? Inshallah.'[19] The resolution of the Court of Directors was confirmed on 14 May by the Court of Proprietors and subsequently by the Board of Control.

As governor-general, Dalhousie was obsessively concerned about organizing and ruling the Indian empire in an 'orderly'

---

[17]Dalhousie's letter dated 4 April 1856, Baird (ed.), *Private Letters of the Marquess of Dalhousie*, p. 373.
[18]Dalhousie's letter dated 20 April 1856, Baird (ed.), *Private Letters of the Marquess of Dalhousie*, p. 374.
[19]Dalhousie's letter dated 3 May 1856, Baird (ed.), *Private Letters of the Marquess of Dalhousie*, p. 375.

manner, which led him to be belligerently expansionist and interventionist. He was a 'workaholic': long hours of work as an administrator in India left him exhausted, and is believed to have hastened his death following a prolonged illness, at the age of forty-eight in December 1860.

∽

Lord Canning was the last governor-general to be appointed by the EIC. The ceremonial for the appointment was, as always, conducted at the Company's headquarters in Leadenhall Street. Accordingly, Canning proceeded to East India House on 1 August 1855 to be formally introduced to the directors and take the oath of office. He would again be administered an oath in the presence of members of the governor-general's council when he officially took up his duties in Calcutta.

The customary banquet for the new appointee was held at the Tavern the same evening. This was the last occasion when a governor-general-designate would be feted by the directors before leaving for India. Writing about the Canning dinner, John Kaye, who had an intimate knowledge of the inner workings of the Company, remarked that, 'Many a gallant soldier and many a wise administrator carried back with him to India the big card of the East India Company inviting him to dinner at the London Tavern, and religiously preserved it as one of the most cherished records of an honourable career.'[20]

Elliot Macnaghten, who was then the chairman of the EIC, presided over the dinner. Among those present were several members of the cabinet. Canning himself was a cabinet minister; he resigned shortly before his departure. Canning did not immediately lay down office after being administered his governor-general's oath because the prime minister wished to delay creating a vacancy in the cabinet.

Although the position of governor-general was not the

---

[20]John William Kaye, *A History of the Sepoy War in India, 1857-58*, Vol. 1, London: Longmans, Green & Co., 1896, pp. 374–75.

most suitable option for aspiring politicians, it was not entirely unattractive to ambitious men (no woman was ever given the post), especially if they were financially hard up. In the roughly fifty years that had elapsed since Minto's appointment, holding a middle-level portfolio in the cabinet had, on occasion, been regarded as an added advantage for aristocrats or would-be peers whose names might be under consideration for the post.

Yet, as Dalhousie had pointed out when he was barely thirty and there was a possibility that he might be nominated as governor of Madras, 'If I go to Madras, who at the end of five years, when I return, will know my name?'.[21] The governor-generalship almost put an end to political advancement at home upon return.

Charles Canning was the same age as Dalhousie. He was the youngest son of George Canning. It may be recalled that the father had been appointed governor-general in September 1822. Before he could go to India, he was offered a place in the cabinet as secretary of state (senior minister) for foreign affairs and therefore, resigned. He was prime minister for a few months in 1827. Following his death in 1827, his wife was created viscountess in her own right. When she died in 1837, Charles Canning succeeded to her title as his two elder brothers had passed away earlier. This gave him a seat in the House of Lords. He had been elected to the House of Commons the previous year and had to give up his membership of that house.

When Peel formed his ministry in 1841, Canning was made under-secretary (junior minister) for foreign affairs. He stayed with Peel when the latter resigned in December 1845. Upon Peel's resumption of office, he was made chief commissioner of woods and forests, a ministerial position. With Peel's resignation in 1846, his second spell as minister came to an end. Canning remained with the Peelites after Peel died in 1850. When a

---

[21]Dalhousie's letter dated 14 December 1841, Baird (ed.), *Private Letters of the Marquess of Dalhousie*, p. 9.

Whig–Peelite government was formed in 1852 under Lord Aberdeen, he joined the new ministry.

Canning was postmaster-general in the Aberdeen ministry. The postal services had recently been revolutionized in Britain with the introduction of the 'penny post'. Letters weighing up to half an ounce (approximately 14 grams) could, from 1840 onwards, be sent from any part of Britain to any other part at the flat rate of one penny. A penny was the 240th part of a pound sterling in the pre-decimal era. Adhesive stamps of the value of one penny were issued by the postal department to facilitate the posting of letters on a prepaid basis. As Asa Briggs, historian of the social history of Victorian objects, puts it, 'Postage stamps, long taken for granted, were one of the first Victorian inventions. Before the first beautiful penny black stamps were sold to the public in May 1840, Rowland Hill, their chief but not their only begetter, had difficulty in defining what was soon to become one of the most familiar Victorian things in use.'[22] Hill had published a pamphlet in 1837 entitled *Post Office Reform: Its Importance and Practicability,* in which he had spelt out his scheme for encouraging the public to use postal services more extensively. This was to be achieved by appreciably lowering rates charged for carrying letters. The prepaid penny stamp was central to Hill's proposal. The penny post was an instant success, with an ever-increasing number of people making use of the mail service.

Growing popular demand for low-price transmission of letters required the expansion of the postal infrastructure, so considerable attention had to be paid by the government to this particular branch of the administration. The carriage of mail registered an increase of 50 per cent within a few months of the introduction of the penny post, and a large number of new post offices had to be added rapidly. Expansion of the network became a matter of priority in the following decade.

---

[22]Asa Briggs, *Victorian Things*, London: Penguin Random House, 1990, p. 328.

Five hundred and fifteen post offices were opened in 1854 alone, when Canning was postmaster-general.

Summing up the impact of the innovation, Briggs remarks that Hill 'was fully content when after 1846, the year of the repeal of the corn laws, the blessings of cheap mail were inevitably compared with the blessings of cheap bread'.[23] The important place that the post office had acquired in the everyday lives of the British people by the early 1850s is reflected in the postmaster-general's report presented to Parliament in 1855, the first comprehensive report on postal services in Britain.[24] The report itself was prepared at Canning's initiative, who stated at the beginning of the report that:

'The service of the Post Office is one which calls for constant expansion and improvement, and its details, as well as its general system, affect the convenience and comfort of every class; but information respecting it is not easily accessible, except by correspondence with this Office, or through questions asked in Parliament; and many misapprehensions and complaints arise from an imperfect knowledge of matters which might, without any inconvenience, be placed before the public. It appeared to me, therefore, that it could not be otherwise than satisfactory to Parliament, if by means of a periodical Report, the general scope and extent of the progress made by the Department were brought under its notice...'.[25]

Aberdeen resigned in 1855, mainly owing to criticism of the Crimean War, which had been dragging on since 1853. Lord Palmerston, secretary of state for home affairs in the Aberdeen government, now formed a predominantly Whig ministry. He retained Canning as postmaster-general and elevated him to

---

[23]Briggs, *Victorian Things*, p. 334.

[24]*First Report of the Postmaster General, on the Post Office*, London: George E. Eyre and William Spottiswoode, 1855.

[25]Ibid., p. 7. The report contains a valuable outline of the history of post office in Britain based on records available in the postal department.

cabinet rank. Palmerston continued to be prime minister till his death in 1865, except for a brief but critical period between February 1858 and June 1859, when a minority Tory ministry was in office, with Lord Derby as prime minister.

Lord Derby (14th Earl of Derby),[26] earlier known as Lord Stanley, had caused the split among the Tories on the issue of the Corn Laws in (1845–46), which we have referred to earlier. He and his followers represented the most conservative and reactionary tendency in British politics. The revolt in India and its suppression occurred when Palmerston was in office. However, during the crucial final phase of military operations against the rebels, there was a minority Tory government in power, and it was Derby who oversaw the initial phase of the transition from Company rule to Crown rule.

Dalhousie's tenure was almost nearing its end when the Palmerston ministry was formed. Whereas, upon assuming office, Palmerston was mainly preoccupied with the conduct of the Crimean War, he had to urgently find someone to replace the incumbent governor-general. Robert Vernon Smith, who had just taken over from Charles Wood as president of the Board of Control (Wood had held the India portfolio in the Aberdeen ministry), put forth Canning's name for the post. Palmerston seems to have readily agreed. The queen was mildly surprised upon learning of the cabinet's choice when she was informally consulted. Canning's name did not figure among those that had been in circulation in the preceding weeks. He had just been inducted into the cabinet as postmaster-general a few months earlier and was doing well in that department. This was an abrupt move.

Moreover, the fifth Duke of Newcastle, secretary of state for war in the Aberdeen ministry, who resigned in January 1855 following serious reverses in the Crimean War, was known to

---

[26]Not to be confused with the 15th Earl of Derby, known as Lord Stanley after his father succeeded to the earldom in 1851. Lord Stanley (later 15th Earl of Derby) became the first secretary of state for India (August 1858) in his father's cabinet, i.e., the 14th Earl of Derby's cabinet.

have shown an interest in going to India. Lord Elgin, governor-general of Canada until recently and eventually Canning's successor in India in 1862, was also being mentioned as a possible candidate.

The appointment of Canning was quickly confirmed, and on 1 August 1855, the governor-general-designate was on his way to Leadenhall Street to present himself before the EIC's directors—the last governor-general to do so. He reached India at the end of January 1856, first disembarking at Bombay. It took him another month to reach Calcutta by sea, with a brief stopover at Madras en route to his destination. The Company's regulations required the governor-general-designate to assume charge immediately upon arrival in Calcutta, without any interval. Canning took over from Dalhousie on 29 February.

Canning's entire tenure, barring the initial months, was spent dealing with the revolt and its aftermath. During his first year in office he had to focus on the situation in Awadh. Dalhousie had left Awadh in an unsettled state, and the former kingdom would be the epicentre of the uprising. The revolt was suppressed ruthlessly, though there were many in Britain who felt that Canning had been too lenient in his treatment of the rebels. He came to be mockingly referred to as 'clemency Canning'. This section of British society clamoured for more brutal retribution.

The revolt commenced with the mutiny of sipahis of the Bengal Army stationed in Meerut, a major cantonment in the upper Doab. Of the three armies of the EIC, the Bengal Army was at this time the most formidable fighting force in the British Indian empire. It was equipped with advanced military technology and had vast combat experience. The 'cartridge issue' (seen by some as a major cause of the uprising), i.e., the resentment among sipahis over new cartridges the paper covering of which was allegedly lubricated with animal fat that was taboo for most of them, was the outcome of the introduction of the state-of-art Enfield Pattern 1853 (P53) rifle. Not surprisingly, the Bengal Army was regularly used by the British in their imperialist wars both in the Indian subcontinent and outside. In the two decades preceding the revolt, the Bengal Army had been constantly engaged in military campaigns. It had fought in Afghanistan, China, Burma, Punjab, and Sind. These campaigns had been exhausting for the sipahis who had shouldered the main burden of fighting. Yet the sipahis were routinely humiliated by their British officers in language that was blatantly racist. Moreover, they had few avenues of promotion. Uninterrupted exposure to fighting for several decades, with the enormous risk and sheer physical toil this involved, combined with the daily experience of having their dignity trampled upon, made the sipahis discontented with the conditions of their service. The introduction of the new Enfield P53 rifle appears to have been seen as further worsening the already adverse service conditions of the sipahis. Opposition to the rifle was articulated in religious terms, the tabooed animal fat used as a lubricant for the cartridges of the rifle being particularly objectionable. There were several incidents at the beginning of 1857 in which soldiers of the Bengal Army declined to use the cartridge. This soon became an emotive issue around which sipahis could be rallied. In the last week of April, eighty-five sawars belonging to the Third Regiment of the Light Cavalry posted at Meerut refused to take part in a practice drill that was intended to train them in the use of the rifle. After a preliminary enquiry they were put on trial, and on 8 May were sentenced to rigorous imprisonment for ten years. This severe sentence aggravated an already tense situation, culminating in a violent uprising on 10 May. British authority was overthrown at Meerut. The sipahis then marched to Delhi, where they arrived the next morning. They put an end to EIC's administration in Delhi, and assumed control of Shahjahanabad and its immediate outskirts. The Mughal emperor, Bahadur Shah Zafar, was urged by the sipahis to bless their cause, which he did. Through this gesture the sipahis were seeking to delegitimize the colonial state; by associating the name of the Mughal emperor with their cause they proclaimed that the Company's rule was no longer legitimate. At the same time they were attempting to gain the widest possible acceptance for their regime.

Canning came to know of these developments on 14 May, and wrote to the Bombay and Madras governments to be prepared for rushing reinforcements. However, he did not as yet realize the gravity of the situation. He refused an offer of the Bombay governor, communicated to Calcutta telegraphically on 17 May, for despatching a fast steamer from Bombay, to England, conveying news of the events in north India. The commander-in-chief, George Anson, was in Simla when the mutiny occurred in Meerut. Four days later he left Simla, and proceeded to Ambala from where he planned to advance to Delhi with whatever European troops he could muster. Canning was unable to communicate with Anson or other officials in Punjab as the postal network and telegraph links had been disrupted. The commander-in-chief succumbed to cholera on 27 May at Karnal, about 120 km from Delhi. Canning appointed another senior officer, Patrick Grant, as temporary commander-in-chief as soon as he learnt of Anson's death. Grant was at that time stationed in Madras, and was asked by Canning to immediately move to Calcutta.

For the next few weeks Canning and Grant together coordinated operations from the capital. In fact, Grant was criticized for staying put in Calcutta. Canning had requested the authorities in London to confirm the appointment of Grant as commander-in-chief. Meanwhile, however, Colin Campbell (later, Lord Clyde) had already been appointed to the post, and was on his way to India. He took over from Grant in August.

Canning remained in Calcutta till January 1858 when it was decided, at his suggestion, that the governor-general should move to Allahabad to be closer to the main theatres of the military operations. The other members of the supreme council stayed on in Calcutta, and a senior member of the council, J.A. Dorin, was appointed deputy governor of Fort William in which capacity he presided over council meetings. Canning's long absence (he did not return to Calcutta till the last week of January 1859) required separate legislation to allow him to be away from the capital and function without his council.

The rebels were in control of Delhi for four months, administering the city with considerable efficiency. The British launched a counter-offensive in the first week of June to recapture Delhi. A Delhi Field Force had been constituted for this purpose, comprising whatever European troops were available in Punjab, and contingents supplied by the princely states of Punjab. The Field Force reached the northern outskirts of Delhi at the end of May.

On 8 June 1857, there was an engagement between the British and the sipahis at a location known as Badli-ki-Sarai, near the village of Alipur on the Delhi–Karnal road. The sipahi force suffered a setback in this battle. On the same day, British troops occupied the northern ridge in Delhi, a hilly stretch (a part of the Aravallis) overlooking Shahjahanabad. The ridge became the base for military operations of the Delhi Field Force against the rebels.

Throughout the summer months the British force remained stationed on the ridge. Then in mid-September 1857, it carried out a major assault to capture the city. From the ridge the (British) troops moved in the direction of the Kashmere Gate of Shahjahanabad. The gate was stormed and taken. By 20 September 1857, the entire city had been occupied by British troops.

Following the 10 May uprising at Meerut and the liberation of Delhi, there were mutinies at several places in north India in quick succession: Aligarh (20 May); Bulandshahr (21 May); Mainpuri (22 May); Etawah (23 May); Bareilly and Shahjahanpur (31 May); and Saharanpur (3 June). This suggests that there might have been some prior consultation among sipahis stationed in the Ganga–Jamuna Doab. The mutinies in this region prompted sections of local elites to join the sipahis, which resulted in putting an end to Company rule in large portions of what is now Uttar Pradesh. Some of the liberated areas remained free for nearly a whole year before they could be reconquered by the British. For instance, the new regime that took over Bareilly with the success of the uprising of 31 May in the city, survived for nearly one whole year. On the other hand Kanpur, located on the banks of the Ganga and along the Grand Trunk Road, was held by the 'rebels' for just a few weeks although this prominent centre of the revolt witnessed some of the fiercest fighting in the Doab in the first few months of the struggle.

Indian troops belonging to contingents of the Bengal Army quartered in the Kanpur cantonment joined the struggle against the British on 4 June. Soon afterwards, charge of the liberated city was handed over by the sipahis to Nana Sahib. British troops, commanded by Hugh Wheeler, were besieged by the sipahis and soon forced into submission. The large European population of the city (most of them civilians) too had taken refuge at the location where the British force was encamped. Towards the end of June, Wheeler agreed to surrender on the condition that civilians were assured a safe passage to Allahabad. In a confusing sequence of events that has been much distorted in colonial accounts, the sipahis began shooting and set on fire the boats in which the British were to travel. Survivors, mainly women and children, were then encircled and interned in a building close to the bank of the Ganga. This building is referred to in colonial accounts as 'Bibighar'.

Meanwhile in Calcutta, Canning had been trying desperately to mobilize an armed force that could restore British control over the Grand Trunk Road connecting the imperial capital with Delhi and Punjab, and carry out the reconquest of Awadh. They eventually chose a ruthless officer from the Madras Army, James Neill, who was summoned to Calcutta to lead a force consisting of European troops and loyal remnants of the Bengal army. On 11 June, Neill reached Allahabad where the death squads he had formed carried out large-scale killings in the city and the neighbouring countryside. Inhabitants of villages suspected to have supported the rebels were killed, irrespective of their age and sex. The troops (led by another military officer,

Henry Havelock, after 30 June) then marched towards Kanpur, destroying entire villages along the way and slaughtering their residents. Nana Sahib's army fiercely resisted the British attempt to capture the city, though it had to eventually retreat and Havelock was able to occupy Kanpur on 17 July. Massive violence, the like of which was perhaps not witnessed in any other centre of the revolt, was unleashed against the local population. The unprecedented nature of the violence at Kanpur was justified as being retribution for the carnage at Bibighar that had preceded the British assault on the city. On 15 July, European women and children held in custody in Bibighar were put to death. It is unlikely that the history of this tragic incident can ever be recovered since all that we have is highly prejudiced, often hysterical, colonial narratives of it. Any narrative that undermined the official colonial version of the incident was systematically suppressed. There is no way, given the lack of evidence, to find out what caused this incident or who the persons responsible for it actually were. In a reappraisal of this issue, Rudrangshu Mukherjee has argued that ultimately the 'rebels' were replicating the violence that the British had used to establish their sway over the Indian subcontinent: 'They "borrowed" from the British and replicated the violence. The terms of their violence were thus derived from that very structure of power against which they had revolted.'[27] Subsequently, the brutal suppression of the revolt was sought to be legitimized by constantly referring to the Bibighar massacre. In the British imagination, Kanpur became a metaphor for the entire revolt. The elaborate memorial built over the well situated close to the site of the massacre, into which the bodies of the European victims were allegedly thrown, became one of the most-visited monuments by British travellers touring India. Lady Canning had taken a keen interest in finalizing the design for the monument. The suggestion for placing an 'angel of resurrection'

---

[27]Rudrangshu Mukherjee, '"Satan Let Loose Upon Earth": The Kanpur Massacres in India in the Revolt of 1857', *Past & Present*, No. 128, August 1990, p. 99.

on top of the well had originally come from her: 'The hope of the Resurrection is the only thought which can calm sorrow or bring comfort in connection with the awful catastrophe which is connected with the place; therefore let a statue of the Angel of the Resurrection be placed over the well.'[28]

The rebels renewed their efforts to liberate Kanpur towards the end of the year. The fresh offensive was led by Ramchandra Tope, popularly called Tatya Tope, who was a confidante of Nana Sahib. By about mid-November 1857 Tatya Tope's troops had brought the countryside surrounding Kanpur under their control. In the last week of November, a major military engagement took place between the rebel sipahis and the British on the outskirts of the city. Initially the British were defeated and had to retreat. The fight for Kanpur continued for several days till eventually Tatya Tope's position became untenable and he had to withdraw to the countryside. Tope then joined hands with Lakshmi Bai who was spearheading the struggle in Bundelkhand. The insurrection was widespread in the Bundelkhand region which lies south and south-west of Kanpur. Here Jhansi, the capital of a small Maratha-ruled principality that had been annexed by Company in 1854 during the aggressive expansionist drive under Dalhousie, had become the main seat of sipahi authority. Lakshmi Bai was the regent of the princely state, ruling it on behalf of her minor son. Her husband, the ruler of the state, had died in 1853. Since his successor was an adopted son the British used this as a pretext for taking over the administration of the territory, and refused to recognize Lakshmi Bai's authority.

Sipahis of the Bengal Army stationed at Jhansi overthrew their European officers on 6 June 1857. They then placed themselves under the leadership of Lakshmi Bai, and British rule in the erstwhile state came to an end. The insurrection spread rapidly throughout Bundelkhand with both local elites and

---

[28] Augustus J. C. Hare, *The Story of Two Noble Lives: Being Memorials of Charlotte, Countess Canning, … etc.*, Vol. 3, London: George Allen, 1893, p. 60n2.

peasants combining to fight the British; the entire countryside was in a state of upheaval. Villagers spontaneously organized themselves to oust the British and their Indian collaborators, arming themselves with any weapon they could lay their hands on—spears, lathis, or wooden rods to which sickles or knives had been tied. Tehsil offices and police stations were attacked and official records burnt. It was firmly believed by the people that the colonial rulers had fled, never to return again. Much of Bundelkhand remained a liberated zone till the beginning of 1858. A British force sent to recapture Jhansi launched an offensive against the city in March. Lakshmi Bai coordinated the efforts to resist this military onslaught. It was with great difficulty that the British were able to force their way into Jhansi by 3 April amidst heavy fighting. Lakshmi Bai managed to escape to neighbouring Kalpi where she joined Tatya Tope who had been on his way to Jhansi to assist the rebels. The two of them proceeded in the direction of Gwalior where they joined the rebel sipahis of the Gwalior Contingent.

The Gwalior Contingent of the Sindia state, formed after a brief military occupation of Gwalior in 1843-44, had mutinied in June 1857. The contingent was officered by Europeans, and was subject to the overall control of the EIC. The sipahis had been growing restive since the last week of May. As news of events at Meerut and Delhi as well as other centres of rebellion reached Gwalior, the capital of the state, the troops geared themselves for an offensive against the British. By 14 June, British officers had been expelled. Several Europeans were killed or had to flee the city. The full potential of the strategic advantage gained by the Gwalior soldiers was never realized. They were pre-empted by the ruler Jiyaji Rao (r. 1843-86) who announced that henceforth, the troops would serve directly under him. The maharaja undertook to pay their salaries regularly. It has been argued that this robbed the troops of their autonomy and on the other hand, gave the beleaguered British some breathing space. The contingent remained confined to Gwalior.

For a whole year after the uprising of 14 June 1857, the Gwalior Contingent did not actively participate as a body in the campaigns of the rebels. It was only after the fall of Jhansi and Kalpi in 1858 that Gwalior became the base of rebel leaders. At the end of May (1858), Tatya Tope and Lakshmi Bai, accompanied by Nana Sahib's nephew Rao Sahib, and nawab Ali Bahadur of Banda (another prominent centre of the revolt in Bundelkhand) assumed leadership of the Gwalior troops. Jiyaji Sindia fled to the protection of the British. In mid-June, the British army launched a major operation to capture Gwalior. In the intense fighting that ensued, Lakshmi Bai died while fighting. On 20 June 1858, Jiyaji was escorted back to his capital by British troops. This was the last major military engagement between the British and the rebels. Tatya Tope carried out a series of guerrilla-style campaigns in central India during the latter half of 1858 and early 1859. He was betrayed, captured, and executed in April 1859.

In Awadh, or 'Oudh', the most important development during the first phase of the revolt was the siege of the Lucknow residency by the rebels. A decisive battle between the sipahis and the British had taken place on 30 June on the outskirts of Lucknow, at Chinhat. The rebels won a resounding victory. With this triumph they were in a position to take over the capital of the province. European soldiers and civilian officials in the city retreated to the compound of the residency and were besieged. Other European inhabitants of the city also rushed to seek shelter in the residency. In all there were about 3,000 persons within the residency compound at the beginning of the siege (apart from the residency itself, the compound included several neighbouring buildings). The epic siege of the Lucknow residency commenced on 1 July 1857.

The siege of the residency compound had an important political significance. This was the seat of the Company's hated administration in Awadh after the annexation of 1856. The erstwhile kingdom was reconstituted as an administrative unit, the province of Oudh, following its annexation, and placed under a chief commissioner.[29]

The rebels proclaimed the overthrow of the EIC's regime and set up a government of their own as the legitimate government of Awadh. They recognized the authority of Begum Hazrat Mahal who remained their foremost leader throughout the duration of the siege. Hazrat Mahal was a former wife of Wajid Ali Shah, the last ruler of Awadh, who was exiled to Calcutta after the annexation. She continued living in Lucknow after Wajid Ali was exiled. When the uprising began, she declared her minor son Birjis Qadr as the ruler of Awadh with the approval of the sipahis. Birjis Qadr was accepted as the nominal head of government by the rebels. On 5 July, he was installed as ruler in a formal ceremony. Hazrat Mahal was the regent for her son. Henceforth, all official orders were issued in the name of Birjis Qadr. Recognition for Birjis Qadr was also sought from the Mughal emperor. The sipahi regime in Delhi acknowledged him as the governor (subedar) of Awadh.

The rebels concentrated their military strength around the residency. It is estimated that initially the strength of the rebel forces surrounding the residency was about 6,000. The British were led by Henry Lawrence, who had assumed the office of chief commissioner in March 1857, shortly before the outbreak of the revolt. Lawrence was killed in the first few days of the siege, on 4 July.

As the uprising progressed and British administration in the entire province of Awadh collapsed, a large section of the landed aristocracy, namely the talluqdars, came over to the rebel cause. Around the middle of November 1857, British forces

---

[29]The spelling 'Oudh', for Awadh, is the result of confusion arising out of mispronunciation of the word when written in Urdu. This is somewhat surprising when we realize that there were quite a few English administrators who knew Hindustani and Persian very well. One can only say that this spelling was perpetuated due to the carelessness of colonial officials towards 'native' languages. Oudh, and its variant Oude, continued to be used very extensively in official records, and the province itself was named 'Oudh'.

led by Campbell launched a major offensive to recapture the city. Canning regarded the re-establishment of British control over Lucknow as the foremost military objective after Delhi had been occupied in September. At this stage there were over 53,000 rebel combatants in the city, of which roughly 32,000 were listed as 'tallukdar's men'. These were armed retainers of the talluqdars, sent to assist the sipahis.

The Company had adopted an anti-talluqdar policy since the annexation of Awadh. Initially the newly appointed chief commissioner of the province, James Outram, had moved a little cautiously in the matter of dispossessing the talluqdars of their rights. When, however, Outram proceeded on leave in May 1856, his successor embarked on a harsher policy, extinguishing the rights of a large number of talluqdars. This gave rise to discontent among the powerful landowning classes in Awadh, and one of the reasons why Henry Lawrence had been brought in as chief commissioner was because he was perceived to be somewhat more sympathetic to the landed elite. But by the time Lawrence assumed office in March 1857, things had already gone too far, and then within a few months the revolt broke out. Although the talluqdars were reluctant to join the rebels when the uprising began, once the Company's rule disappeared in Awadh, a large number of them shifted their allegiance. The British were somewhat surprised that even the peasants whom the talluqdars oppressed had joined the rebel cause under the leadership of their respective talluqdars. Colonial officials seem to have assumed that the peasants would appreciate the EIC's anti-talluqdari measures, since these were supposed to be in the interests of the peasants. However, the structure of rural society, and an instinctive comprehension of the exploitative nature of the colonial regime which ultimately targetted the surplus produced by the peasant, made peasants fight side-by-side with the talluqdars in Awadh.

As the monsoon season came to an end in 1857, the British made a concerted attempt to regain Lucknow. By this time, they had already brought the stretch between Banaras and Kanpur under their control. British troops commanded by Havelock attempted to break through the siege. Havelock was accompanied by Outram who had returned from leave and was now asked to assume charge of the province. On 25 September 1857, Havelock and Outram, along with a small contingent, managed to reach the residency, but they in turn were besieged. The siege of the residency continued.

Then in November 1857, another attempt was made to lift the siege. We have referred to this offensive that was led by Campbell. Campbell's military action on this occasion was only a partial success. What Campbell was able to do was to evacuate the besieged inhabitants of the residency. However, Lucknow itself still remained under rebel control. Eventually a massive offensive was launched in March 1858. The recapture of Lucknow was a matter of urgency; without control over Lucknow, British rule could not be restored in Awadh. Campbell's contingents occupied Lucknow on 21 March 1858.

With the military occupation of Lucknow, there was swift and cruel retribution against the inhabitants of the city. The barbarities of Kanpur were repeated. Further, the layout of the city was transformed to do away with the possibility of popular armed resistance. The task of reshaping Lucknow was entrusted to military engineers led by Col. Robert Napier. A large part of the densely populated area around Macchi Bhawan, the traditional centre of the city, was demolished. Nearly two-fifths of the entire city was destroyed and the residents uprooted. The socio-religious and cultural life of the city was severely affected by colonial vengeance. The military occupation of the Jama Masjid robbed the area of its life and vitality. Veena Talwar Oldenburg in her study of colonial Lucknow observes that the area 'dwindled into a picturesque ruin on a barren eminence with an unpeopled esplanade around it. Periodic attempts at rehabilitating have failed since it now stands on the periphery of what remains of the old city and is no longer the convenient locus it once was.'[30] What is more, narrow winding streets that made military operations difficult were replaced with broad avenues, as for instance, Victoria Street. This broad avenue, running from north to south, made it easy for the army to march from one end of the city to the other without having to encounter barricades. Thus, the post-1857 policy left a permanent mark on the urban configuration of Lucknow. The city was never the same again.

In eastern India, a rebellion had broken out in Bihar as early as July 1857. There was an uprising in the city of Patna on 3 July 1857, which was swiftly crushed. Then on 25 July British troops stationed at Danapur cantonment near Patna mutinied. Subsequently, a bigger mass struggle emerged under the leadership of the famous Kunwar Singh, a landed aristocrat of Jagdishpur in the Bhojpur area of western Bihar. Incidentally, Kunwar Singh himself was a very old man at this time, but he actively led the rebellion in Bihar. He continued to do so right till his death in April 1858. After Kunwar Singh's death his brother, Amar Singh, continued to lead the struggle. In the case of Bihar, the period from April 1858 till about the end of 1858 is a period of intense struggle and resistance. Amar Singh launched a guerrilla war which the British found difficult to contain. The most crucial phase of this guerrilla war was the period following the death of Kunwar Singh in April, right up to the end of the monsoon of 1858, when the British launched a counter-offensive which destroyed the resistance. Amar Singh was captured in December 1859. He was imprisoned by the British at Gorakhpur, and died in January 1860 while in captivity.

Following the recapture of Lucknow, the British attempted to restore their authority in the Awadh countryside. For this purpose they initiated a policy of reprisals against the talluqdars,

---

[30]Veena Talwar Oldenburg, *The Making of Colonial Lucknow: 1856-1877*, Princeton: Princeton University Press, 1984, pp. 36–37.

hoping at the same time to gain the support of the peasantry. In March 1858, Canning issued a proclamation confiscating the estates of the talluqdars. Only five talluqdars who had remained loyal were exempted. This measure of Canning led to a serious crisis. Talluqdars throughout Awadh promptly mobilized themselves against the British. This was a desperate struggle on their part to hold on to their land and feudal privileges. Even fence-sitters now joined the fight. Canning's proclamation prolonged the revolt in Awadh by several months. There was no British administration in Awadh for most of 1858, except in a few prominent towns. Canning's policy led to a complete breakdown and there were sharp differences among colonial policymakers, both in England and in India, over the proclamation. These differences almost led to the fall of the minority Tory ministry in Britain headed by Lord Derby. In India, there were serious differences between Outram and Canning on this question.

Canning eventually agreed to a policy of reconciliation, and Outram was authorized to negotiate with the talluqdars, assuring them that they would not lose their estates if they gave up the path of rebellion. It was obvious that the Awadh countryside could not be won through a military conquest. The revolt of the people was defeated through a compromise between the colonial rulers and the indigenous landed elite. In the post-1858 period the landed elite became the main support of the colonial state. Their participation in the revolt ended with their capitulation as a class. This capitulation was at the cost of the toiling people in villages and cities who had played such an important part in the anti-colonial struggle of 1857–58.

In July 1859, Canning declared that peace had been restored: 'War is at an end; Rebellion is put down; the Noise of Arms is no longer heard where the enemies of the state have persisted in their last Struggle; the Presence of large forces in the Field has ceased to be necessary; Order is re-established;

and peaceful Pursuits have everywhere been resumed'.[31]

The concluding phase of the suppression of the revolt coincided with a change in the manner in which the Indian empire was governed. In August 1858, Parliament enacted legislation that brought to an end the era of Company rule. Following the 1858 Act, whereby the Crown directly took over the government of India, the queen issued a proclamation in November 1858 announcing this change. The governor-general was henceforth also the monarch's representative in India, with the title of viceroy. Canning, who was named in the proclamation, was the first viceroy.

჻

Canning's tenure ended in March 1862, when Lord Elgin arrived to relieve him. He left India in the *Feroze*, the same vessel that had conveyed Dalhousie to Egypt. Canning was afflicted with a fatal disease of the liver and died within two months of his arrival in England. Elgin was in office for just over a year; he died in November 1863. He was buried at Dharamshala (in present-day Himachal Pradesh).

Since November 1858, governors-general had the additional title of viceroy, though the official title was the older one. The 1858 Act has no mention of the term 'viceroy'. Canning, the first governor-general with the additional official designation of viceroy, had decreed that the title was to be used sparingly, only on solemn occasions 'or when the fullest degree of ceremony was required'.[32]

John Lawrence was appointed governor-general (and viceroy) following the death of Elgin—the first direct appointee of the Crown as governor-general. Unlike all his nineteenth-century predecessors, Lawrence had lived in India throughout his career. He began his life as a writer, or junior clerk, in the

---

[31]Michael Maclagan, *'Clemency' Canning: Charles John, Ist Earl Canning, Governor-General and Viceroy of India, 1856–1862*, London: Macmillan & Co., 1962, p. 232.

[32]Ibid., p. 228.

EIC's service and gradually rose to be the principal colonial official in Punjab before he was appointed governor-general. The family to which he belonged was a few rungs lower in the social hierarchy than those of Clive and Hastings. John's father, Alexander, had spent nearly twenty-five years in India as a 'volunteer' officer in the royal army in the last quarter of the eighteenth century. The royal army at that time allowed young men seeking a military career to enlist as 'volunteer' officers. These soldiers did not have a commission and had to subsist on their own. Booty acquired by troops in successful campaigns was the main incentive for these officers to join the army. Once they had accumulated sufficient resources from the sharing of plunder, they could purchase commissions.

Alexander had fought in the Third Anglo–Mysore War in the early 1790s, and later participated in the British invasion of Ceylon. He was present at the Battle of Seringapatam in 1799. Alexander was subsequently posted in Ceylon, where Henry, John's elder brother, was born. Henry would become the Company's resident at the Lahore court after Hardinge invaded Punjab; and later, chief commissioner of Oudh. We have noted that he was killed in the fighting between the rebels and the British at Lucknow in July 1857. Six of Alexander's twelve children were born in India or Ceylon. John, the eighth child, was born in England.

Alexander was able to purchase a commission as lieutenant, was then promoted to major, and eventually retired as a colonel after having briefly fought in the wars against France. He sold his commission for £3,500, a substantial one-time lump sum earning for the family. In addition to this sum, he received a meagre pension from the royal army, which was supplemented by a small allowance sanctioned reluctantly by the EIC for his service in India.

Five of Alexander's sons were employed by the Company, either as officers in its army, or in the civil service. Three of John's elder brothers (Alexander William, George, and Henry) and his younger brother (Richard) joined the army. John entered the

EIC's service as a writer. All these appointments were made on the recommendation of a family friend named John Huddleston.

Huddleston happened to be related to John's mother through his marriage to one of her cousins. He had been a Company employee posted in the Madras presidency in the years immediately after Plassey. Starting his career as a writer, as did all civilian employees sent out to India, Huddleston rose to be a member of the Madras council. The Lawrences came to know the Huddlestons well while both were stationed in the Madras presidency. Soon after his return to Britain, Huddleston became a director of the EIC. As we have seen, cadets in the Company's army and writers in its civilian establishment in India could only be nominated on the recommendation of a director. Every year, nominations were distributed among members of the Court of Directors, each of whom could recommend cadets or writers out of their quota. Cadets were admitted to the EIC's military seminary at Addiscombe, near London, for their training and prospective writers to the East India College at Haileybury.

The East India College had been in existence since 1806. Candidates nominated by the Company's directors had to undergo training as probationers at the East India College for two years before proceeding to India. Cadets received their commissions in the EIC's army after passing out from the Addiscombe Seminary.

Whereas John's elder brothers joined Addiscombe, he was not nominated for a cadetship, much to his disappointment. No vacancy was available for a cadetship in the quota allotted to Huddleston (or to his friends) in the year in which John Lawrence's nomination was due. Thus he had to join the civil service, for which a recommendation was obtainable. A biographical sketch of John's patron emphasizes the role of Huddleston in promoting the young Lawrences:

> His great work was the wisdom he showed in giving
> the Lawrences, cousins [sic.] of his wife, commissions

in the East India Company's service. John Lawrence was appointed in 1827... Dozens of others received appointments, and old John [Huddleston] rarely made a mistake. [He died in 1835, at the age of 86.] His five sons were all in the E.I.C.S. [the Company's civil service]; one grandson, William ... acting Governor of Madras 1881. Four grandsons were in the Madras Army, one in the Bengal Army; one great-grandson in Indian railways, and another, in the 5th Gurkhas.[33]

The Company lived on in the careers of descendants of its officials long after the Crown had taken over.

John Lawrence passed out of Haileybury in 1829. He reached Calcutta in 1830, where he had first to clear his language examinations in Urdu and Persian. Lawrence was initially placed in Delhi as one of the commissioner's assistants, mainly attending to revenue matters, before being transferred to Panipat. The commissioner looked after administrative matters relating to Delhi. Lawrence was then transferred to Gurgaon as joint magistrate and deputy collector. Gurgaon was part of the Delhi Territory administrative unit. He gained most of his early experience as an administrator in what is now the state of Haryana, in areas adjoining Delhi. From Gurgaon, he was shifted to Etawah (in present-day Uttar Pradesh), where he was a land settlement officer for a while, returning to Delhi as civil and sessions judge. Before taking up his post in Delhi, he was granted leave for a short vacation in England. By the time the First Punjab War began, he was collector and magistrate of Delhi.

At the end of the war, he was appointed commissioner of the Jalandhar Doab. The territory was annexed under the provisions of the Treaty of Lahore. His appointment inaugurated a long association with colonial Punjab.

After Dalhousie's Punjab War of 1848–49, Lawrence

[33]George Huddleston, *The Huddlestons*, Part I, Bristol: St Stephen's Press, 1928, p. 17.

emerged as the key colonial official in the territories of the erstwhile kingdom (Kashmir and Jammu had already been detached from these territories). He was one of the three members of the Board of Administration constituted by the governor-general to govern British Punjab. Henry Lawrence was made president of the board without any overriding powers. Henry differed sharply with both Dalhousie and John regarding policies to be adopted for stabilizing the EIC's control over the region. Finally, he was shunted out of Punjab.

As Dalhousie's great favourite, John was appointed chief commissioner of Punjab in 1853, when that post was created upon the dissolution of the board. He would remain in office for six years, the last two months as lieutenant governor. Lawrence was the main instrument of Dalhousie's aggressive policies in the province. His lengthy tenure made him synonymous with Punjab in a way that no other colonial official was identified with any specific region of the Indian empire.

He came to be idealized as the model colonial bureaucrat who was supposed to be strong, manly, benevolent, and just. The image of Lawrence was of an administrator loved and feared by the Punjabis, dispensing instant justice and ruling with a firm hand.

When the revolt began in May 1857, Lawrence was called upon to mobilize troops to recapture Delhi. He strenuously sought to enlist soldiers for the Delhi Field Force. The recapture of Delhi made Lawrence famous in colonial writings as one of the most prominent 'saviours of India'.

It needs to be emphasized that the chief commissioner had found it extremely difficult to recruit soldiers from Punjab for the Delhi Field Force. In the post-revolt period, colonial historiography, monopolized by administrators, propagated the myth of 'loyal' Punjab willingly supplying troops to fight against the rebels. Since, in the last decades of the nineteenth century, a disproportionately large number of Indian soldiers began to be recruited from Punjab into a reconstituted Bengal Army, it became necessary to carefully nurture this myth, which also reinforced Lawrence's reputation.

Lawrence returned to England in early 1859, after having spent nearly thirty years in India, most of them in Punjab. He was back in India in January 1864 as governor-general. His tenure lasted till January 1869. The same year, upon his final return home in 1869, he was made a peer—Baron Lawrence of 'Punjaub and Grateley'. His sister had a small estate in Grateley, near Southampton, for which reason he included this obscure location in his title, making him a territorial peer.

It may be recalled that Shore, too, had been raised to the peerage with a rank at the lowest level of the hierarchy. Shore and Lawrence were created peers rather grudgingly, in both cases at the end of their respective tenures as governor-general. The reluctance to raise them to the peerage was a reflection of the aristocracy's disdain for their relatively humble social origins and elite displeasure over their having been made full-fledged governors-general (and viceroy in the case of Lawrence), notwithstanding that they had begun their careers as lowly copying clerks in the Company's employment.

VIII

LAST OF THE OLD-TIMERS

The East India Company had a long afterlife. Apart from the several other ways in which the colonial state of the post-1858 period was shaped by Company rule, the administrative and military personnel recruited by the EIC in the second quarter of the nineteenth century continued to be in service in the latter half of the century, many of them occupying high office. Of these, Lawrence alone reached the topmost level of the hierarchy within the Indian empire. At the same time, like several senior officials of the Company era, he continued to be associated with policymaking while living in Britain in retirement, thereby influencing colonial policies under Crown rule.

During the years he was home from 1859 onwards, and before he was appointed governor-general, he was a member of the Council of India. The council (not to be confused with the supreme council in Calcutta, styled under the 1858 India Act as the 'Council of the Governor General of India') was a body constituted under the provisions of the Act of 1858. The function of the Council of India was to advise the secretary of state for India. The ministerial portfolio too was a product of the same Act, which abolished the Board of Control, and gave the responsibility for administering India to the secretary of state, a minister in the British cabinet. The cabinet minister was to be advised by the fifteen-member Council of India.

In accordance with the Act, the first council was composed of seven members elected by the Court of Directors 'from among the Persons then being Directors of the said Company or having been theretofore such Directors'. The Charter Act of 1853 had changed the composition of the Court of Directors by reducing its members from twenty-four to eighteen, one-third of whom were to be nominees of the government. This gave the government a formal presence in the court for the first time in its history. Therefore, the members elected by the court to represent the EIC on the Council of India when it was first constituted, had the prior approval of the government as they were endorsed by its six nominees in the Court of Directors.

Lawrence was one of the eight other members of the Council directly nominated by the government. He joined the Council in April 1859, within a few days of his arrival in London. Membership of the Council had been offered to him by Secretary of State Lord Stanley. Stanley (later, 15th Earl Derby) was the first secretary of state for India. His father, Lord Derby (14th Earl), headed the government, which had secured the passage of the Act of 1858 in Parliament.

Membership of the Council of India was a full-time occupation for Lawrence, requiring regular attendance at the secretary of state's establishment, which came to be known as the India Office. The Company's sprawling Leadenhall Street complex, its head office, was shut down and eventually dismantled. Over the years, the EIC had acquired several buildings adjacent to its original offices in Leadenhall and incorporated them into its labyrinthine East India House headquarters.

While its new premises were under construction in central London, the India Office was temporarily located at a prestigious hotel named the Westminster Palace Hotel. One wing of the hotel was leased by the government for this purpose. The India Office operated from the hotel until 1867. The structures that comprised East India House were demolished. Hunter provides a description of the desolate state of the East India House while it was being dismantled by the orders of Charles Wood. Wood had taken over as secretary of state for India when Derby was replaced by Palmerston as prime minister in June 1859. He showed great impatience in disposing of the EIC's former headquarters. Hunter had travelled from Scotland to London in 1862 to appear for the public examination for the civil service in India (under a new system introduced in 1855, under provisions of the Charter Act of 1853), and was dismayed to find that the most important symbol of the Company's power was no longer extant:

> 'That wretch, Sir Charles Wood, has broken up the venerable tenement; the beautifully painted but now bare walls and black fireplaces stare through the dismantled windows, and auctioneers' bills, in red and blue, are stuck over the whole building, inside and out. When I thought of the great dead who had written and schemed within the rain-streaked, gilded chambers, my heart swelled within me with indignation.'[1]

Lawrence was also given a baronetcy upon his initial return in recognition of his role in the suppression of the revolt. However, he was disappointed that he had not been made a peer. The chairman of the EIC, Frederick Currie, had lobbied hard for the peerage but was not successful. Currie and Lawrence had been colleagues in Punjab in the 1840s and had been part of the group of EIC servants entrusted with the political and diplomatic aspects of the plan for the subjugation of the Lahore kingdom. Currie had negotiated the 1846 Lahore Treaty at the end of Hardinge's Punjab War. Following his homecoming at the end of a long career in the Company's civil service in India, he became a member of the Court of Directors and was subsequently elected its chairman, a position he held when the Act of 1858 was passed. He was appointed vice-president of the Council of India (the secretary of state was ex-officio president). One of his final acts as chairman of the EIC was to get a resolution passed by the court in the last week of August 1858, granting an annuity of £2,000 to Lawrence.

---

[1]Francis Henry Skrine, *Life of Sir William Wilson Hunter*, London: Longmans, Green & Co., 1901, p. 47.

In 1860, while Canning was still the governor-general, a position he would hold for another two years, Lawrence was approached with the offer of going to India as the governor of the Bombay presidency. With the emergence of Bombay city as a centre of industry and finance, and with the addition of Sind to the territories of Bombay, the Bombay presidency was no longer the inconsequential administrative unit it had been until the end of the eighteenth century. However, Lawrence was not inclined to accept the position. Accepting the offer would not necessarily have implied consenting to a demotion, as some of his biographers have suggested. We must bear in mind that he had retired as lieutenant-governor of Punjab. The office of the chief commissioner of the province had been upgraded to that of lieutenant-governor a few weeks before he left Lahore (in the colonial system, a lieutenant-governor had more powers than a chief commissioner). Governorship of a presidency was a step higher in the hierarchy.

It is unlikely that Lawrence aspired to be governor-general at this stage. He seems to have been quite satisfied with his work as a member of the Council of India, seated at his desk in Westminster Palace Hotel in close proximity to the secretary of state. In the previous sixty years, there had been no precedent for a Company employee to be given the top post in the Indian empire. There had been only one exception since Warren Hastings—John Shore. Furthermore, the EIC had ceased to govern the empire. How could the government set aside the maxim 'which had come almost to have the force of law' prior to 1858, that no 'circumstances could justify the Company in approving one of their servants to the highest dignity in their gift'?[2]

Lawrence's biographer, R. Bosworth Smith, suggests that the deaths of three governors-general in quick succession (Dalhousie, Canning, and Elgin) between 1860 and 1863, the

---

[2]R. Bosworth Smith, *Life of Lord Lawrence*, Vol. 2, Sixth Edition, London: Smith, Elder & Co., 1885, pp. 268–69.

first two immediately at the end of their tenures and the third within a year of assuming office, made the government nervous about sending out a minister or senior politician to Calcutta. To them, Lawrence seemed to be the best choice both due to his extensive experience and long exposure to the climatic conditions prevalent in India. Surely, he must have been very surprised when, quite unexpectedly, on the morning of 30 November 1863, Sir Charles Wood looked into his room at the India Office with the significant announcement, 'You are to go to India as Governor-General. Wait here till I return from Windsor with the Queen's approval.'

It was not until long after office hours that Sir Charles returned with the warm approval which he had sought and obtained; and now the '"imperial appointment, which is the greatest honour England has to give, except the government of herself," belonged to John Lawrence'.[3]

Lawrence, the obedient bureaucrat that he was, was expected to dutifully implement Woods's policies for the restoration of British authority in India. British authority had collapsed in a large part of the subcontinent between 1857 and 1859. Canning and Elgin did not have sufficient time to bring about a semblance of normality (mopping-up operations had continued till the beginning of 1860).The new governor-general arrived in Calcutta in the second week of January 1864. He was received at Government House by William Denison, who was governor of Madras and had been asked to officiate as governor-general following Elgin's death.

Hunter's hagiographical account of Mayo's life has a romanticized description of the formal welcome accorded to Lord Mayo by the outgoing governor-general, Lawrence, in January 1869 at the end of his five-year term. Hunter himself was present on the occasion: 'The reception of a new viceroy on the spacious flight of steps at Government House, and the handing over charge of the Indian Empire which immediately

---

[3]Ibid., pp. 269–70.

follows, forms an imposing spectacle. On this occasion, it had a pathos of its own. At the top of the stairs stood the wearied veteran viceroy, wearing his splendid harness for the last day; his face blanched and his tall figure shrunken by forty years of Indian service, but his head erect, and his eye still bright with the fire which had burst forth so gloriously in India's supreme hour of need.'[4]

He then compares Mayo's reception with that of Canning by Dalhousie thirteen years earlier, thereby bringing all his heroes together in a group portrait. 'The toilworn statesman [Lawrence],' he writes, almost quivering with emotion, 'who had done more than any other single Englishman to save India in 1857, was now handing it over to an untried successor; and, thirteen years before, Lord Dalhousie, the stern ruler who did more than any other Englishman to build up that empire, had come to the same act of demission on the same spot, with a face still more deeply ploughed by disease and care, a mind and body more weary, and bearing within him the death which he was about to pay as the price of great services to his country'.[5]

As we have seen, a peerage awaited Lawrence upon his return. For the last ten years of his life, as Baron Lawrence of 'Punjaub and Grateley', he was a member of the House of Lords, where he spoke occasionally. He had the privilege, like many of his predecessors who had sat in the same House, of defending his actions in India.

It is worth mentioning that Dalhousie, upon his return, was never able to attend Parliament, though he was a member of the House of Lords. He was convalescing in Malta when Derby's India Bill was being debated and could contribute nothing to the debate, even though he had strong views on the proposed legislation.

Lawrence, when he was made a peer, could speak about and justify his conduct while he was still in Punjab as chief

---

[4]Hunter, *A Life of Earl of Mayo*, pp. 177–78.
[5]Ibid., pp. 178–79.

commissioner prior to his governor-generalship. On one particular occasion, he intervened forcefully to defend himself in a debate on the treatment meted out to the Mughal emperor and his family on his instructions.

Bahadur Shah was made captive towards the end of September 1857, while the Delhi Field Force was engaged in final operations in the city against the rebels. The emperor was then put on trial on the orders of Lawrence. The Punjab chief commissioner's jurisdiction extended to Delhi when the British troops occupied it. In early 1858, the EIC invoked martial law and arraigned Bahadur Shah. The arraignment and trial coincided with the launch of a major military offensive against rebels in large parts of northern, central, and eastern India.

It took the British nearly eight to nine months after the 1858 offensive was launched to restore their authority in what had effectively been liberated zones. The trial seems to have been an afterthought and was primarily a propaganda exercise. It had no legal or constitutional basis, nor can it be regarded as an attempt by the British to show that they were willing to adhere to the rule of law even amid all the turmoil of the 'mutiny'.

The Company could easily have taken punitive action against Bahadur Shah, even execution, without the fuss of a trial. The ruthless military occupation of Delhi and its environs after the city had been recaptured made it unlikely that anyone would intervene to demand justice for the emperor.

The proceedings, conducted within the royal palace, in the hall of special audience or Diwan-e-Khas where Bahadur Shah and his predecessors had held their special durbars, were intended to send a message to rebels who had pledged their loyalty to the emperor. The British sought to demonstrate, through the trial, that the actions of these rebels lacked any legitimacy.

The Mughal emperor, now referred to as 'the ex-king of Delhi', was put on 'trial' four months after the British reconquest of Delhi. This sham show, for which provisions of martial law were invoked, lasted from 27 January to 9 March 1858. Martial law had been initially proclaimed by Canning immediately after the outbreak of the mutiny at Meerut and subsequently was extended to a large part of the subcontinent. Authorization for imposing martial law was provided by the Company's charter. The martial law imposed by the colonial authorities was based on the draconian provisions of Bengal Regulation X of 1804.

In his study of the legislation, Troy Downs notes that 'The importance of Regulation X for the maintenance of British rule in India accounted for its long-standing presence on the colonial statute books with its statutory powers remaining in force for more than a century. As an extreme and well-entrenched instrument of state violence, it had the capacity to inflict widespread death and destruction because it seemingly combined both law (Regulation X's legal powers that overrode ordinary criminal law) and lawlessness (the physical operation of martial law as carried out by the military)'.[6]

David Dyzenhaus, in an essay on what he calls the 'puzzle of martial law', writes that 'the state—that is, the officials who act in its name—is legally authorized to act without any legal controls' by the imposition of martial law. He considers martial law an indispensable instrument for upholding imperial interests. He perceptively observes that 'one way of conceiving empire was as a raw projection of power, in the sense of power unmediated by law. However, the advocates of empire conceived what it was to govern through law, they saw no option but so to govern, in part, because governing through law legitimized empire'.[7]

Orders for constituting a military commission to try Bahadur Shah had been issued by Lawrence under Act XIV of June 1857 ('Military and State Offences Act'). The Act contained

---

[6]Troy Downs, 'Bengal Regulation 10 of 1804 and Martial Law in British Colonial India', *Law and History Review*, Vol. 40, No. 1, 2022, p. 2.
[7]David Dyzenhaus, 'The Puzzle of Martial Law', *University of Toronto Law Journal*, Vol. 59, No. 1, 2009, p. 58.

provisions for setting up courts martial to try 'state offences' that were punishable under Act XI of 30 May 1857 or Act XIV of June 1857. Section I of Act XIV stated: 'All persons owing allegiance to the British Government who, after the passing of this Act, shall rebel, or wage war against the Queen or the Government of the East India Company, or shall attempt to wage such war, or shall instigate or abet any such rebellion or the waging of such war, or shall conspire so to rebel or wage war, shall be liable, upon conviction, to the punishment of death, or to the punishment of transportation for life, or of imprisonment with hard labor for any term not exceeding fourteen years; and shall also have forfeited all their property and, effects of every description.'

The commission comprised five members, the minimum required under the act, with Lieutenant Colonel M. Dawes as president and four other members. Three of these members held the rank of major and one of captain. All were European officers. The opening statement of the deputy judge-advocate general, Major F.J. Harriott, repudiated the long history of the EIC's acknowledgement of the Mughal emperor's de jure authority:

'For that he, being a subject of the British Government in India, and not regarding the duty of his allegiance, did, at Delhi, on the 11th May 1857, or thereabouts, as a false traitor against the State, proclaim and declare himself the reigning king and Sovereign of India, and did then and there traitorously seize and take unlawful possession of the City of Delhi, and did moreover, at various times between the 10th of May and 1st of October 1857, as such false traitor aforesaid, treasonably conspire, consult, and agree with Mirza Moghal, his own son, and with Muhammad Bakht Khan, Subadar of the Regiment of Artillery, and divers other false traitors unknown, to raise, levy, and make insurrection, rebellion, and war, against the State, and, further to fulfil and perfect his treasonable design of overthrowing and destroying the British Government in India, did assemble armed forces at Delhi, and send them forth to fight and wage war against the said British Government.'[8]

The proceedings of the trial were published from Calcutta in 1858 with the title *Proceedings on the Trial of Muhammad Bahadur Shah, Titular King of Delhi, Before a Military Commission upon a charge of Rebellion, Treason and Murder.*

Significantly, in a private letter of December 1857, Dalhousie had succinctly outlined the history of the Company's relationship with the Mughal court, even though he disapproved of the respect accorded to the emperor by the Company in recognition of his status as sovereign. 'In early days, the East India Company always recognized the King of Delhi as their sovereign,' he candidly admitted, 'from whom they received the grant of the revenues of Bengal. Warren Hastings, when Governor-General, took his place in the howdah [seat on the back of an elephant] *behind* the King when they were seated on the elephant together; and even as late as my father's time, high officers always presented a *nuzzur* in money to the King when they were presented to him. The Governor-General, however, gradually assumed his proper position. At last, when Lord Hastings [Moira] was to visit the King at Delhi, he claimed equality so far as a chair on the same level with the King's chair was concerned. It was refused. The visit has never since been paid by a G.-G.'.[9] The otherwise well-informed Dalhousie seems to have overlooked the 1827 audience of Amherst. Yet the point he was making did not lose any of its validity for all that.

The verdict delivered by the military commission was that 'the Prisoner Muhammad Bahadur Shah, ex-King of Delhi, is

---

[8]*Proceedings on the Trial of Muhammad Bahadur Shah ... etc.*, Calcutta: Calcutta Gazette Office, 1858, p. 2.
[9]Dalhousie's letter dated 2 December 1857, Baird (ed.), *Private Letters of the Marquess of Dalhousie*, p. 390.

Guilty of all and every part of the Charges preferred against him'.[10] He was convicted and sentenced to transportation, along with his wife, Zinat Mahal, and two of his sons, Jawan Bakht and Shah Abbas (Shah Abbas was Bahadur Shah's second-youngest son, Jawan Bakht the youngest). The three of them were never put on trial, even in the phoney sense that the emperor was. For seven months after the conclusion of the trial, the four prisoners remained in British custody in Delhi. In the first week of October 1858, they were sent to British Burma, reaching Rangoon by the end of the year. Bahadur Shah passed away on 7 November 1862.

Bahadur Shah and his immediate family were not the only members of the royal family sentenced to transportation and banished to Burma. At the beginning of the 1870s, a hitherto suppressed story of Mughal exile suddenly came to light. This was a story that seems to have been concealed so effectively that senior colonial officials were themselves somewhat taken by surprise. In 1872, the House of Lords received a petition from a member of the royal family exiled in the remote Burmese town of Shwegyin in the Pegu region. The petition originated from Mirza Ali Qadr, a nephew of Bahadur Shah (Ali Qadr was a grandson of Akbar Shah). We do not know how Ali Qadr was able to locate someone familiar with the procedure for presenting such petitions or drafting them. There certainly were networks that enabled the Mughal exiles to maintain contacts, albeit intermittently, with the outside world. The petition stated that Ali Qadr had been transported to Burma because he was allegedly implicated in the violent occurrences at Delhi in 1857. No specific charge had ever been brought against

---

[10]*Proceedings on the Trial of Muhammad Bahadur Shah*, p. 160. Mirza Mughal was the eldest surviving son of Bahadur Shah at the time of the revolt. He headed the sipahi regime after the liberation of Delhi, till the beginning of July (Bahadur Shah was the nominal head). Mirza Mughal was killed in cold blood by a British officer, William Hodson, shortly after his surrender at the end of September 1857. Bakht Khan succeeded Mirza Mughal as the head of the government, a position he retained till the British recaptured the city, when he left Delhi to continue with the struggle in other areas of north India.

him, nor had his participation in the revolt been established. Having dumped him in Shwegyin, the British Indian government seems to have completely forsaken him. Ali Qadr asserted in the petition that he had nothing whatsoever to do with the rebels. He had remained in hiding throughout the revolt, and when the British troops captured the city 'was compelled and driven by the reckless and vengeful fury of the British Army to follow the steps of other fugitives to seek safety out of Delhi'.[11] He subsequently surrendered at Panipat, was tried by a military commission, and was sentenced to transportation in June 1858. Drawing attention to the plight of Ali Qadr during a debate on the petition in the House of Lords, the Earl of Derby (the title by which Lord Stanley, 15th Earl, was known since 1869), formerly secretary of state for India and now in the opposition, pointed out 'that no charge was made against … [the petitioner], either then or afterwards, and that the officer conducting the inquiry before whom he was examined admitted as much, but said, that as a relation of the ex-King of Delhi it was necessary that he should be sent out of India. He was accordingly kept in strict confinement in the gaols, successively of Agra, Allahabad, and Alipore. He was thence sent to the Andaman Islands—where … several of his companions died on the way from the rigour of their imprisonment—and subsequently to British Burmah, where he now is. He further affirms that he has never been informed of the nature of the offences imputed to him and believes that there is nothing against him beyond the facts of his being the nephew of the ex-King and being in Delhi when the rebels held it.'

Derby endorsed the petitioner's appeal for an enquiry into his case, adding that 'it is monstrous to detain men now for an obscure and doubtful share—even if they had a share—in a civil war 16 years ago'.[12] It may be recalled that Derby himself had

---

[11]Mirza Ali Kadr to House of Lords, 24 April 1872, NAI, FDP, 'A', February 1873, No. 94.
[12]Hansard, House of Lords Debates, 18 July 1872, Vol. 212, Cols.1352–56. The name is misspelt as 'Kadir' in the official record of the debate.

been president of the Board of Control, and secretary of state for India in his father's cabinet in the crucial period between June 1858 and June 1859. He was, therefore, responsible to a large extent for the persecution of the Mughal family.

The Duke of Argyll, secretary of state in Gladstone's first ministry, which was in office from 1868 to 1874, was unable to shed any light on the case in his response, admitting that 'every endeavour had been made at the India Office, without success, to find some trace of the process under which the person on whose behalf the Petition had been presented ... had been sentenced to imprisonment'.

All he could do was forward the petition to the authorities in India. He then turned towards Lawrence, who was present in the House, and sought his assistance as a member 'who had been recently Governor-General of India, and who was, of course, much better acquainted with the facts'. He requested Lawrence to enlighten the House about the circumstances in which the royal family had been banished to Burma.

Before the former governor-general could rise to speak, the atmosphere of the house was vitiated by Argyll's concluding remarks on the petition, which were calculated to prejudice members against the royal family as a whole. He linked Ali Qadr, since he belonged to the Mughal family, to the misfortune that befell a 'considerable number of our countrymen and countrywomen [who] were ... cruelly slaughtered in Delhi, and even in the Palace in that city'. The peers were reminded that, allegedly, 'not one of the members of the Royal Family, although they were all pensioners of the Government of India, extended his hand for their protection'.

He then went on to make a general point about the culpability of the entire Mughal family, implicating Ali Qadr as well: 'Indeed, as he was informed, they were universally believed to have evinced a sympathy with the murderers. They were not, then, in the position of ordinary political offenders; but there was strong ground for the presumption that they had really taken an active part in the insurrection, and had given their concurrence to the organization of plans resulting in the outrageous cruelties that had been committed in the city in which they lived.'[13]

Lawrence, like Argyll, was not interested in Ali Qadr as an individual or the merits of his case. Reflecting the deep-seated animosity in official circles towards the royal family, he upheld the harsh punishment meted out to its members. They were collectively guilty and deserved no mercy: 'It had been proved beyond all doubt that almost every member of the ex-Royal Family of Delhi had taken an active part in the Mutiny. There were certainly two or three exceptions, and those cases were fully inquired into and dealt with accordingly. Indeed, *every prominent case was investigated and reported to him*. He could not, therefore, understand how this particular member of the Family who had petitioned their Lordships could have been imprisoned without just cause' (emphasis added).

He was firmly opposed to ending their exile: 'Bearing in mind what those men did, and what would be the evil effects of allowing them to come back to Hindostan, he thought it would be an unwise and injudicious course to permit them to return to India.'[14]

Many of the leading Tory members had some sympathy with Ali Qadr. The petition itself had been introduced in the House by Derby. Lord Cairns, a Tory legal luminary who was solicitor-general during the prime ministership of the senior Derby (1858–59), advised the government to refrain from proceeding on the basis of a 'general presumption of the guilt or complicity of the ex-Royal Family of Delhi as a whole'.

As for the petitioner, 'no horror which was naturally entertained at the acts committed at the time of the Mutiny, ought to deprive that person of the ordinary right of having an investigation made into his case if none had been made already'.[15] Lord Salisbury, soon to become secretary of state

---

[13]Ibid., Cols. 1356–58.
[14]Ibid., Cols. 1357–58.
[15]Ibid., Col. 1358.

for India in Benjamin Disraeli's government formed in 1874, and who knew something of the matter, retorted, when Argyll mentioned that Ali Qadr 'was in the Palace of Delhi when they [murders of Europeans] were committed', that 'the Palace of Delhi was a large place'.[16]

Ali Qadr's offence was that he was a member of the royal family and was present in Delhi when it was under sipahi rule. In his petition, he pleaded 'for the granting of a free pardon for any and every offence (if any) that may have been imputed' to him.[17] The government was in no mood to entertain his appeal.

The official correspondence that Ali Qadr's petition gave rise to would suggest that the colonial state deliberately pursued a policy of making no public acknowledgement of the presence of several Mughal exiles in Burma—and perhaps elsewhere. The surfacing of Ali Qadr caused no embarrassment or pangs of conscience. Rather, it provided an opportunity to concretize a comprehensive hardline policy towards the Mughal family, cynically spelt out by C. U. Aitchison, who was at that time secretary in the Foreign Department of the British Indian government.

Aitchison had earlier been lieutenant-governor of Punjab, where his name survives in an institution established originally for schooling young princes, Aitchison College of Lahore, which is now a prestigious 'national school'.

'However insufficient the evidence may appear at this distance of time to bring individual guilt home to individual persons,' Aitchison argued, 'it must be remembered that the conduct of the Delhi family as a body was so notoriously hostile, and their participation in the murders and atrocities perpetrated, particularly the cruel massacre of a large number of women in the palace, was so general, that the two facts, 1st, of belonging to the family, and 2nd, having been in the city throughout the siege ... were considered sufficient evidence to

---

[16]Ibid., Col. 1359.
[17]Mirza Ali Kadr to House of Lords, 24 April 1872, NAI, FDP, 'A', February 1873, No. 94.

justify the inference that the person identified himself with the rebel cause'.[18] Aitchison was echoing the view of Lawrence, his illustrious predecessor at Lahore, who had initially articulated this opinion in Parliament.

In the wake of the petition, an enquiry was initiated to determine the exact number of such exiles. It was discovered that there were nine prisoners at various locations in Burma besides the four in Rangoon. Two more (excluding Zafar) had already expired. There were another two in Karachi, in Sind. These exiles received paltry allowances, ranging between ₹18 and ₹25 per month, from the local authorities. Zinat Mahal and Jawan Bakht were the only prisoners who received a relatively large sum—₹250 and ₹300 respectively.[19] Shah Abbas got ₹35. There might have been a few other exiles who did not receive a pension and therefore do not figure in colonial records.

Jawan Bakht died in 1884 of 'cirrhosis of the liver, jaundice, and dropsy', in the Burmese town of Moulmein, where he had been allowed to go for convalescence.[20] He had become an alcoholic in captivity. Jawan Bakht predeceased his mother, Zinat Mahal. Zinat Mahal passed away in 1886. She had been struck by 'an attack [of colic] of some severity' in 1884, and 'again in November 1885; she had an illness lasting for about a month, suffering from similar symptoms which nearly terminated fatally'. Zinat Mahal had been addicted to opium for nearly seventeen years, 'consuming as much as 10 grains—about 650 mg—of the drug in 24 hours', generally considered a fairly high dose.[21]

Jawan Bakht's wife, Shah Zamani Begum, who had shared his captivity, had lost her sight, not having been allowed to

---

[18]C. U. Aitchison's Note, NAI, FDP, 'A', February 1873, Nos. 94–116.

[19]Government of British Burma to Government of India, 2 July 1873, NAI, FDP, 'A', August 1873, No. 230.

[20]Deputy Commissioner, Moulmein Town, to Commissioner Tenasserim Division, 23 September 1884, NAI, FD, Internal 'B', November 1884, No. 12.

[21]'Report of the Civil Surgeon, Rangoon', 17 July 1886, NAI, FD, Internal 'B', August 1886, Nos. 140-41.

avail herself of medical treatment in Calcutta. She died in 1899.[22]

☙

By the 1850s, the Indian empire had reached its greatest territorial extent. The only territory added to it in the latter half of the nineteenth century was the kingdom of Ava (Upper Burma). The empire governed by Dalhousie and Canning encompassed the entire subcontinent.

The conventional view on the question of sovereignty in the context of the EIC has been that the Charter Act of 1813 proclaimed the sovereignty of the British Crown over the Company's territorial possessions in India, and this had been recognized by European powers by the 1814 Treaty of Paris. More recently, it has been argued that acquisitions of the Company were sanctioned by the authority of the English king to make war and peace, which, in turn, was based on prize laws with roots in naval prize distribution, the sharing of plunder, and booty on the seas. The subcontinent was thus 'fixed in a permanent state of martial law, while the [British] Isles were not'.[23]

As early as 1756–57, the king's law officers had emphasized, when opinion was sought in the context of the recapture of Calcutta in January 1757, that 'all such places, as may be newly conquered in this expedition [the confrontation with Siraj-ud-Daula before the Battle of Plassey], accrue to the sovereign, and are vested in His Majesty, by right of conquest'. Further, that 'by stronger Reason, all moveables and Plunder ... from the Enemy, are vested in His Majesty, subject to his power of disposing, by virtue of His own Prerogative'.[24] These could be

---

[22]Government of Burma to Government of India, 4 July 1899, NAI, FD, Internal 'B', August 1899, No. 283.
[23]Rahul Govind, 'The King's Plunder, the King's Justice: Sovereignty in British India, 1756–76', *Studies in History*, Vol. 33, No. 2, 2017, p. 3.
[24]Barun De, 'Early Manifestation of the Colonialist Premise in the British Occupation of Bengal', *Proceedings of the Indian History Congress*, Vol. 38, 1977, p. 477.

restored/disposed to the EIC as a subject of the king.

The EIC's status within India was complicated by the sanction it sought and received from the Mughal emperor. The matter remained unresolved when Bahadur Shah Zafar was tried for 'treason'. In an important essay published in 1922, F. W. Buckler argued persuasively that 'the source of the Company's authority in India lay not in the Charters of the King of England, nor in the Acts of the British Parliament, nor in the sword, but in the farmans of the Mughal emperor'.[25]

Two years later, Douglas Dewar and H. L. O. Garrett published a critique of Buckler's essay, deriding his argument. Douglas was a lawyer and a colonial official, while Garrett was a historian and vice-principal of Government College, Lahore. He was later appointed by the Punjab government as keeper of records. While holding that position, he published an edited version of the proceedings of Bahadur Shah's trial, making it readily accessible to the public.

In their critique of Buckler, Dewar and Garrett focused on the powerlessness of the Mughal emperors of the early nineteenth century.[26] Buckler's understanding challenged the prevalent view in post-revolt colonial historiography regarding the political role of the last three Mughal emperors. It became embarrassing after 1857–58, to acknowledge the relationship between the Company and the emperor, which included a recognition of Mughal sovereignty. The history of that relationship was completely erased.

In his recent study of the colonial state and its processes of legitimation, Sabyasachi Bhattacharya comments that the 'stout defence of the imperial point of view' by Dewar and Garrett 'completely misses the point made by Buckler that the point at issue is, who was the de jure sovereign, there being no question

---

[25]F. W. Buckler, 'The Political Theory of the Indian Mutiny', *Transactions of the Royal Historical Society*, Vol. 5, 4th series, 1922, p. 74.

[26]Douglas Dewar and H. L. Garrett, 'A Reply to Mr. F. W. Buckler's *The Political Theory of the Indian Mutiny*', *Transactions of the Royal Historical Society*, Vol. 7, 4th series, 1924, pp. 131–65.

about the situation of the "powerless House of Timur" since 1803 nor about the superior coercive power exercised by the East India Company'.[27]

While Bahadur Shah languished in confinement in Rangoon, Victoria proclaimed her sovereignty over the inhabitants of the Company's territories in the Indian subcontinent. Victoria's proclamation, issued in November 1858 following the Act of August 1858, was an assertion of the sovereignty of the Crown over the British empire in India.

It declared that all inhabitants of the EIC's territories, which were now directly to be governed by the British government, were subjects of the Crown, though subsequent deliberations, especially in the context of the amnesty provisions of the proclamation, made it clear that what was available to Indians was an inferior subjecthood—not equivalent to that of European (British-born) subjects.

The queen's Indian subjects were to be ruled by her personal representative bearing the grand title of viceroy, a title that many later governors-general preferred to use in place of the insipid designation of governor-general, which they were given in constitutional documents.

Twenty years after the revolt, the queen's Indian subjects had once again to be reminded that Victoria, now styled queen-empress, or Qaisar-e-Hind (the Indian Caesar), was their sovereign. The title was added to the other titles of the monarch by the Royal Titles Act of 1876 and was announced at a grand imperial assemblage held in Delhi in January 1877.

In 1887, on the occasion of the golden jubilee of Victoria's accession, a bronze statue of Lawrence was erected on the Mall in Lahore, outside the High Court. The statue's chequered history reveals much more about the reputation of Lawrence than do colonial hagiographies of the viceroy-bureaucrat. The statue was commissioned by friends and admirers of Lawrence

---

[27]Sabyasachi Bhattacharya, *The Colonial State: Theory and Practice*, New Delhi: Primus, 2016, p. 72.

shortly after his death, originally for installation at a prominent public place in London. However, when it was ready, his fans were dissatisfied with the sculpture.

The statue was made by the prominent Vienna-born sculptor, Joseph Boehm. Boehm's first Lawrence statue was stowed away, and he was asked to make another version. The new statue, completed in 1882, was installed in London at Waterloo Place, where it still stands. The first statue was shipped to India in 1887 to be put up in Lahore.[28]

Lahore, the premier city of Punjab and the capital of the province emerged as a major centre of the anti-colonial struggle at the end of the First World War. Punjab was at the forefront of the nationalist agitation against the Anarchical and Revolutionary Crimes Act of 1919 (Rowlatt Act), which was introduced to crush radical movements.

From the 1920s onwards, amidst the intensification of the freedom struggle, there was a sustained campaign by nationalists for the removal of the Lawrence statue. The statue bore an inscription on its pedestal—'Will you be governed by the pen or the sword?'—which was particularly offensive to Indian subjects. The Boehm statue depicted Lawrence with a pen in his right hand and a sword in his left hand.

A number of protests were organized against the presence of the statue in 1921–22. Several agitators were sentenced to imprisonment for terms up to six months or even more. As the demand for removing the statue gained popular support, the Lahore municipality adopted a resolution in 1923 to replace the Boehm work with another statue depicting Lawrence with a pen in one hand and a tax roll in the other—referencing his supposed reduction of taxes during a famine.

Then, in 1925, the figure was seriously damaged, and the 'pen for the right hand of the statue [went] missing and half the

---

[28]The brief outline of the history of the statue which follows is mainly based on Tommy Maddinson, 'Repatriated Colonial Statues', *Cast in Stone* project, University of Exeter; John Heasley, 'The Statue of John Lawrence in Lahore', *Foyle College Former Pupils Association Magazine*, 2021, pp. 60–63.

sword in the left had broken'.[29] The statue was again disfigured in 1932. Four activists—Hazar Singh, Chanan Singh, Ojagar Singh, and Bindar Singh—were apprehended for mutilating the Lawrence sculpture and sentenced to imprisonment for two years.

Following Independence, the statue was relocated to Lahore Fort by the provincial government of Punjab in 1950, where it remained for over a decade. In the late 1950s and early 1960s, a group of retired colonial officials, along with a few British institutions, became active in the drive to relocate various imperial commemorative objects from India and Pakistan to Britain.

One such institution, Foyle College in Londonderry (Northern Ireland), where Lawrence had spent two years as a pupil, negotiated the transfer of the Boehm statue from Lahore Fort to Londonderry to be erected on the school campus. Lawrence had studied at Foyle College, which was earlier named the 'Free Grammar School of Londonderry', between 1823 and 1825. Lawrence's parents were originally from the northern part of Ireland.

Eventually, the statue was transported to London in 1962, where it underwent repairs at a foundry, before being sent to Londonderry for installation in Foyle College. It was unveiled at its new location in 1963. It was moved yet again, and installed in the new campus of Foyle College in 2018.

As for the second Boehm statue, it remains at the site where it was erected in 1882, though the inscription on its pedestal has been partially obliterated to protest against his role in the suppression of the revolt. The words effaced refer to Lawrence as 'ruler of the Punjaub during the Sepoy mutiny of 1857'. The sentiment among people of the subcontinent, including the diaspora in Britain, remains hostile to his memory, making it difficult to sustain his image as a hero.

As a corporate entity, the East India Company ceased to exist in 1874, five years before the death of Lawrence, the last of its old-timers to rule over the Indian empire.

---

[29]'"Pen or Sword?"', *The Sun*, 17 October 1925.

ACKNOWLEDGEMENTS

I would like to express my gratitude to my colleagues in the Department of History, University of Delhi, discussions with whom over the years have helped shape this work. Interactions with my students, whom I have had the opportunity to teach courses dealing with many of the themes discussed in the book, have been invaluable for me. Conversations with Sohail Hashmi, Anirudh Deshpande, and Eshan Sharma, especially on various aspects of the history of the nineteenth century in the context of colonial India, have been immensely useful for me. I am beholden to them for their insights. I am grateful to Prabhu Mohapatra, S. Irfan Habib, and Neera Chandhoke for their support, comments, and suggestions while writing this book, and for encouraging me to reflect on the purpose of writing a book on the lives of governors-general.

I am thankful to the librarians and other staff of the India International Centre Library, New Delhi, and archivists at the National Archives of India, New Delhi, for their assistance and cheerful cooperation.

Aienla Ozukum's persistence kept me focussed on the book. My sincere thanks to her and the editorial team at Aleph, especially Nandini Devdutt Tripathy, for all the hard work that has made the text comprehensible, and for helping me avoid several pitfalls. Responsibility for errors and omissions is mine alone.

SELECT BIBLIOGRAPHY

Andrews, Kenneth R., *Trade, Plunder and Settlement: Maritime Enterprise and the Genesis of the British Empire, 1480-1630*, Cambridge: Cambridge University Press, 1984.

Baird, J. G. A. (ed.), *Private Letters of the Marquess of Dalhousie*, Edinburgh: William Blackwood and Sons, 1910.

Banks, Alfie, 'The Imperial Afterlife of Warren Hastings, 1818–1947', *The Journal of Imperial and Commonwealth History*, Vol. 50, No. 3, 2022, pp. 498–531.

Bhattacharya, Sabyasachi, *The Colonial State: Theory and Practice*, New Delhi: Primus Books, 2016.

Bhattacharyya-Panda, Nandini, *Appropriation and Invention of Tradition: The East India Company and Hindu Law in Early Colonial Bengal*, New Delhi: Oxford University Press, 2008.

Brittlebank, Kate, *Tipu Sultan's Search for Legitimacy: Islam and Kingship in a Hindu Domain*, New Delhi: Oxford University Press, 1997.

Burnage, Sarah, 'Commemorating Cornwallis: Sculpture in India 1792–1813', *Visual Culture in Britain*, Vol. 11, No. 2, 2010, pp. 173–94.

Butler, Iris, *The Eldest Brother: The Marquess Wellesley, The Duke of Wellington's Eldest Brother*, London: Hodder and Stoughton, 1973.

Cannadine, David, *Victorious Century: The United Kingdom, 1800-1906*, London: Viking Press, 2018.

Chatterjee, Partha, *The Black Hole of Empire: History of a Global Practice of Power*, Ranikhet: Permanent Black, 2012.

Chatterjee, Rimi B., *Empires of the Mind: A History of the Oxford University Press in India under the Raj*, New Delhi: Oxford University Press, 2006.

Chattopadhyay, Swati, *Representing Calcutta: Modernity, Nationalism, and the Colonial Uncanny*, London: Routledge, 2005.

Chaudhury, Sushil, 'The Road to Plassey: A Reappraisal of the British Conquest of Bengal, 1757', *Proceedings of the Indian History Congress*, Vol. 59, 1998, pp. 734–50.

Cohen, Ashley L., 'The "Aristocratic Imperialists" of Late Georgian and Regency Britain', *Eighteenth-Century Studies*, Vol. 50, No. 1, 2016, pp. 5–26.

Colley, Linda, *Britons: Forging the Nation, 1707-1837*, London: Pimlico Books, 1992.

De, Barun, 'Early Manifestation of the Colonialist Premise in the British Occupation of Bengal', *Proceedings of the Indian History Congress*, Vol. 38, 1997, pp. 474–88.

Dirks, Nicholas B., *The Scandal of Empire: India and the Creation of Imperial Britain*, Ranikhet: Permanent Black, 2006.

Downs, Troy, 'Bengal Regulation 10 of 1804 and Martial Law in British Colonial India', *Law and History Review*, Vol. 40, No. 1, 2002, pp. 1–36.

Feiling, Keith, *Warren Hastings*, London: Macmillan, 1966.

Fisher, Michael H., *Counterflows to Colonialism: Indian Travellers and Settlers in Britain, 1600-1857*, Ranikhet: Permanent Black, 2004.

———*Indirect Rule in India: Residents and the Residency System, 1764-1858*, New Delhi: Oxford University Press, 1991.

Gordon, Stewart, *Marathas, Marauders, and State Formation in Eighteenth-Century India*, New Delhi: Oxford University Press, 1994.

Guha, Ranajit, *A Rule of Property for Bengal: An Essay on the Idea of Permanent Settlement*, Hyderabad: Orient BlackSwan, 2016.

Hunter, William Wilson, *The Marquess of Dalhousie and the Final Development of the Company's Rule*, Oxford: Clarendon Press, 1890.

Jenkins, Roy, *Gladstone: A Biography*, London: Macmillan, 1995.

Khan, Abdul Majed, *The Transition in Bengal, 1756-1775: A Study of Sayid Muhammad Reza Khan*, Cambridge: Cambridge University Press, 1969.

Maclagan, Michael, *'Clemency' Canning: Charles John, Ist Earl Canning, Governor-General and Viceroy of India, 1856–1862*, London: Macmillan, 1962.

Major, Andrea, *Pious Flames: European Encounters with Sati, 1500-1800*, New Delhi: Oxford University Press, 2006.

Malcomson, A. P. W., 'The Irish Peerage and the Act of Union, 1800–1971', *Transactions of the Royal Historical Society*, Vol. 10, 2000, pp. 289–327.

Mani, Lata, *Contentious Traditions: The Debate on Sati in Colonial India*, New Delhi: Oxford University Press, 1998.

Marshall, P. J., 'The Personal Fortune of Warren Hastings', *The Economic History Review*, Vol. 17, No. 2, 1964, pp. 284–300.

Mehta, Uday Singh, *Liberalism and Empire: India in British Liberal Thought*, New Delhi: Oxford University Press, 1999.

Moreland, W. H. (ed.), *Peter Floris; His Voyage to the East Indies in the Globe, 1611-1615*, London: The Hakluyt Society, 1934.

Nelson, Paul David, *Francis Rawdon-Hastings, Marquess of Hastings: Soldier, Peer of the Realm, Governor-General of India*, Madison: Fairleigh Dickinson University Press, 2005.

Newman, Ian, 'Edmund Burke in the Tavern', *European Romantic Review*, Vol. 24, No. 2, 2013, pp. 125–48.

Ogborn, Miles, 'Writing Travels: Power, Knowledge and Ritual on the English East India Company's Early Voyages', *Transactions of the Institute of British Geographers*, Vol. 27, No. 2, 2002, pp. 155–71.

Oldenburg, Veena Talwar, *The Making of Colonial Lucknow: 1856-1877*, Princeton: Princeton University Press, 1984.

Range, Matthias, *Music and Ceremonial at British Coronations, From James I to Elizabeth II*, Cambridge: Cambridge University Press, 2012.

Rocher, Rosane, *Orientalism, Poetry, and the Millennium: The Checkered Life of Nathaniel Brassey Halhed, 1751-1830*, New Delhi: Motilal Banarsidas, 1983.

Rosselli, John, *Lord William Bentinck: The Making of a Liberal Imperialist, 1774-1839*, New Delhi: Thompson Press, 1974.

Roy, Tirthankar, 'The Permanent Settlement and the Emergence of a British State in Late-eighteenth-century India', *Economic History Working Papers*, London School of Economics and Political Science, No. 355, 2023, pp. 1–32.

Singh, Radhika, *A Despotism of Law: Crime and Justice in Early Colonial India*, Oxford University Press, Delhi, 1998.

Spear, Percival, *Master of Bengal: Clive and His India*, London: Thames and Hudson, 1975.

Subrahmanyam, Sanjay, and Shulman, David, 'The Men Who Would Be King? The Politics of Expansion in Early Seventeenth-Century Northern Tamilnadu', *Modern Asian Studies*, Vol. 24, No. 2, 1990, pp. 225–48.

Wagner, Kim A., *Thuggee: Banditry and the British in Nineteenth–Century India*, South Asia edition, New Delhi: Primus Books, 2014.